REVIE

This is an illuminating book; a work of fiction that became provable fact! It tells a story of historical intrigue, spanning time-lines and lifetimes. More than a beautiful story, it relates a mission which answered Rachel and Hannah Myer's call for justice, from 1663.
Unshriven should help all who read it; it opens minds and inspires!

Karin Barnes
Silva Method Training Instructor

A fascinating paranormal novel, the content of which later proves to be historically accurate.

This story is about historical, psychic remnance crying out for healing and is wonderful evidence of the unseen realms fusing with earthbound reality.

Josephine Sellers
Author of *Parallel Worlds* and
Director of the *AwakeningTVChannel*

Forthcoming titles by June Kidd:

"A Dance of Masks"
(A sequel to *Unshriven*)

"You Can't Stop the Waves – But You Can Learn to Surf"
(So Fake It 'til You Make It – Pretend 'til You Mend!)

See website for details of events and talks:
junekidd.com

THE AUTHOR

June left the pace and excitement of working in and around New York to be married in New Orleans, before moving with her husband, a physician, to Saudi Arabia.

There she spent the next ten years, savouring the exotic Middle Eastern culture, living, working and enjoying the company of people from all over the world and also co-founding the first school for children with Down's Syndrome.

She also travelled extensively to Europe, China, Australia, America and the Caribbean.

It was during a home visit to England that June began her intensive study of 'Imagination, meditation and mental discipline,' eventually becoming an advanced graduate of The Silva Method.

The decision to take this course was to transform and enhance her life, particularly as a writer, freeing her from a lifelong handicap with dyslexia, learning to spell virtually overnight at the age of 40, and developing a heightened 'Spiritual Sensitivity,' that enabled her to write *Unshriven,* her first book.

Unshriven

1663 - 1963

Unshriven

1663 - 1963

June Kidd

cover illustration
Patricia Stevens

Talking

Whoever holds the talking
stick has within their
hands the sacred
power of words –
only the one
who holds the
stick may
speak

but
must
speak the
truth about
personal
understanding
and experience

Stick

First published in Great Britain by
Talking Stick
an imprint of Archive Publishing
Wimborne Dorset BH211HB England
01202 848352

Text © 2012 by June Kidd
The rights of June Kidd to be identified as the Author
of this Work have been asserted by her in accordance with the
Copyright, Designs and Patents Act, 1988.

www.junekidd.com

A CIP Record for this book is available from
The British Cataloguing in Publication data office

ISBN 978 1 906289 20 1 (Paperback)

Content I.D. 11159741

Printed and bound by
Lightning Source

DEDICATION

This book is dedicated to
JOSE SILVA

Founder of the
SILVA METHOD

In 1966, Jose Silva's advanced thinking presented to the public a revolutionary scientific approach to self hypnosis, self mind control and self development. This resulted in him becoming one of the most creative scholars of his time and without these teachings this book could not have been written – an experience that changed my 'Concept of Reality', for life!

and

J.K. LAURA SILVA QUESADE (U.S.A)

Director of the
SILVA METHOD

(The Silva Method was formerly known as Silva Mind Control)

ACKNOWLEDGEMENTS

My love and thanks to my dear husband Roland, for his wisdom, constant support and for never complaining about the hours that I spent at the keyboard, and to my dear family for their never failing encouragement. Special memories and thanks to my dear mother who also loved to write and to my father, for encouraging my early interest in history and antiquity.

To the multi-talented Dr Gerald Moore, whose mentoring and encouragement freed me to write, in those formative and difficult years. To my dear and constant friend Barbara McDonald, who in the early days when PCs were 'user unfriendly', steered me through the minefields and stopped me from throwing a machine out of the window on several occasions! and Neil Wellington who took over the technical support and always answered SOS calls. To Felix Morris-Duffin, for creating my website: www.junekidd.com. To my friend, the artist, Patricia Stevens, for the front cover. To Lindsey Jordon Evans and Clare Ledingham (Penguin Books) for their kind, professional and constructive advice. To Janis Hall, Karin Barnes and to Eve Burdge, my sincere thanks. To the late Beryl Giles who was 'meant to be' at the right place at the right time. (We will meet again, dear Beryl.) To Catherine, Gilly and their families for opening their homes (the featured manor houses) and manorial records, for my inspection, and for making me so welcome. To all friends from Saudi Arabia now scattered across the globe, many of whom lent typewriters and PCs, proof read my manuscript, (suggesting I was dyslexic!) and who gave generously with time and friendship. I do remember and I do thank you.

To Diane Turner for the pen, which I still treasure.

Special thanks also to actress (and fellow dyslexic) the elegant and talented Susan Hampshire, always encouraging over so many years. And last but by no means least, my representative and friend in the USA, Maureen Lowbridge.

www.silvamethod.uk.com

CONTENTS

INTRODUCTION

1663 UNSHRIVEN 1963

"To die without absolution from sin by the Church"

Unshriven is a true account of an extraordinary happening in my life. As a writer with dyslexia, having completed a course on Imagination, Meditation, and Mind Discipline (The Silva Method) I found that not only could I now spell but had also developed a heightened 'Spiritual Sensitivity'.

Living in the Middle East at the time and working on a 20th century novel set near Shakespeare's Stratford-on-Avon, this most extraordinary gift was to result in my writing the 17th century biographies of Rachel and Hannah Myer.

I initially assumed this saga had emanated from my free-wheeling imagination but, on returning to the United Kingdom, I found myself following a most bizarre trail of 'coincidence', and discovered that my 'fictitious' story was provable and previously unknown 17th century history! I then had to accept the fact that a miscarriage of justice committed at that time was reaching across the centuries for resolution by the Church, through me.

I hope you enjoy the developing story of *Unshriven* and notice how the 17th century fact slowly interweaves with 20th century fiction. It was written as it came to my deeply relaxed and receptive mind, while sitting in the shade of the bougainvillea and cooled by breezes from the Red Sea.

The second part has the historic details of my work of 'fiction' as they were revealed as provable fact on my return to England. For the sake of clarity, some general background historical data and the use of old place names etc., were put into the novel *Unshriven* in retrospect, but I assure you that nothing of importance was changed.

PART ONE

*1663 Unshriven 1963
The Novel*

Monday 5th August 1963 – 1-4 Brook Cottages

There it was again – the strangest of feelings – like the touch of a finger pressed, oh so discreetly, on a bare shoulder. What was it? Preoccupied and tying back shoulder length fair hair with a fine silk scarf, Stella searched her memory but like the thinning fragments of a fading dream, it was gone. 'Three hundred years of people living and dying in this terrace,' she shrugged; 'Just a feeling.'

The four stone cottages, isolated, too small for a family and not pretty enough to invite speculation, had been bypassed by time, and 'weekenders' looking for a second home. Until this moment, Stella had always appreciated the isolation and the solitude. Now though, somehow the solitude felt more like loneliness.

As a college lecturer, for her the start of the August break meant good walks over the surrounding hills, time to relax, time for yoga and reading and whole glorious days when she could paint, uninterrupted while Uncle John worked on some watercolour or other, next door. 'I'll miss you, old friend,' she whispered, reaching out to touch their dividing wall, grey eyes brimming first tears since the funeral. 'And I am going to make room for your easel even though I really haven't got room for it. I just want something tangible, something I can touch every day to remind me of you,' she said sadly.

Nearing 50, Stella had a generous smile and a languid elegant walk. A love of long earrings, silver painted nails and an interest in herbal complementary medicine, had earned from her lover Josh, the epithet 'sophisticated bohemian'.

His much younger sister Cynthia (early forties, "Spinster of this parish and proud of it") who lived alone at the far end of the terrace, openly scorned anything arty.

'Stop criticizing, it's just her way, and she's the first there if anyone needs help.' Stella smiled, remembering how grateful they had all been when Cynthia, a born organizer, had taken on the arrangements for the funeral. Now it was all over and Cynthia was back at work, convinced that the Post Office in the village couldn't function without her. Josh had meant to stay on for a couple of days but duty called, and he was back in Cheltenham, where he lived above his bookshop.

Abby, gentle and kind, who lived at the other end of the terrace, was John's niece, though everyone had called him uncle. Bewildered by his sudden death, Abby had been persuaded to go and stay with relatives in Devon. That had thrown Cynthia off balance; Abby never ever went away; never had the confidence to do anything of importance without consulting Cynthia. They had grown up together like book-ends, at either end of the terrace and Cynthia, two years older, had always been boss; a benign dictator.

So with Abby still in Devon and Cynthia back at work, Stella was the only one at home. 'It's no wonder the place feels strange,' she whispered. 'I feel deserted, a bit like an orphan!' It was such a ridiculous thing to say that she laughed out loud and felt better.

They would all have appreciated more space but all four cottages, roughly the same size, had been one long dwelling in the 17th century. Stella had made the most of hers, housing the studio in the attic where the north light was perfect for painting aspects of the garden. Winter was a good time for that, when the brook ran hard and grey, when fat clumps of grass squatted like sagging pillows and bare-boned trees with pretended life of ivy, beckoned the grey folding clouds. Yes, winter was a time for observing how the earth coped without the sun.

This morning however, was beautiful; warm with a soft breeze, a clear blue sky above the surrounding tree-lined hills, perfect for having all the doors and windows open. She had planned a full day; a book to enjoy, time for yoga, then she could take Cynthia's dog Napoleon, for a walk – first however, there was something that had to be done. Something she could no longer put off. 'All right, no more excuses. I'll go in, now,' and taking a deep breath she reached for the key and stepped onto the back path.

* * * * * *

The scent of lavender and mint, mingled with fat old roses sprawled across the length of the cottage walls; branches intertwined, thick as a gnarled wrist and noisy with the hum of foraging bees. Anxious, hesitating for a moment outside his back door, Stella was moved beyond comprehension by the sudden remembered feel of John's hand on her shoulder. It was warm and reassuring – and encouraging? 'You want me to go in, don't you, old friend?' She spoke the words as people often do to a loved one, recently departed. 'I know I must, but actually seeing your home empty – will make it all so final.' She looked at the sky, blinking hard again. 'Finished.' Then with a shake of her head, 'but then as you always said when faced with the inevitable: "*This is life. It is the way of things*". And strengthened by the old man's wise philosophy, Stella turned the key and pushed the door open, slowly.

The shocking nakedness! That's what first registered. The door, now wide open, let in an interrogating search-ray of sun that whipped over her shoulder; shooting ahead through the kitchen, flashing scratch-sharp across the tiny hall, laying everything bare and tired, old and lifeless.

The walls divested of most of his pictures, the stone floors of the rugs, this cruel exposure gave her a feeling of embarrassment; like a person caught dressing in an ungainly position. Through to the sitting room, his easel, propped in a corner, redundant without canvas or the usual multi-coloured bunting of oily, paint-covered rags. Books and mounds of painting magazines and torn scraps of articles that had filled the corners – that had filled this emptiness – all now gone. The table that had never seen the light of day, apart from a corner where he ate his meals, had been cleared and smelled of polish but the resistant wood was scratched and stained and not a thing of beauty; a working surface that had been used, not admired. Even the line of jars kept along the sill, filled with brushes and varying colours of turpentine had been thrown away.

Vera had done a preliminary clearing out, bless her and the up- stairs and the attic were still to be done. They were fortunate to have her as cleaner for all four cottages, fussing over John, like a mother hen, popping in to have coffee with him while she was working in the terrace and often cooking his lunch when they were all at work.

That attic was still to be cleared and that would be a big job. Abby would have to organise it and sort through a lifetime of John's private family papers at the same time. And no one can do that for her; Stella shook her head.

We used to laugh at those jars, she smiled. Both of us reluctant to throw unusual ones away. She still had shelves of them in the kitchen filled with things she had gathered for herbal remedies. Of course it all had to go, for without John's vital energy, the creative mind behind the activity, the house had folded in upon itself – had stopped living; and Uncle John had gone. 'And that's why you wanted me to come in,' she whispered. 'It's time to move on, eh?' Stella closed the door gently, turned the key and, deep in thought, went home.

Stella's sitting room was welcoming and comfortable with an overstuffed sofa, two easy chairs, cushions and curtains in rich browns, apricot and ochre, the shades of leaves in autumn. With shelves filled with books and bric-a-brac of which only she knew the significance, it was a room in which to live, read, work and to think – and she was thinking now and reminiscing too much.

Needing to regain composure, she placed a folded blanket on the floor and sat down, back straight, legs crossed, hands on knees and with measured timing began the yoga breathing exercises: Breathe in for the count of eight, hold for the count of four, out for the count of eight and hold for the count of four; concentrate, mind and body, slow the rhythm – until, 'Oh no!' the rhythm was broken. Cynthia's old Labrador, claws scratching the stone floor, had ambled in from the garden, stopped just inches away from her face and was watching closely, waiting for her eyes to open. Stella could feel his penetrating stare and it was all she could do to stop herself from laughing and ruffling his head. 'Out.' Eyes tight shut, she pointed. No response. 'Out!' – more fiercely this time. Still no response, then with a resigned puff that meant no walkies, Napoleon plodded off down the garden, drank from the ford where the water was shallow, wandered back and flopped down on the back step in the shade to wait.

Gradually, steadily, one controlled movement followed another, stretching, holding, stretching, holding, visualizing the intake of air spiralling high and the outflow of energized breath flowing deep into the earth – and into its stillness she merged, mind clear of all thought. The big clock ticked on, a zephyr carried perfumes in from the roses round the open window and, as if she were moving into a bubble, the membrane of peace closed around and she sank into the centre of silence and perfect harmony.

How long had she been there, ten minutes, an hour? No matter. Time was irrelevant, time had stopped, as though the pulse of the earth had stopped and Stella was at one with everything – until, like the silence in the forest before a storm, hushed, expectant and still as stone, even before the first murmured sound was heard through ancient and long gone trees, her sixth sense became aware of change. *And here it was again, that strange feeling. She shivered, but this time she did not resist.*

The pressure increased like the pressing of a thumb in the centre of Stella's forehead, the 'mind's eye' a clearing window as vague mental pictures polarized and strange brown smudges became... hoods... became monks... became a procession of monks in brown habits following closely on each other's heels. They came over the hill and down the path between the lines of hazelnut trees above the manor, crossed the cart track and headed on down the gully to the ford outside; an unstoppable force, the power of the Church, its armour. An unbroken line, evenly paced, faces concealed, hands together, chant hypnotic, marking time as sandaled feet relentlessly slapped the dry earth. Their plainsong, like the dead words of old spells, strengthened by belief and repetition, holding minds in tight, unwavering, unquestioning bias. It was a force that would suffer no interruption as it marked ecclesiastical boundaries and cleansed all evil in its way. Outside by the ford now, shallow with summer drought, waving incense and chanting rituals, they formed into a power-filled circle on the ground of a ruined cottage. Desolation was rife, with weeds clawing over charred stumps and a big brick fireplace scarred, standing defiant, the iron door of its big bread oven wide open and beckoning. 'No!' an instinctive reaction and at once the focus of attention was swung on her, instantly followed by a most dreadful smell of burning as she felt herself being pushed into a small suffocating space.

'No light, for God's sake, where am I?' Then in an instant, free again, fighting, sucking air, but the monks were chanting again, and she was totally outraged; outraged without knowing why. 'Stop this; you have no right, no right!' Yet still they sang, with controlled monastic breath as the ceremony progressed relentlessly on and on, sprinkling the holy water, ringing the bell, sealing lies into history by accepting outrageous injustice as truth and leaving the burned flesh stain of bloody belief on this poor strip of land, pulling Stella, still protesting, back into a time that was not hers, as they cleansed the ground of evil, where she knew, deep in a past mind, that there had been none.

'Stop, stop this charade!' Her voice had a weak echo and as though pulled by a powerful magnetic force, she was back in the chill of the closed-in place, drifting, semiconscious, accepting a fate, futile to resist.

Out there she had been witness to the progress of the monks, in here, in here she could not see, could not move or feel her body; this small, small body – and what did it matter? What did anything matter? Stella was drifting, losing sensation of 'Self'. Why struggle? Then again the primitive instinct for survival kicked in and she screamed, '*No!*' Now it was a battle of wills, now she was fighting hard for separation from whoever's small body this was – but willpower alone was not strong enough to break free of this suffocating stone chamber – the bread oven? It's not real, it's illusion. '*Let me out!*'

Her mind was groping for a grip on current reality but her body, as though suspended somewhere in long gone time, was giving up the fight; accepting a fate that seemed justified... '*No, dear God, please don't leave me in limbo*', she begged, surfacing again, dragging for breath as a wave of sheer terror began to engulf her.

Then into that wave a voice called her name and as if distracted, the nightmare scene halted, then quickly faded, leaving her alone, still with the sensation of being physically trapped and unable to move or make herself heard, yet less threatened. No one could reach her and now the fear of abandonment was like no horror she could ever have imagined. All was deathly, everything waited, even her heart seemed on hold, as she strained for sound, listened for seemingly eons, willing the call to come again.

'Laundry. Anybody at home?'

Napoleon padded into the hall, woofed half-heartedly at the man, wagged his tail and plodding over to Stella, gave her a nuzzle and couple of big licks that brought her spinning back to consciousness.

'Must be in the back garden,' a voice mumbled.

'No, no, I'm here. Please wait,' Stella called, coughing, trying to disguise the tremble.

'OK, back in a minute. Your clean laundry's here in the hall. I'll get Miss Cook's first, she's left it on the step.' And whistling, he walked off along the path to pick up Cynthia's bag.

Stella gave Napoleon a big hug, struggled to hold back tears of relief. She hadn't heard the laundry van and now, staggering upright, she picked up the laundry bag from the kitchen and dropped it outside. With a quick wave to the driver she picked up the brown paper parcel, darted back and closed the door. Leaning her back against it she heard him walk past, then start the van. They usually had a little chat but conversation was out, she was trembling too much from shock and fright that still cloaked her.

'What just happened? Oh, I need a drink!' Panting, she reached for a glass, hands trembling, spilling some, she poured a very large whisky, drinking it in one go. The harsh spirit stung the back of her throat and, still coughing as she rinsed the glass under the running tap, Stella nearly shot out of her skin as Cynthia marched in and sat her well-corseted Post Office hips on a stool.

'Morning, Stella. A quick word before I go to work.'

'Ah, I thought you had already left,' Stella spluttered...

'Business; things to tell you first.'

Cynthia's short black hair was combed fashionably forward,

circling the face like a monk's; she smoothed it down, ran a tongue over strong white teeth, then reached over and shook the kettle. 'Empty,' she said, almost accusingly. Plonking it down she perched back on the stool, looked pointedly from wrist watch to kettle to Stella, then ran a judgemental eye along the shelves at the jars, their contents neatly labelled with what looked like dried up bits of leaves and stick. She rolled her eyes, 'The rubbish this woman keeps!'

Moulded by elderly parents, running the Post Office or anything else that needed a leader, meant complete fulfillment in Cynthia's life. At least it did until the eligible Rev. Andrew had come on the scene. As Post Mistress, she knew everything that was worth knowing, just as her mother, the district nurse, had done. Fortunately for all concerned, she was discreet and looked upon the gleaning of private personal information and influencing most village committees, as a sort of caring public duty; an extension of the parish council, and now it seemed, Church affairs!

Shoving the wedge under the door with her foot, Stella's eyes narrowed in frustration. The last thing she wanted was company but taking a deep calming breath she picked up the kettle. 'Coffee?'

'Tea. Now I'm already late, so let me do the talking. I know it might seem a bit insensitive to talk about Open Gardens Day, in view of recent events.' She nodded towards John's wall. 'However, that is our private grief and we have to put that to one side, there's work to be done. Pity Abby is away, it's most inconvenient. I know she's upset but she needs to be kept busy and there's plenty to do here. This open day is a whole village venture and as we are combining it with local history this time, and as a special favour to me,' she gave a coy smile, 'the vicar, dear Andrew, has allocated the centre spread of "The History of Sennington" booklet, to this very terrace, just our four cottages.' She paused for Stella to get the full impact. 'So now that I've managed to get prime position, we have to find something to put in it. The posters have already been done so even if we wanted to we couldn't have changed the date. The 31st is only three weeks away. Did you see the rough draft, before John.....' Eyes suddenly glossy, she waved a hand and rushed on. 'Good thing they were already printed. I'm getting them distributed round the villages, Josh said he will put one up in the shop and pass more round the town. I've had big posters done and here's one of the small ones. As you can see the charge for entering the gardens plus map and order of touring, comes underneath the title.

OPEN GARDENS DAY CELEBRATION
300 Years of Local History

To read about the history they will have to shell out again for a booklet. Clever, eh? It's a reasonable amount and all for charity. Anyhow, we don't want them traipsing round for nil and gratis, do we? This place is last on the itinerary, so with natural selection, the lazy ones not bothering, we should be spared most of the dross.'

At times, Cynthia's audacity took Stella's breath away but not wanting to prolong the visit she didn't interrupt; an argument would take up precious time when she just needed space to think.

Cynthia was off again. 'So, they either get public transport out of here – if they wait long enough…' She shook her head at the inefficiency of the transport department of the council. 'I've put the number of the bus in for the simple minded who can't look it up at the depot – or…' she took a breath and shuffled her notes, 'they can drive and park up top, along The Avenue, and walk down the track. We've no room for parking. We hardly have room to turn our own cars and I don't want them going round the back and driving across the ford to explore. We don't want the brook access opened up again, do we? Got to maintain some privacy, can't be expected to sell our souls to swell church funds.'

She drummed finger tips as Stella put the cups out. 'And another thing; refreshments. There won't be any,' she followed with greater emphasis, lifting the lid of the tea pot and vigorously stirring the leaves. 'I've said there are to be no picnics. They'll be knocking on the door asking to use the lavatory if we allow refreshments. Anyhow, I don't want them sitting on the lawn with their thermoses, scattering biscuit crumbs and sandwich papers around saying, "Oooh, isn't it lovely," and taking their shoes off and having an afternoon nap.'

Cynthia was prone to exaggeration.

'Anyhow, must be off. Don't forget, top priority, find some something interesting about this terrace. Oh, one more thing. Sometime this week, again as a special favour to me,' her tone softened, 'Andrew has said he will come over and open up the parish records in our little church. Maybe you could help him. You've got the time. Six weeks of it!'

'Actually, I have got a few ideas, already.' Feeling guilty, Stella tried to muster enthusiasm.

'You can tell me later. Oh, and you might take Napoleon for a walk. I wish I could,' she lied. 'All the summer off; perks of the job I suppose. I have no such luxuries, I'm a mere civil servant,' and draining the cup, she left.

While Stella, nerves charged like electric wires and irritated beyond endurance, was using the slow routine of clearing away and washing the cups to help calm down, Cynthia was driving past the vicarage which she planned to be her future marital home.

A gentleman by nature and upbringing, ordained in his youth, the Rev. Andrew had moved swiftly away from the pulpit and out to his chosen field and passion, history in church archives. His research and reputation had gained him access to the Vatican. Not married, widely travelled, with the added attraction of a private income, he was in his fifties, a bit old for Cynthia. Not that that mattered.

'Don't look a gift horse in the mouth,' she muttered. A stroke of luck the old vicar retiring suddenly.

'This stint back in the dog collar' as Andrew laughingly called it, 'is going to be short and, undoubtedly, my last.'

'That's what he thinks.' Cynthia's chin went down. She loved a challenge. She would be an ideal vicar's wife. Not the romantic stuff of course; she wasn't interested in that kind of thing and neither should he be, given his calling, but with his connections and her push, they could have a good working relationship. 'From strength to strength,' she hummed the hymn. Together they could get to the top!

* * * * * * *

Stella had made another pot of tea and, taking it out into the back garden, put the tray on the table in the shade of the pear tree that she and Cynthia shared and sank down on the bench. Time passed. She didn't move. Sitting here was quiet and warm and comfortingly familiar; secure somehow.

The gardens weren't divided, just little paths running down to back gates, yet they each commanded privacy; only John had pottered at will, pulling weeds, tidying, planting vegetables enough for them all. He had been a kind of security blanket, always there, always available and, arms crossed, she bent over as though to ease ache of loss. With no one to talk to, the courage to go over what had happened was slow to return.

'All right,' she said eventually, lifting her head, 'Now, what the hell was that all about?' She spoke in a fierce whisper, needing to hear the words.

'I've had similar experiences all my life and I've always been in charge, able to come back to the present, at will; my will! Not today though. This time it was very different. It was really frightening, and it's not over, it's not cleared. If the laundry man hadn't called at that moment I might have been forced to go on with it. Maybe that would have been a good thing,' she reflected slowly, then, 'Who am I fooling? Thank God he called when he did. I hate to admit that I'm out of my depth but it's true and I really need someone to talk to, someone to advise me.' She sat up, hands clenched. There must be religious connections, or why would monks be involved? More to the point, what happened here to attract special attention from a monastic order? She thought of talking to the vicar, and then backed off. 'Perhaps I'll talk it over with Josh, first,' she cautioned herself. 'Then maybe I'll call Andrew. A bit of guidance from the Church would put my mind at rest, of course. A sort of insurance, a stiffener should it ever happen again.'

Tuesday 6th August

It was barely daybreak when Cynthia woke. Ten minutes later she was in the kitchen, tea poured, pencil and pad at hand, working on the layout for the Commemorative Magazine (in fancy italics) Local History 1663–1963. She had already finished the programme for the Gardens Open Day, an event which she usually organized with her eyes closed! Cynthia scribbled furiously, chewing the end of the pencil as if she were leaving teeth marks for posterity, proof that she, Cynthia Cook, pillar of this community, had been here doing 'good works'. 'Open Day' was always held on the last Saturday in August and this year, (she checked the calendar), would be the last day of the month too. Very neat. Cynthia liked tidy ends. The only fly in the ointment was collating three-hundred years of boring history in time to get it printed. Everyone was talking about it, thinking about it, doing research for it, not noticing that she was the one doing most of the work. This is a prime example of how much Andrew needs a wife, Cynthia thought, as impatience and edginess surfaced like acid bile. Then I can nip these daft schemes in the bud. Andrew's idea had been the easy part; the members of the Women's Institute, all anxious to please the nice-looking new vicar, had enthusiastically accepted his idea of the project to benefit church funds. 'It's left to me to do the donkey work and Abby's not here to do the running around,' she moaned on, hooking a bit of pencil wood from between her teeth.

'On top of that I have to keep the printer on standby, beg traders to pay for advertising they don't want, organize the publicity and worry about deadlines! The problem is we still haven't found anything special on Brook Cottages, so what kudos and thanks am I going to get out of it? Josh is no help. What a brother!

'A shop full of books, ancient and modern, and he's come up with nothing. Wait till he gets here. Oh, damn it, it's Vera's morning for cleaning. I'll have to whisper so she doesn't eavesdrop, and that means he won't take any notice.'

'Come on Napoleon,' Josh snapped. 'A daft bloody name to give a dog.' Not in the best of moods and glad to be out of ear-shot of his sister and her moaning on about this Open Day, he crossed the shallow brook rippling its short way to the derelict mill at Syreford and headed up the steep hills at the back of the terrace.

Stella had called late last night sounding really stressed, making sure he would be over this morning. What was that all about? He had driven very early to miss the traffic but her curtains were still closed and rather than be subject to Cynthia's probing, Napoleon was being taken for an unexpected bout of exercise.

In his early sixties, thick set with dark graying hair, handsome in a comfortable sort of way, Josh attracted people to him; especially younger women though he never seemed aware of it and that too was part of his charm. Now, though, his thoughts were on his second love: golf. This time in the morning the course would be aloof, manicured and pristine; a virgin awaiting the suitors. 'Later, my mistress, have patience,' he grinned.

Not slowing the pace, Josh soon reached the old Drovers' Track along the high ridge where he stood admiring the view. As a young man, he had often scrambled up to the top on summer nights, the silence thick with history and suspense. He imagined how, once the geese or wool-heavy sheep had been sold at market and money stowed in the bag, these solitary men then had to make it home safely, some as far away as Wales. More than a few had lost their lives, plundered and shallow-grave buried, their families hearing no more.

Sometimes bodies had been found, though with no mourners, unidentified and with no coinage to give them a respectable end, they warranted only a pauper's grave in St Andrews' tiny churchyard. A man would have to be soulless not to feel the atmosphere up here.

'Hey,' he said to the dog, 'It's something for the magazine that happened right here above our terrace.

'They came along this track and then carried on to the mill and the sheep dip over there.' He shaded his eyes and looked into the distance. 'The drovers would have had a good night's sleep in the barn and time to tar the feet of the geese before the last long walk or cart ride to Lechlade market or the barge trip to London. What a relief, something to get Cynthia off my back.'

Directly below was the terrace, then across the cow pasture (which Cynthia was now calling a meadow) was St Andrews with its tiny churchyard, separated from the Jacobean Manor it would once have belonged to, by a high stone wall. The manor was for sale. Burying the owner, a recluse for more years than Josh or anyone else could remember, had been the last official duty the old vicar had performed. Josh liked the new chap, they had become friends almost immediately; the same sense of humour helped.

'When I buy a house here, I'll have to find a house keeper,' he had nudged Josh. 'Or I might even find myself a wife, someone bright and warm, a lady with a sense of style; any ideas?'

'I can't say anyone springs to mind in this catchment area, Andrew.' The 'certainly not my sister' went unsaid.

Andrew had started off on the wrong foot in the parish. Thrown into the role unexpectedly and hardly knowing the area, the new man had gladly accepted Cynthia's guidance, thinking that her interest was in parish affairs. Almost right. Cynthia Cook was Parish Affairs! Soon after they had met him, Josh had asked Stella why a guy so well set up wasn't married.

The answer surprised him, then on reflection he realized the truth of it; Andrew was at heart a shy and very modest man. The nature of his work would have restricted his social circles and there wasn't much of a social life or many females in dusty old church vaults.

The Labrador wandered back, flopped down and began to snore softly as Josh relaxed on the grass and looked down at John's empty cottage. Abby had inherited and would obviously sell it. So, strangers would be coming in. That would take some getting used to. Stella had been the last to arrive; he could see her now, an attractive and very mature teenager, moving in with her aunt to finish her education at the prestigious Cheltenham Ladies' College. They had both been aware of it, an instant and mutual attraction, but her next few years were mapped out and he was carving a career and enjoying a very active social life, so he had kept things light. Then came the chaos of the war and he was away for years. All bad timing; life, you couldn't regulate it. So, over the years he had become instead her close friend, confidant and lover. She would never marry. That young Canadian soldier stationed locally, had been her first love and when his plane crashed, she had never considered anyone else. 'And she never will,' Josh thought ruefully, 'but perhaps after all these years the arrangement suits us both.' His twist of a smile was philosophical.

The early sun was picking out the back garden of the so-called New Houses along The Avenue just above the hamlet; pre-war ribbon development, white walls, pan-tiled roofs, impeccably mowed lawns hidden behind high laurel hedges, all so out of keeping with the area. On the plus side, the tarmac road had been upgraded for the bus, and a street lamp put near the top of the gully, so some good had come of it. Checking his watch he lay back, linked fingers with palms outward and laid them across his eyes.

Only eight o'clock. I can't go down yet, Cynthia will still be there. That cottage is half mine yet I feel like an interloper and he thought longingly of his flat, of good music, of time to read and a place to make leisurely love when Stella came over. 'I am a normal bloke with a regular appetite and sleeping with Stella at her cottage, with a disapproving sister next door isn't exactly conducive to relaxation,' he muttered, drifting into a light sleep.

Napoleon, whimpering and flicking his golden paws, probably dreaming of chasing rabbits as he had in his younger days woke as Stella's call broke their reverie.

'Morning, darling. Thanks for coming over. I saw you leave,' she said a little breathlessly. 'Had to sneak up. Cynthia is on the war path this morning, goodness knows why.'

Josh nodded and smiled a welcome, showing his pleasure, taking in at a glance the softly tanned limbs and the curve of her breasts under the fine cotton shirt; feeling the stirrings, his usual reaction.

'It sounded urgent. What's happened?' he asked.

With a serious expression, she sat down, leaned over to kiss him then, elbows on knees and needing no further prompting, began to tell him of the unnerving flash-backs she had experienced. 'I'll come right to the point. Josh, you know that from time to time I have what I call 'out-of-body journeys' – mostly when I'm asleep or meditating,' she began.

'Yeeeeees…' He waited.

'Oh, I know it's never happened to you, though it's quite common and well documented. It's just that people who don't recognize the difference assume it was a vivid dream. Well, the point is, I'm used to them and it's usually a joy, probably because I'm in control of the situation and I can come back to my body, in an instant.' There was a long pause. 'Not this time though,' she sounded far away as though reliving something. 'That's not the way it was yesterday and that's why I called you, Josh. I want to tell you all about it and have your opinion – but don't interrupt.'

'Do I ever?' He feigned injured feelings then listened as she unburdened herself.

'It was like watching a frightening film and actually being ensnared in it. I was reliving the hellish happenings from another time, and I was damned frightened,' her voice broke, then she steadied herself. 'So now, I'm absolutely sure that in the past, something dreadful happened, down there,' she pointed to their cottages below. And I've been asking myself what. Josh, this is really confusing me because if I'm right, I then have to ask what it has to do with me. If it's history, it's gone. Why involve me or even present it to me?'

He was thoughtful for a few minutes then shrugged. 'At a guess, it's because you are clairvoyant, but it's the isolation of this place that feeds it.' His voice changed to a groan. 'I never noticed when I lived here. Now though, living in Stratford-on-Avon with its culture of theatre-going, boating on the river, visitors from all over the world, well, I find the hamlet claustrophobic. So, my darling, what you need, what *we* need is a break – a holiday in fact.'

'We,' she emphasized the plural, 'can't go anywhere until Cynthia has something for that centre spread.'

'You're right,' he agreed reluctantly. 'I've thought of something. It won't be enough to pacify her though it might get you off the hook for a while. She's really on edge, isn't she? Bashing cushions as soon as I move, throwing my coffee cup in to the sink before I had finished, and poor old Napoleon's not allowed over the threshold.'

'That's understandable,' she said. 'One rub against the couch and you could stuff a cushion with the dog hairs.' She managed a smile and stood up. 'Let's go. I'll make coffee.'

'OK, but I'm not staying long. Without Abby to take her orders, my sister thinks I'm next in line. By the way, that's not the only reason I'm anxious for us to get away.'

His voice had dropped. 'We need time together, Stella.' He held up a hand to silence another protest. 'First, let's get your worry into perspective. Darling, I'm not dismissing what happened to you because you've been right too many times about some amazing things. This is different though and it's really got to you, hasn't it?'

She nodded. 'Josh, was there ever a fire in our terrace?'

'Fire? You mean one that burned the place down? Not in the present building, not that I know of, there's no record of it. Fire could have destroyed the previous cottage I suppose; sparks from open fire on a dry thatch.' He carried on strolling down the hill side. 'It was a common occurrence until the Chimney Law was passed, after Wood Street and High Street in Stratford-on-Avon were burned to the ground. That was in Shakespeare's time.' When he turned she was still several paces back, one hand on her throat, face tight with shock. He came back and she gripped his arm.

'Josh, what cottage, what are you talking about? Tell me, please tell me.'

'Estelle!' he used her full name sharply and she stopped. 'Take it easy.' He was surprised by her intensity but knew from experience that telling her to calm down would only increase her irritation. 'Let's sit for a moment.' He pulled her towards a grassy hollow. 'You're always doing yoga, so use it now and calm down. Please!'

'All right, all right.' Leaning back on elbows, face up to the whitish cloudless August sky, she closed her eyes and began to regulate her breathing. 'OK I'm listening. Now tell me,' she said eventually.

Josh was smiling, feasting his eyes and imagination on her.

'There's nothing earth-shattering to tell. Our terrace, once one long house and built, I would think, in the early sixteen hundreds, was sited over the foundations of a small cottage. It's the history of this place and I assumed you knew.

'When it was divided, the hearthstone, fireplace and the built-in bread oven from that original dwelling were left in Abby's wall, the one that divides her house from John's. For some reason lost in time, whoever built our terrace actually designed the place around them and they are still there, in situ. So, God only knows what stories they could tell. Get more information about that for the centre page of the magazine and Cynthia will be all over you like Napoleon's dog hairs. Ah, there is another interesting thing. I would think that whoever lived there originally must have made and sold bread. You see, that oven is bigger than most cottages would have had at that time, and it would have needed a lot of wood to get it up to heat. Being by the ford, they would have been in the right spot for passing trade; a little cottage industry serving travellers who would rest here before crossing the water to continue their journeys.'

'Yes, of course.' She opened her eyes. 'Even though I didn't recognize anything, the place felt familiar. That's where I was, by the ford at the bottom of our garden. It was densely wooded and that's why I didn't realize it. Now it's making sense. It must have been the old cottage and the bread oven that I saw. Why was it burned?' she frowned. 'And why did the monks think of it as an evil place and why, more importantly, was I being directed to witness it?'

The questions were left in the air and they didn't talk for a while, uncomfortable possibilities hovering on the horizon.

'If something really bad did happen,' she went on, 'there must be a record of it. It would surely have come to the eyes of the law or the Church?'

'Knowing where to look and how to gain access to records, private and church, that's the difficulty,' Josh replied. 'And yes, Andrew would be your best bet.' He brightened at the prospect of handing the problem over. 'Monks, monasteries, church history, all that stuff is right up his street.'

'I've thought of that but what would I say? "Hi Andrew, I think I'm tuning into life here in the 17th century?" Come on Josh, he would think I've lost my marbles!'

'You might be right.' He scratched his chin. 'He doesn't know you yet; whilst I, on the other hand, am used to you coming off the wall with daft ideas. I'll tell you what I'll do,' he continued, warding off a thump, 'after lunch we'll go back to the shop and I'll help you find any books that might hold a clue. You can bring them back and read them at your leisure. I was going to play golf but I'll cancel it. See how I look after you?' He gave an exaggerated sigh.

'Give up your game of golf? That's an offer I can't refuse.' She smiled and he looked relieved.

'Is that all you can't refuse?' He lowered his voice, nuzzling her neck and placed an enquiring hand on her thigh. 'You're all wound up Stella, you need to switch off and we haven't been together for over a week, have we?' And Stella lay back and stretched herself out in the sunshine, glad of the comfort, glad of the distraction when he finally eased himself on to her.

Wednesday 7th August

Now the light was fading and for Stella, most of the day had been a waiting game. She could have used the time, caught up with things, gardening for instance, but she couldn't settle or couldn't apply herself. She and Josh had arranged to meet the vicar over at St Andrews, though Friday was the earliest he could make it.

Concerned that she might forget some aspect, she had already typed a detailed account of the happenings in the cottage – but had she captured the intensity? She hadn't imagined it, yet even as she wrote the words, like reading a book for the third time, the power of the drama was fast fading. By Friday it might read as though she had been dreaming. 'Perhaps I'm over-reacting. Perhaps I should wait and see…. Oh, damn it,' she exploded. 'How can I hope to convince him of its importance, when even I am losing conviction?'

Cynthia had called in earlier expecting some positive input for the magazine and, unable to sleep, Stella had spent the early hours typing all the information Josh had given her about the Drovers' Track. Although her own gleanings didn't amount to much more, by combining the two, she had enough written to pacify Cynthia, at least for the time-being.

"The Manor of Sennington was a gift from Elizabeth 1st in 1590. Everyone in this area would have been economically involved with the Manor in some way or other, so it stands to reason that even after her death, people in this hamlet would have remained Royalist in sympathies; through the Civil War, the battle of Worcester, all in the 17th century; 300 years of local history."

Cynthia was nodding in all the wrong places. Nodding was a habit that surfaced when she was getting impatient or if she was over-anxious to agree with someone important, particularly Andrew.

'This is all very interesting though you're still missing the point, Stella dear,' she said, looking at the ceiling. 'What does it do for us, for Brook Cottages? Find something important about us. Give that snooty lot up there in The Avenue something to think about.'

Stella soldiered on: 'OK *The Ford* here is marked bold. On old maps, it was important as the shallowest point to cross for a couple of miles either way, even when it was flooding in winter. So geographically we have the Manor House on this side, Witetune House on the other and Sudeley Castle little more than a morning's horse ride away. It doesn't take a lot of imagination to realize how uniquely situated we were. This was a resting place for everyone, from scruffy strolling players from Stratford-on-Avon, here to perform to crowds on market day, to the landed Gentry crossing the country on business. Now, what would people have done while they rest? Eat, drink and – gossip.'

Gossip! Cynthia had stopped nodding.

'With the political intrigue of the time, the owners of Sennington Manor and Witetune House would have been fools not to have laid on simple refreshment to encourage these people to rest longer; cheese, fresh bread baked in that big oven in Abby's cottage, and homemade beer. Plenty of it to loosen tongues, and there would surely have been spies posing as travellers, encouraging confidences and reporting back to the Lord of The Manor; ours, here.' A sudden ripple of fear and Stella stopped abruptly, remembering the charred skeleton of a burned down cottage, but Cynthia, inspired by success, wasn't sensitive to her sudden change of mood.

'Good work Stella,' Cynthia's praise was a relief. 'Keep digging along those lines, it's getting a bit exciting.

'Now, Open Day. Let me bring you up to date. We, Andrew and I, that is, are quietly confident of getting the manor grounds opened for the visitors. There should be no objection because the sale hasn't been finalized yet. They can tour the garden then perhaps go through the gate into the churchyard and take a peep into our own dear little St. Andrews. It is one of the smallest churches in England, did you know? I read that in the Official Guide Book. It's in black and white so must be true.'

'You hypocrite,' Stella thought, biting her lip. 'Our own dear little church!' No one would believe that Cynthia rarely put a foot inside these days. The one in the village attracting the local big-wigs was more her style now. She had her teeth into the vicar, so evening service there was priority.

'It's been a full time job I can tell you,' Cynthia sucked her breath. 'Oh, I wish the so-called garden lovers would just send a donation and not bother coming,' and she left without a goodbye.

Cynthia was fast going off this history project and, apart from the vicar, didn't care who knew it.

With a sigh, weary of it all but not ready for an empty bed, Stella went up to the attic and pushed the window wide; woodbine and lavender wafting intoxicating scents over the window-sill as she settled down in the high-backed chair – then suddenly it was back again, that strange feeling.... The clock ticked. Shadows played fleeting tricks across her tired face as, turning away from the rising moon's critical search, Stella entered that state between sleep and awareness where, in some corner of the subconscious mind, the search for answers never ends. Now only the shadows moved, shrinking back into corners as the moon spread distorted light through old glass and reached across the antique table, thick-sliced from the heart of some ancient oak, glossy with beeswax and the toil of forgotten hands.

Hardly being aware of the change, Stella found herself sliding out of her physical body once again; drifting a few feet above the ground, along streams, across pasture with fat, contented cattle and fields heavy with grain. It was like watching a film and sometimes completely furnished rooms or huge, intricately-carved buildings would be presented.

Other people's memory pictures, she assumed, picked up in their passing, rather like small meteorites going out into the corridors of silent outer space. Tonight was a little different in that everything was exceptionally sharp in outline. A big purple cloud gathering over hills to the west looked threatening – and time had moved backwards...

The village on market day! Stella recognised the picturesque Alms Houses. The rough-beamed cottages with over-hanging gables looked new and prosperous but the people had more on their minds as they went about their business, shoving and bartering, wiping away sweat and the buzzing flies crawling on the chunks of meat and dead-eyed rabbits. Drought was making people irritable and the summer old before it had run its time. The talk was of the plague, spreading out again from London, and of two sisters who mixed herb cures and lived in the hollow down by the ford. Stella moved closer to the women gossiping around the well, as the subject expanded:

" *'Tis a great comfort to know they have the gift of healing. I met the little one, Hannah, out gathering herbs for her sister Rachel. She gave me a bunch, said they cured bleeding. I had no bleeding, but then the next day I lost the child! Bless Heaven, thanks be to God I had those herbs or I might have died too.*"

The woman was grateful – until a shadow voice whispered slyly.

"*So ask yourself, was it the girl who started the bleed? They say there's no smoke without fire....*"

And so Stella witnessed the start of the poison, the wickedest of insinuations.

Anyone could spread the vilest of lies and at least part of it would be accepted as fact. It was a rumour, a creeping apprehension that was to stretch out, spreading its malignant tendrils wide as it grew in distance and strength.

Speculation now rolled like grey smoke from the empowered gossips' slandering mouths, and the sisters were the target. They were only daughters of the miller, yet the young girl was learning to read and write like her sister. Why did a wood-child need such things? What did she read? Spells? They joked, but with malice. And she was so different. There was no hiding the flame hair, the pale skin and that narrow nose. Where does that come from? Was she sired by one of the passing Gentry? They laughed raucously then stopped, eyes narrowing; Or was she what some suspected – a changeling? Even Master Lawrence of the Manor had been heard to call Hannah, his "*Little Witch of the Woods.*"

Such sayings spread fast on market day...

For no apparent reason, Stella was suddenly presented with a mental picture: a young man on horseback, finely dressed, and a young girl with red hair and a fine pale skin looking up at him; adoration in her eyes, kind amusement in his…

Time was moving on and Stella's attention was redirected: Hot days and black nights flashed across the fields, people gathering on the Nut Walk; a dirt track that ran down to the manor from a settlement of crude cottages on the hill, made from wattle and daub.

'There's no record of this place,' Stella registered.

Aggressive gesturing, harsh whispers, the huddled group gathering tight, suddenly split to give hat-tipping subservience to the fresh-faced parson as he strode past.

"*Good day to you Parson. We were talking about the young wenches who live down the gully there in the thatch, by the ford. Rachel Myer, and that young Hannah. They're daughters of the miller, just along the stream at Syreford, you know. Don't mix much, do they? Too good for the likes of us, with their reading and writing.*" They laughed with false modesty. "*Suppose you've met them – in your official capacity like?*"

"*Yes I know of them.*" The young man, new to the isolated hamlet and the narrowness of country life, nodded and walked swiftly on, yet his agreement was enough to strengthen their prejudice.

Confirmation! The Parson already had his eye on them. He knew where evil could lurk. Forewarned was to be forearmed – and so the cruel accusations spread, fuelled by an innocent remark.

Was it at this point, Stella wondered later, that she had become privy to their thoughts and aware, and alarmed, at the hardening of their attitudes? Yes indeed, the Parson did have his eye on the girl, though he wouldn't tell them more. He wouldn't let them know that he often sought Rachel's company and that her sharp questionings delighted, and surprised him. They wouldn't understand that the freshness of spirit, the stimulation of an enquiring, intelligent mind from a lovely young woman, had kindled his longings. What did they know of respectful and restrained feelings? How could they know of the dreariness he experienced serving them, feeding them, trying to enlighten their uneducated minds? He had few to relate to here, no one and nothing to fill his dark lonely hours, until he met Rachel. Then, joy, relief from the tedium. In the last few months, delightful prospects had kept his sanity as he ministered to the drudgery of everyday life. One day he might have a wife to share his walks and his bed and his hopes – and while he dreamed, the energy of darkness grew strong.

Now, gripped by unease, farmers abed pulled fat wives closer when the dogs howled across the moon; not that they were frightened – but no one was quite sure what was happening. Stealthily, rumours of witchcraft grew wings as black nights and unvoiced terrors nibbled at their guts.

Then two children died, followed close by a labourer.

Then it came – *Plague!*

Plague struck the village and moved out into the hamlet. Now, thinking minds that had dismissed the hand of sorcery gave way in quiet dismay to a malignant growth of fear that night intensified. Hands reached across the crib as comfort trembled with the vice-like grip of a growing alarm as rumour was accepted as stark fact: People were dying and there could be two witches alive in their midst!

With opposition crushed, fear, like a vengeful demon, laid its thick cloak on receptive minds and from the settlement above the Manor there came a crescendo of panic-driven rallying shouts:

"*Stop the evil. Kill the sisters, kill the witches!*"

'No, no!' Stella's hands banged flat palms on to the little oak table. 'Stop, for God's sake. I can't control it,' she heard herself shout, then, 'What is going on? Did I make that up? Damn it, I'm so tired I can't think straight – and I don't want to think. I just want my bed and deep uninterrupted sleep.'

Pushing the attic window wide, she leaned on the sill, gulped in the fragrant air of the night. An owl hooted, white-faced flowers flirted with pale dancing moths and everything was as tranquil as it had been. Only disinterested time and the all-observant moon had moved on, but what she had witnessed had surely been more than a dream, more than co-incidence. Now there was no doubt, she had to talk to Andrew.

Sleep was out of the question until she had recorded every last detail while it was still fresh in her mind – though it was several minutes before Stella, ears nervously pricked, one hand on the stair rail, one foot pointed as though ready to descend, felt inclined to break the puzzling, trance-like pose. This sense of being pulled back in time, was it empathy with someone who had once lived here; stood here and waited on these stairs, listening?

Thursday 8th August

Too early to go to work, Cynthia Cook walked upstairs deep in thought, automatically checking the seams on the new floral wall paper in case Bertie hadn't done a good job, and picking up microscopic pieces of fluff from the landing carpet. 'Bits, bits, bits, I wish I hadn't chosen this plain stuff,' she grumbled. 'I'll have to watch Vera, it's never vacuumed to my satisfaction; another irritation. Why don't people do a job properly? I do.'

Strolling into the back bedroom she spotted Stella closing the garage door and leaning straight-armed on the window ledge, Cynthia peered through the net curtain, careful not to move it.

'So what's she up to now? Wasting time, that's what. Andrew's coming over on Friday. So she could be going through those books that Josh lent her. Oh, would you believe it, I think she's talking to the flowers!' Her voice shot up an octave then dropped to a confiding whisper. 'Must be saying something stupid if you need to be that close. Oh my; now it's leaf-stroking time.'

It was a running commentary the BBC would have been proud of. 'What's she doing, praying for their eternal souls, or apologising, before she pulls them to bits and bashes them into paste for the feeble-minded to swallow? Herbal medicines, my foot. Her kitchen shelves are full of junk; dried leaves, rose hips, lavender, bits of old, probably poisonous, mushrooms. I think it's a health hazard. Why doesn't she chuck it all out and get some hygienic wipe-down Formica units like mine? I could report her if I were the interfering type. I blame it all on that meditating. Inactivity, it's bad for the brain.'

Cynthia was on the landing when she caught sight of her face; tight-lipped and frowning. She didn't move, making herself look at the miserable reflection and wondering why.

Why was she dissatisfied, why was she being so critical about dear Stella and why was she feeling irritated with almost everyone?

'It's partly because I'm feeling uneasy, as if there's something I should know,' she said, and with a shake of the dark glossy hair, left for work.

Stella wandered to the end of the path to check on Abby's cottage and stood for a few moments enjoying the shade of the huge willow tree that hid the side door; remembering Uncle John's funeral and wondering how Abby was faring in Devon. Everyone had crowded back to Abby's cottage where Cynthia had arranged for refreshments. Cynthia had also arranged the funeral service, cars, flowers, dealt with all the paper work and knew just whom to contact. This was Cynthia at her best; she came in to her own, fully occupied, organizing things that needed an efficient guiding hand, and she had carried it out most splendidly. The cottage was small, the vicar spoke in turn to everyone, and a smiling Cynthia had shadowed him so closely they could have been joined at the hip!

Desperate for a few minutes' break from voices droning and drilling through her temples, Stella had slipped, unnoticed, down the back garden and through the little gate to find some peace by the brook where the air was always cool under the weeping willows.

Poor Abby, barely five feet tall, had been lost to sight behind a flank of backs. Pale at the best of times, she had been staring unseeing through the open window, eyes glossy with tears that did not spill, small hands folded around a mug of coffee as if to warm them. She looked so vulnerable, her plump body squeezed into a formal black frock, fair fuzzy hair crammed under a little black hat, both borrowed. They made her look like a lost child in grown-ups' cast-offs. Abby wasn't good at social chit-chat at the best of times and the strain of meeting all those people was painfully clear to anyone who knew her well. Cynthia's habit of taking charge, and telling her what to do was security to Abby.

She needed it and always had. Her first and only job as shared secretary to the local infants and junior school suited her need for quiet routine.

It was the bewilderment on her face that had prompted Stella to take Abby's only relative aside, a distant cousin, and make the suggestion: Abby needed a break. So, as the last mourners left, Abby's protests had been firmly overridden, a few things packed hastily into a bag and she was bustled out into the car. 'We will see you at the end of the month. There's no need to come back before term starts,' Stella called as they pulled away. Abby, who never went away even for a day, was now sleeping in a strange bed somewhere in Devon. And I sent her packing, Stella cringed. Did I do the right thing? Everything had happened so fast...

Cynthia had driven off to work, already planning her day. The Women's Institute committee was meeting at lunch time, to hand in any more historical snippets. Andrew had not wanted to attend, insisting he trusted her judgement, but he wasn't getting out of this one so easily. Cynthia intended to keep him closely involved and he had finally agreed to spare her ten minutes after the meeting, to discuss the layout of the stalls on the vicarage lawn, all ready for the big day. Attention to detail was the key to a smooth running operation, military precision. He could have sounded more enthusiastic about it. She had managed to get another appointment in his diary for a working lunch at her cottage on Sunday, by saying that Josh and Stella had already agreed. 'OK, if it's just a light snack,' he had conceded,

Light snack, on a Sunday? She already had the food in and the menu planned. The vicar coming to Sunday lunch would give the women on the committee something to talk about. 'Not long now and we will be going back to the vicarage together.' She gave a self-satisfied smile. The Reverend and Mrs Andrews, and it wouldn't be in that flashy Jaguar either.

He had given her a lift in it with the top down, and her hair had been all over the place. They would have something with a bit more dignity. She fancied a Bentley and he could well afford it. The move couldn't come quickly enough for Cynthia who was getting increasingly frustrated. She was used to getting things done fast, getting the wheels in motion and Andrew hadn't made a move yet; nothing that could be the start of a more personal relationship. She manoeuvred things so that they spent a lot of time alone but he hadn't held her hand or asked her to tea. She didn't have much experience in this sort of thing, so being efficient and showing how well they worked together seemed the best way forward, especially given his mature years. He probably didn't want to rush things because of the age difference, so what he needed was a shove in the right direction, and Cynthia was getting ready to give it.

Friday 9th August

Josh and Stella found the vicar, delighted to be free of the tedium of parish duties, waiting impatiently for them by the gate to the churchyard. 'I can't tell you how much I'm looking forward to this.' They shook hands and he walked ahead. 'We've records here I've barely glanced at and think of this, I'm taking an afternoon off to indulge my hobby,' he enthused while unlocking the church and standing aside. 'Incidentally Stella, if we're going to work together please call me Andrew, everyone does. I'm only a stand-in, and this reverend stuff is a bit of a mouthful. I don't want to be likened to the Saint himself; too much to live up to.'

'Some Saint!' Stella eyed his fine cashmere jumper and the expensively cut trousers. Yet he was so… she searched for the word; understated.

Inside, the church was surprisingly small; a dozen short pews each side of the centre aisle, with a few more in the arms of the cruciform. A thin stiletto of sun through a high narrow window highlighted fine dust particles drifting lazily around the beams, as though the opening of the door had disturbed a long, long slumber. Once closed, all was hushed again, apart from the twitter of a few birds outside on the stone sills. A slight dank smell crawled a shiver up Stella's arms as she stopped at the altar. 'Remember the Harvest Festivals when we were children, Josh?' then, turning to Andrew, 'The whole church would be crammed with people and autumn produce. Money and food were in short supply until well into the fifties yet there was an offering from every garden or kitchen and no one in need went without. There was a generosity in the giving and no pride was lost in the receiving. Sorry, no offence intended but now we have to share a vicar.'

'It comes down to economics in the end; the collection plate,' Andrew said philosophically, then laughed aloud. 'Talking of cash flow, did you know that Chancels were originally built for priests who got paid for praying for the souls of the rich who didn't have the time or the inclination to do it for themselves? It was a thriving business, stopped when the priests were found to be spending the money on loose living. Though, there's no reason why Men of the Cloth shouldn't appreciate a little luxury,' he added, savouring the thought of an evening run in the navy blue E-type Jaguar Coupe he had recently taken delivery of, the smell of new leather briefly replacing that of the musty church. He was glad of a private income but would have liked some female company.

A pity Stella was spoken for...

'Time to work.' Josh propelled Stella on towards the cramped vestry; a few well-worn surplices on hooks, a long choir pew against the side wall, a narrow oak table under the window piled with box files, a few books and a couple of dog-eared registers that Andrew had already spread out ready for their inspection.

'I came early and, before we start, I think you have something you want to discuss?' His voice rose to a question and pushing the books to one side, he sat down, looking at Stella. 'The little you told me on the 'phone was very interesting, though it wasn't like you to sound anxious. Not like you at all.'

He didn't mention the informative call from Josh that morning. It wasn't easy for her. She had only ever confided in Josh and opening up to Andrew required a big leap of trust. Where to start, how far back? Premonitions, or that she had always been aware of another dimension? They did not interrupt until, holding out an envelope containing her typed notes, she finally told Andrew of the unnerving development of the last few days. 'Perhaps you can find some connection, some reason for this dramatic surfacing of an old energy. It's eluding me.' Her voice was pleading.

'So, have you always been spiritual, clairvoyant?' Andrew asked softly, carefully monitoring her reaction as she nodded.

'It's what came from living with your batty old aunt for years,' Josh cut in, taking a step back out of her reach.

'My aunt had the gift of healing and she was also a respected clairvoyant,' she said indignantly. 'A lot of people in this area used to consult her and they wouldn't have done that if she had been batty; the word would soon have got around.'

'All right, I'm sorry. Actually, Andrew, she was the one who taught Stella to use divining rods to locate water, and she can find things that are lost.'

'Don't look so uncomfortable, Stella.' Andrew laughed at the penetrating glare she was giving Josh. 'I've seen rods used to find water in Africa and in the desert. I know they work. I just don't know how. An interesting and perhaps relevant story is that after the war, a group of us who had the appropriate training had ex-service men referred to us for help; men who were having difficulty coming to terms with traumatic experiences. We found that by putting them into a deep state of relaxation they were often able to revisit and deal with situations they had mostly blanked out. It is fear of the 'unknown' that frightens most people, it's the anticipation. Procrastination makes it worse. However,' Andrew shook his head slowly, 'an interesting side effect was that several of these veterans talked of things that were not of this period in time. They spoke in dialects hard to understand and one, a different language. Strangely, they did not recall these experiences when they woke. Not so unbelievable if we accept what is written in the Bible, that there is life after this one. If that's the case – what about a life before this one and one before that? So, bring it on. You might find that I am surprisingly open-minded.'

She was encouraged by his frankness but still hesitant. 'Andrew, please understand that although I come to this church, I'm not religious. I'm more – spiritual. I don't think that God is religious; not Catholic or Protestant, Muslim or Buddhist or any other denomination. I think it doesn't matter to Jesus, whether you think of him as the Son of God, or a prophet, or just a wise man. In my opinion, he didn't go through what he went through to start a fan club or another religion. What he said was common sense, and I try to live it. Do unto others as I would have them do unto me. That's the basis of it really. Having this awareness of, and sometimes interaction with, another dimension is just part of my life and I have always been comfortable with it – until now.

'Now… something, …the dynamics seem to have changed and for my own peace of mind, I need to know why. After all these years,

I'm actually nervous about letting go or what might happen next.'
She ploughed on. 'You see, I know how that child felt when she was
in the bread oven. I know because – because I felt that I was encased,
trapped in that small body.'

'You didn't tell me that!' Josh exploded.

'Hang on,' Andrew cautioned. 'No need to get alarmed. Stella,
nothing more has happened since Wednesday, has it?'

'No – it's as though everything is on hold, waiting. What for and
why me, I don't know. I'm interested but not obsessed by this history
project.'

'Who knows?' he said. 'You being a clairvoyant, receptive to
collective thought; it must come into the equation.' It was the only
link he could come up with. 'Everyone's talking about, preoccupied
with, concentrating on, three hundred years of history that's got to
be typed up, ready for the printers. They won't wait. On a lighter
note, if nothing untoward has happened since Wednesday, perhaps
it's over.'

'Following that train of thought, if everything is energy, and no
doubt Science will one day say that it is, then our thoughts, our focus
of attention must be energy too. Your extra-sensory ability could be
attracting other people's focus of attention, creating a kind of entrain-
ment, everything joining to and affected by, the strongest energy.'

'It can happen,' Josh agreed. 'Some people can walk into a room
and drain everyone's enthusiasm without saying a word,' he finished,
thinking of his sister's present mood. 'Now look, I know we shouldn't
rush this but on a practical note, time is money and I'm short-staffed
at the shop. If we are going to get any work done, we have to press
on.' Andrew opened a file and by the time they had each selected a
few items for themselves, he was already sorting through packs of
hand-written papers. There were several bundles of them, large
rough-edged sheets of thick paper and parchment held together by
tape though holes punched along the top. Some were four and five
hundred years old and in amazing condition. Trying to understand
them was another matter and mostly beyond the scope of Stella or
Josh. The elaborate styles, whirls and hoops, the spelling and words

of the period made them almost illegible to the untrained. Fortunately Andrew had the eye of experience and enthusiasm. 'This parochial register is quite straightforward and dates back to 1588.' He showed it to them.

Ye register booke of all weddings, buryings and christenings which have been in ye parish of Sennygton, from ye yeare of our Lord one thousand fyve hundred and eighty eight. A.D.1588.

'I've already taken a quick look through it and there was nothing of particular interest to us, no mention of Brook Cottage, so to save us being holed up here for weeks, I've spread the net a bit wider. I suggest we start at 1600 onwards,' he said, squatting on the table. 'Not getting much are we?' he said over an hour later. 'Let's trust something really riveting turns up soon to put your place on the map or Cynthia will be very disappointed, and I don't want to be on the receiving end.'

'Hey, just listen to this,' Josh called. 'It will be interesting enough if we need to fill space in the magazine. Notice the subtle change in spelling from Sennygton, with a 'y' in 1588, to Sennington, as we spell it today, by 1634.'

"Reverend S.W. Symonds. Sennington 1634. In the end of January did fall the greatest snowe that was ever seen in the memory of man and it was soe extreme colde violent and tempestuous that some coming back from market were smothered and starved to death. Snowe lay until August deep in the quarry at Brockhampton."

'Good, and here's another,' Stella called out, excitement mounting. 'It's a list of Parsons from 1531 to 1879 and the time they served.' She studied the paper intently. 'That's a bit odd. There's a gap from 1623 to 1634, the time when Rev. Symonds wrote that weather report. I wonder what happened.'

'Hmm. it had to be something pretty drastic to leave a gap that wide.' Andrew thought for a moment, 'Could have been an outbreak of plague, common in those days. If the population was dropping like ninepins, who cared about keeping records that probably no one would survive to read. Priorities. You can tell a lot by the gaps in these lists and – hang on, there's something I marked this morning that ties in with that period. It wasn't written until the eighteenth century but it caught my eye,' Andrew's voice trailed as he reached for a book from the cupboard, opened it at a marked page, put his foot on the bench and, book in hand, began to read.

"It is said that there once stood a small village on the high ridge known as "Old Sennington" about half a mile to the north west of and above the present church of St. Andrews. The path up to it, known as 'Church Walk or Nut Walk', was between two rows of hazel trees that grow to this present day. As it was not a prosperous settlement, comparatively unimportant and remote from the big villages around, a brick or stone building would have been unlikely. However, remains of solid foundations can still be traced over the high ground during summer drought."

'That fits with what you say you saw, Stella,' Josh said, punching a palm with his fist. 'A village housing the peasant labour was just above the manor house. Church Walk is the track opposite the manor, just up the hill, and there are still hazels growing in the hedges there. I wonder how long a hazel lives? They could be offshoots from the original; a direct line back. Nice thought, isn't it? It could of course, all be coincidence.'

'I don't believe in this many coincidences,' said Andrew, shaking his head. 'As unlikely as it seems, Stella's attention could be being directed so that we look for something, some evidence – though evidence of what?'

'I wonder why they abandoned the hill, Andrew?' Josh came back.

'Well, perhaps it was plague as Stella suspects, and the survivors came off the hills and down here, to what used to be referred to as The Bottom, to be near flowing water.' Andrew stood for a moment in thoughtful silence, then, 'If this coincides with the break in the records perhaps the clergy were wiped out even as they came to officiate over the dead. And, if you think it through, it's more than likely that only young and inexperienced clergy, with few social connections, would have ended up ministering to a small and scattered population like this. There was no worthwhile money to be made here. This kind of area would have been a calling for the truly dedicated, not just a job for the youngest son of the titled gentry, a Lord's son for instance. Younger sons without a chance of inheritance yet armed with an education would look for a respectable living with a good stipend. They would have had their eyes on richer pickings, namely Sudeley Castle and the big houses around the area. Rich land-owners would not have sought guidance for their eternal salvation from ordained ministers unless they were high up the church ladder, I would hazard a guess. All a question of politics, keeping in with the influential, who could pull a few strings when you died.' His laugh was ironic.

'So, how would a young Parson have managed in a drop-dead crisis?'

'God only knows, Josh,' Andrew frowned. 'Some good did come out of it. The plague hit so hard that the clergy couldn't cope and the Bishop gave an order: Laymen, men who were involved in running the church and were conversant with the Bible and the way it was taught, but had little or no Latin, could hear confessions of the dying and give absolution from sin, in English. Bibles and prayer books written in English became generally available and that move had amazing repercussions. It liberated the common man from the confines of the Latin text and from words he had never understood. Suddenly, anyone who could read could understand what he had been responding to, parrot fashion, all of his life. From then on people started to interpret the teachings for themselves and not accept unquestioningly the dictates of the church. They realised that words thundered from the pulpit weren't necessarily direct from God, and human nature being what it was, they could be threatened with eternal damnation by a preacher who had a vested interest in manipulating them. Remember what I said about the chancel and monks spending the money on pleasures of the flesh.'

Josh looked doubtful. 'I know they were powerful yet even a seasoned veteran would have had difficulty keeping sway over a congregation being wiped out before his eyes.'

'With such odds stacked against them, I'm sure you're right. So much was expected of them, so much expected of ordinary chaps like me who started out with high ideals, just wanting to help people lead happier lives. Oh, the optimism of youth! Things haven't changed. I'm glad I've taken a back seat.'

Getting anxious about the time, they worked on steadily for little reward, as only insignificant and mostly unconnected scraps of information came to light. Josh mumbled, 'I've really got to go' .

'So have I,' Andrew seconded, carrying on until Josh spoke again.

'Hang on, I think I've found something important,' he said slowly. 'It's a deed of some sort tied to an itemised bill. The date's right though the writing's difficult. Fancy having a go?'

Andrew took it and, standing close to the window, peered intently at the faded ink. When he did begin, it was with some hesitation. 'Well this is interesting. It won't be word for word but here's the gist of it.'

"On land in Sennington, situated in the Bottom, sided to the ford at Lower Brook, once the home of Rachel and Hannah Myer and owned by Lawrence Roberts, Gent., of the Manor in Sennington, one long dwelling to be built to instruction. This to be held in readiness for Hannah Myer, my housekeeper at the aforesaid Manor House, for her retirement from my service and to be rent free for the length of her life, and to revert to my estate upon her demise.

Until that time, the Long House will be used as an hostelry as it was afore, providing refreshment of all travellers and water for horses. Entertainers, jugglers and players of Stratford-on-Avon theatre may rest and perform, but not on the Sabbath."

'Yes, at last,' Josh punched the air. 'We've got something. Pity the rest is missing. It could just be misplaced of course. Keep an eye open for it. Nice though. Now we've got an actual reference to Brook Cottages and it is pretty conclusive isn't it; *sided to the ford*? So our terrace is older than we thought and as a bonus, there's a direct link to Sennington Manor. How about that? We've gone up market!' Josh laughed. 'That should thrill my sister and keep her off our backs for a bit.' Andrew laughed too; they understood each other where Cynthia was concerned.

'No other place fits the description. It's yours,' he agreed, 'And it mentions only one dwelling, so Brook Cottage must have been divided much later. I wonder when that was done?' Then, as an afterthought, 'This Hannah Myer must have been very special to Lawrence Roberts, or why would an important chap like him be taking such care over her welfare?'

'Maybe she was a comely wench,' Josh offered with a grin.

'Maybe, though, I'm more interested in why he decided to build a place down by the ford,' Andrew said, gathering the papers together. 'She must have been more than just a faithful retainer, so you could be right, Josh, there could have been a personal relationship.

'If this was the reason, he didn't hit on a choice spot for her retirement did he? You only have to look at the drawbacks for an old person. Apart from anything else it's in a hollow and by a stream that would have flooded most winters, so the place would have been damp at the best of times.'

Andrew was making the points, at the same time watching Stella's face, speculating on what was going on in her worried head. 'There's no direct road to the manor, so access would have been across the meadow just as it is now, or up that steep gully to the track at the top that would have been deep in mud after a heavy rain. And wouldn't it have been on the big side for one person, even if a couple of servants had lived in?

'Think of an old lady trapped down in the bottom of these hills in winter, cut off by heavy snow. If he thought so highly of her, why didn't he build something in his grounds? Or, why didn't she just stay on in the house? It looks big enough to separate the modest quarters she would have required. Big enough surely to house his own family in spacious comfort and still have room to bed the servants up in those attics running the length of the house. From the look of the place they must be vast with fantastic views, especially at full moon or with deep snow. What a sight!'

Stella caught her breath; she was searching the past again, uneasy, unsure, aching to catch something as fine as a drift of scent; bitter sweet, a loss, a shadow, ah, she had it…

…then it was gone, falling just below the surface of thin ice on a winter pond. She nearly grasped it – almost remembered – but what?

Andrew looked at his watch, 'Hey slaves, I've got to go right now.'

'Would you like me to carry on?' Stella offered, pulling herself together. 'We're getting somewhere at last.'

'No, I'm sorry. I have to lock everything up. In fact, I'm surprised that these original documents have been allowed to stay here; there's no real security. Things like these, even pages torn from old registers, are being framed and sold – mostly to the American market.

'You can't blame the buyers, not really. They don't know the provenance of what they buy and, as hand-written examples of local history, they do make interesting reading.

'Oh, thanks for this Stella,' he waved her envelope. 'I'll study this tonight. We can arrange the next meeting over the weekend and start where we left off. OK So I'll see you on Sunday at Cynthia's?'

'Oh, Andrew,' Stella stopped him. 'Please don't mention anything about my personal interest to Cynthia, when we meet, will you? She's such a practical person and I don't want an interrogation, so let's just keep it between ourselves for the time being.'

'Of course, Stella. I realise it's confidential,' he smiled warmly. 'Thank you for your trust.'

Sunday 11th August

The day was close and humid; nearly 70 degrees in the garden where a shimmering heat haze made everything seem illusory. Cynthia had all the windows and doors, back and front, wide open and thanked God for the breath of breeze every time she got a heat blast from opening the oven door. The smell though was mouth-watering. It was Sunday and she was doing a roast. She did this summer and winter, if there was company or not. If it were a day as hot as this, Cynthia would usually have left it until the cool of the evening, especially if it had been, as it sometimes was, just for herself and Abby – and Uncle John..... This Sunday however, right on track, the vicar was coming directly after morning service, ostensibly for a working lunch, or so he still thought, silly man. Cynthia had worked out that the housekeeper didn't go to the vicarage on Sundays so the man would be hungry and this meal was going to be a taste of home cooking he would remember. Cynthia was pulling out all the stops. "Slowly slowly, catchee monkey" had been the idea when she suggested it. 'Josh and Stella are staying on after we've eaten so that we can co-ordinate our work and do a basic layout for the Special Edition. Time is marching on. Why don't you join us, combine forces? We could do with your help. Come to think of it, why not eat with us?' It was thrown in like an after-thought and he gave in because she was aware that he knew, that she knew, that there was nothing in his diary to make him say no, and that he would have to get lunch for himself or go, as he often did, to the hotel in the village.

'The four of us together for a few hours will break the back of it, really lick things into shape and by your being away from the vicarage, Andrew, you won't be at the beck and call of the door-bell or the telephone. You won't be disturbed at Brook Cottage, I can guarantee it.' Not many people telephoned Cynthia unless it was very important and never, never on a Sunday. They wouldn't dare unless it was a matter of life or death. 'An army marches on its stomach.' She had prodded him playfully in the middle. It had sounded reasonable even to her ears. How could he refuse? He hadn't!

Roast rib of beef and Yorkshire pudding she was famed for; potatoes and onions roasted alongside the joint, with fresh vegetables; all from Uncle John's garden. He would be delighted, God bless him. Now, a gravy that you could stand a spoon up in and to finish off, homemade horseradish sauce. Josh had dug the root fresh that morning from by the compost heap, thumping it on the kitchen table, moaning on that they would all prefer salad. What rot, who remembers salad? If the way to a man's heart was through his stomach, she was home and dry. On second thoughts, she could do without the heart stuff. Life as the vicar's wife and his right hand help would do for starters.

Cynthia took a break, went to the open back door, now shaded by the pear tree, and fanned the sleeves under her arm pits, grateful for a cooler.

What to do next? The water jug was filled and in the fridge with sliced lemon, mint and ice cubes floating in it. The picture had been in a magazine and looked very swish. A bit of style to show Andrew she wasn't an old stick. If push came to shove, she would even pretend to enjoy trips in that open-topped Jaguar.

The cold lemon soufflé had almost set to perfection. She opened the fridge door and gave the mould a shake. A nice light pudding to cleanse the palate and liven them up a bit. She didn't want them stuffed mindless and have Josh cut the meeting short so he could take an afternoon nap – in Stella's bed!

They would be here any minute. Time to put the Yorkshire pudding in. The pudding was Abby's favourite. Strange not to have her at the other end of the terrace coming in with Uncle John as the meat came out, and to have her eulogizing over the meal.

'It will never be the same again.' Cynthia stopped for a moment, saddened at the loss of the old man more than she could admit, then, 'enough of that.' She breathed deeply a couple of times.

The heat from the oven gushed out like a wave. Stepping back, Cynthia let the smoke clear then poured the batter mixture into the spitting fat, slammed the tray back on the shelf, banged the door shut and, straightening up, dragged the back of her hand over her face. Phew, it was hot in here. Never mind, it would be worth the sweat, Andrew needed to know what an excellent cook and homemaker she was; one capable of entertaining dignitaries from the church.

The table was already laid in the sitting room and it looked impressive with the best water glasses on the starched white cloth. It was nice and cool in there, the front of the terrace lost the sun late morning so they could sip their sherry in a civilised manner and, with any luck it would make Andrew start to think how nice it would be to have her at the vicarage taking care of his social entertaining and domestic life. She hoped Josh wouldn't let her down by asking for beer. What now? Turn the vegetables down low, don't want them soggy. Nothing else, was there? Oh yes, the coffee. This was real coffee specially bought for the occasion. Little coffee cups went on the side board; she couldn't actually remember ever having used them before. It was usually a beaker; take it or leave it.

Taking a minute off she flew upstairs and gave her hair a final brush. Glossy and dark, the monk's style suited her face, very suitable for someone going to live in an ecclesiastical setting she thought, approving the reflection in the mirror and smoothing down the navy blue and white spotted dress.

Pity she had to wear this elasticised corset underneath; called a Roll-On, it kept rolling up and she felt strangled with it in this heat and it itched but without it she looked a bit too hefty round the back side.

At the sound of a car pulling up by the back gate she looked out of the open window. It was Josh with Stella and they would come in through the kitchen. Then the added grind of tyres twisting to a fast stop on the track at the front of the cottage had her down the stairs and at the door in record time. That was Andrew; he always drove like a teenager in that sporty thing and it was time he grew up.

Cynthia readjusted her face into a smile, smoothed the dress again, and was standing framed in the doorway, beaming a relaxed welcome. Lunch for four, nothing to it.

Josh raised an eyebrow to Stella, noting Cynthia's affected casual pose. 'It smells nice, Cynthia,' Stella said, noting that they hadn't warranted so much as a backward glance as they came in past the bubbling veg.

'God, it's boiling out there, I need a drink. Fancy a beer Andrew?' Josh called down the hall. Familiarity breeds a thick skin so, ignoring Cynthia's paralysing look, he went to the pantry and lifted a couple of small bottles from the stone floor. 'Nice and cold on those slabs.' He reached for two glasses and the opener. 'No need to put it in the fridge; not that it would have been allowed,' he said pointedly, starting to pour.

'I'm sure Andrew would prefer an aperitif.' Cynthia held up the bottle of sherry and shook it like a cocktail mixer. 'It's cream.' Andrew was treated to her flirtatious look.

'Err,' he read the label, controlled a shudder. 'I think a beer. That's perfect Josh. I could do with a long cool drink after all that sermonising. I'm a bit out of practice.'

It was a sort of apology to Cynthia who had to smile back understandingly, though she didn't understand. He was a refined man, so why did he want beer? Beer was so common. 'Or you could try my dandelion wine?' Cynthia wasn't one to give up easily and turning her back on Josh, she tried to block his eye contact with Andrew. 'Mother's recipe,' her voice tinkled. 'No one knows what's in it; the magic ingredient.' She flashed the pearly-whites.

'Tempting, Cynthia,' he responded backing a pace, 'Fortunately I know how potent these homemade wines can be. I've got evening service to do, so I'll give it a miss if you don't mind.'

'Very wise; it's been known to slay lesser mortals,' Josh muttered as Andrew reached for the long glass a little too eagerly and they moved into the sitting room. Stella would also have preferred something long and cool like her home-made lemonade but it was too late to ask. Cynthia was already filling two small glasses with something thick and dark brown that looked a bit like cough mixture.

Josh had carved the joint and the vegetable tureens were being passed round when the knock came on the kitchen door.

'Cooeee!' There was a well of silence as Stella, Josh and Cynthia exchanged wide eyed looks and Andrew put down his napkin. 'Abby?' three voices echoed in unison.

'Back from Devon – and so soon? You missed us, didn't you?' Cynthia couldn't keep delight from her voice.

'Yes I did, and oh, what a lovely Sunday smell. I know I'm home now. Is there room for a little one?' Small fists pushed together under a soft ample bosom, pleading for, and sure of a welcome. Abby came into the fold with a hug from Stella and Josh, a warm hand shake from Andrew and a nod and a pleased smile from Cynthia that she couldn't hide. With Abby's return the terrace seemed balanced again. Life was getting back to some sort of normality.

Routine could be re-established.

'Nice to see you back. Pull up a chair.' Cynthia directed operations with a serving spoon and everybody shuffled to make space. 'Sit down, you can tell us all about your holiday, later,' she called, bustling into the kitchen for another plate. Andrew's full attention needed to be on the table and not on Abby's sudden appearance. 'Don't let it get cold.'

'No chance of that in this heat.' Josh waved a hand over the rising steam, laughing at Andrew's alarmed expression. 'It's a challenge, man. Get on with it,' he hissed, as Cynthia came back in, already organising.

'Now you're home we can set a date for our AGM. What about this Thursday? All agreed?' There were nods all round.

'Good, that will give us something else to think about. No point in moping. Uncle John wouldn't have liked that. He was very philosophical about death, Andrew,' Cynthia passed the vegetable dishes round. 'Do have another roastie.'

She held the hot potatoes right under Andrew's nose. 'It's short notice…' she sat down and addressed the others. '…so if Bertie has to do some work before the open day he'll need to assess the job, sharpish. I'll try to get him up here tomorrow; he can tell us what's needed when we have our meeting. Leave it to me. I'll call him later.'

Cynthia never cared who *she* called on a Sunday!

Abby didn't care if Cynthia was being bossy, that was Cynthia, and familiarity was security. She was happy to be home again and it was nice, being seated next to Andrew. 'You see, I've not been away from here since Mom died. Dad died in the war,' Abby explained to him. 'I never wanted to go anywhere and anyhow, Uncle John liked me to pop in after school each day.' She piled her plate and added an extra piece of Yorkshire pudding. 'I couldn't leave him, could I?'

It was an excuse and Cynthia was having none of it. 'Stuff and nonsense,' she boomed, then turned down the volume, seeing Andrew's startled look. 'He never lacked for company and anyhow, he liked his quiet times as we all do.'

'Well, I know,' Abby fidgeted, filling her fork with obvious relish. 'The truth is, Vicar, I don't like being away even for a day. I don't even like being back late from school. I'm a home bird,' she giggled, her eyes anxious, searching their faces for understanding.

'My cousin was very nice to me and made me welcome. Your Mum and Dad came over, Cynthia, Josh. They looked well. And Devon is a lovely county. It was just that I just got – I just got home sick. I felt lonely,' she admitted. The soft voice petered out as she filled her mouth. 'Oh, I was so hungry on the journey; I hoped I would be in time.' A trace of a smile.

'But it's strange not to have Uncle John...' The mouth trembled, eyes brimmed with tears. 'Coming back here – it's just becoming sort of real, that he's gone,' her voice wavered. 'This is lovely Cynthia, thank you,' she said, choking back a sob.

'Yes it is. You really are a splendid cook.' Andrew joined in to stem the tide. 'Let me congratulate you, Cynthia. A perfect Sunday lunch. I don't ever remember having better. You are a darned good cook.' He meant it and Cynthia beamed her delight.

'Thank you, Andrew, it's just the usual; no trouble at all. Abby is the better pastry cook, aren't you dear; light as a feather and melt in the mouth.'

It was true, though nevertheless a kind thing to say.

Monday 12th August

Carrying a couple of piles of books Stella and Josh paused while Vera, putting her bucket of cleaning materials on the ground, locked Uncle John's back door.

'I've more or less finished in here now.' She turned the key then gave it three pushes to make sure. 'He never locked up, did he; now, though, it seems important, respectful, sort of like giving the place time to settle, time to adjust. There wasn't much and I had already stacked the crockery, cutlery, and glassware in the kitchen, ready to be collected. It will only take a day to clean any marks off the walls where the pictures were hanging, then it's the attic and that will be a big job. There's so much up there and Abby will need to go through it with me. It all belongs to her now. I don't know what's important; what to throw or keep. I'll give the place a final dust and a going over when the removal men have been to move that piano into Abby's place.

'It all seems to be moving too fast; we've only just buried him. But,' she gave a sigh, 'the more we do, the less Abby has to face. The legal side will be demanding. Once that's finalised she can take her time, deciding when to sell. She always has Cynthia to call on, of course. You've been through his books and taken what you want haven't you Josh?' He nodded. 'Good, don't want them taking things personal to anybody. Is everything that's left going to the auction rooms?'

'Mostly,' Stella confirmed. 'Apart from a painting I've already taken, that one of the front garden, all lawn and roses climbing over the rustic arches. He painted it just after the turn of the century and for me, it is timeless. Oh, and the easel. Cynthia is having the brass ornaments.'

'So I'll have to go on cleaning them,' Vera flicked her head. 'Abby wants the painting that's left in the hall.

'Painting was his life, though there's precious little to show for it; he gave so many away, didn't he? I think that half the village must have them on their walls and Abby's cousin took four. How she's going to move around that front room once that piano is in, I can't think. You can hardly swing a cat round as it is.'

'Don't worry about that. I've talked to Bertie and he and I will go in and make space for it somehow,' Josh assured her. 'Whatever happens she has to have her music; couldn't live without it. Did you know she could have been a concert pianist?'

'No I didn't. What happened?' Vera's brows went up an inch. 'I can't imagine her ever having had the confidence to stand up in front of an audience.'

'That's what stopped her. She had the gift but lacked the push and one's no good without the other. She's not so bad now. When she was young though, that shyness was positively crippling and Cynthia sort of protected her.'

'Vera, tell me, what have you chosen?' Stella changed the subject.

'The coal scuttle. It's better than ours and it's nice enough to fill with flowers in the summer. Thank you. Now listen, I've sorted through his clothes and if you give me a lift when you've got a spare hour, Stella, we could drop them off at the Salvation Army rooms. That was his favourite charity. He said the Salvation Army was one of the few organisations that arranged visits to them in the trenches, in the First World War and they did so much to lift the men's spirits when times were desperate. He'll be glad to know that his things are helping them out. It's what he called, *passing it on*. Someone does something for you and you do something for somebody else along the line.'

'That's a nice memory, Vera. Let's make it early next week. Decorating is the next thing on the list. Bertie will do it of course but it will have to wait until after the AGM and Open Day because the terrace might need a bit of work before the public arrive, so we're talking sometime in September.'

'Then comes the decision about the sale, I suppose.' Vera's face fell. 'It will be a big step when the advert goes in the paper.' No one spoke for a moment, it all seemed so final. 'A lick of paint and it will be ready for anybody to inspect,' she added softly, still looking at the ground. 'You know how I take a special pride in keeping these old cottages up together. I really liked Uncle John. He was a gent – one of the Old School, and it was a real privilege to do what I could for him. There might be a problem selling his cottage though; it's the smallest one, isn't it? Be a squash for a modern couple. They want more space these days and big windows that let out all the heat. And it's a bit cut off down here, wouldn't suit an old person.'

'I suppose not.' Stella hoisted the books. 'We've spent most of the morning researching local history.' There was casual emphasis on the word most followed by a sideways, very relaxed look at Josh, as she tried to adjust the combs in her hair with one hand. 'For now though,' Stella took a deep breath and smiled, 'we're going to have a break and walk the dog over to Witetune House because Miss Jenkins has invited us there for lunch and that's always a treat.'

'Oh, I'll tell you what,' Vera said, ' if you want more information for the magazine, nip up to the sitting room upstairs, the one she calls the snuggery. There are a few books on the little table in the corner, all about this area years ago. It's worth a look. I gives her a few days in the Spring and Autumn, cleaning the place and they're always in the same spot. She won't have me put them away, likes things left where she can lay her hands on them and that's all right with me. It's her own filing system. Which way are you going, through the wood?'

'No, the direct way, just over the hill. We're a bit pushed for time; things took longer than we thought.' Josh answered, patting the books. 'If we had had a free morning we would have gone that way and spent half an hour by the water mill. We love that walk. Did you know that the mill pool, the top one that over flows down into the sheep dip, has a base of Fuller's Earth? I don't know of another one in the area. The old drovers washed the sheep in it before the final long march to market in Lechlade. They would have got a better price if the animals looked well cared for and it killed the ticks, took the grease out of the wool, and fluffed it up a bit. Fuller's Earth was mixed with lanolin to keep it moist. Interesting, isn't it?

'It was rumoured that it was also used as a paste to paint the face of Elizabeth the First. It would have dried white you see; stayed flexible and it was supposed to make her resemble the plaster models of the Virgin, in the churches.' He raised his eyebrows. 'She was called *Elizabeth the Virgin Queen*, wasn't she? The apparent similarity strengthened the loyalty of uneducated country folk, as she travelled in her grand carriage through villages, towns, and hamlets like ours. Just think, the Queen could have had her personal supply replenished from that very pond when she passed through here on the way to Sudeley Castle. Hey, that could be another claim to fame. Cynthia will be delighted.'

'More evidence of our Royal connections? I'll make sure to ask Miss Jenkins for those books you mentioned, Vera,' Stella said.

'I bet you find them exactly where I said. By the way, now we're all thinking about village history, I've always been curious as to what that moat round her house was used for; it's too shallow for fish.' Vera manoeuvred the bike out of the back gate.

'Yes I know', Josh replied. 'That particular one was fed from an underground spring and provided extra water for the kitchens. Bigger ones, called stew ponds, were for breeding fish; fresh food to feed the household and visitors plus Royalty and their entourage who could drop in unannounced, on the way to Sudeley Castle and would have expected to be fed. The Church had ordained a lot of meatless days and that created a problem for the monasteries too. The monks had to be self-sufficient, feed themselves, pilgrims, travellers, and any church dignitaries who just turned up, so those fish reserves were invaluable. Just think of sitting down to a nice fat carp or pike, stuffed with herbs and crushed cob nuts then roasted over wood, and no problem in catching it.'

'Hey, where did you learn all this stuff?' Stella looked amazed. 'I know you like to dabble in cooking but I've never known you to be enthusiastic about history. Whenever I've tried to talk to you about it, you glaze over.'

'With all due modesty,' Josh looked anything but modest, 'when I tackle a subject, I do it thoroughly. Take Orchard Street, for instance. The orchard was owned by the church and honey from hives kept in the orchards gave them fresh fruit and vegetables of some type or other, all year round. They had a healthy diet and a plentiful supply

of mead wine made from the honey. It must have been a good life.'
He looked wistful.

'On the down side,' Vera had to balance the scales, 'a bad spring
would mean no blossom for the bees, a very poor harvest and no
honey to eat, or sell. They lived in a beautiful building that would
have been cold and draughty in the winter and I'll bet they had
chilblains, so it wouldn't have been all quiet contemplation and easy
living.'

'Oh, what a miserable thought. You've killed the romance,' Stella
said. 'Now let's all move or we're going to be late.'

* * * * * * *

Stella had always felt at home in Witetune House; a sort of spiritual
affinity, as though it knew her, as though they had once before known
each other. The massive wood door was propped open and entering
the cool, flag-stoned hall, her fancy turned to a cold gin and tonic;
Miss Jenkins made them the American way – very dry.

Stella took a long delicious sip, and wanting to get through the
afternoon, added a little more tonic. Then she asked Miss Jenkins if
she might just pop upstairs to find the books Vera had told her about,
and, assuring them she wouldn't be more than a couple of minutes,
hurried up the handsome squared staircase.

The sun, hard and high above the trees, streamed in through the
big windows of the upstairs sitting room, easing shadows into dark
recesses and carving mullioned patterned squares across the warm
faded rugs. Leaning on the stone sill, she pushed the iron-framed
window wide. The fragrant air was sucked in as though the room had
woken and was taking a deep refreshing breath; perfume from the
garden's flowering borders already circulating as she walked back
across the "snuggery", hung heavy with quiet and memories of lives
lived and long gone. Sometimes she thought she heard talking out
there on the landing; voices, not quite whispered, not quite audible,
like someone who shouldn't have been there. 'Psychic sensitivity,'
she grinned. 'Good to know I'm not going mad!'

The books were where Vera had said they would be, of course. Nothing much was ever moved. Things had found their own niche over years, so why move them? She chose just one, the date and text promising, idly admiring the worn binding as the minutes ticked by and the tension of the last few days eased its grip. A small breeze ventured in, corner-lifted a few pages from the open book then as though bored, danced away, leaving the air to thicken as she closed the window. The stillness of the sanctuary had been re-established, left as it had been found; an act of respect.

Suddenly, with visions of ice cubes watering the barely sipped gin and tonic, Stella picked the book up, hurried out into the corridor – then for no reason she could afterwards understand, headed for the back flight of stairs which, in more affluent times had been the confine of servants and children.

It was just a brief pause, an ever-so-slight glance through the landing window as a ripple of a shadow crossed the air and stopped Stella dead in her tracks; what was that?

Had the light moved? Tension in the air; then, like a slide in a projector sharply flicked back, hard rain was pricking the glass of the small panes, heralding the downpour that flash-smoked the paths outside and obliterated all traces of the garden... in *winter*? Stella hardly had time to register what she had seen with her own eyes before it was all over, returning the hot sun to a dry summer's garden. But in those brief moments, as though time had warped and stopped, she had looked beyond the garden, through the untroubled eyes of one still very young; one no longer afraid. It hadn't been a flight of fancy. Stella knew beyond doubt that she crossed to another dimension, that she had bonded with someone very much loved and cared for; a very young... Hannah Myer! 'Hannah, I'm here, come back. Let me find you.' An anxious whisper, the yearning for union, a physical ache as she searched the rafters for a breath of the child who needed her. It was an emotion so strong, so powerful, that as she laid her hand on the stair rail, time itself harnessed the direction of that power and warped once more.

As clearly defined as sinking into an imprint left in a deep feather bed or of a hand, pressed into newly risen dough, the position her body eased itself into, was so engraved in time that the very air could not erase its outline. Stella offered no resistance as arms and legs gently repositioned themselves. Her fingers stretched wide on the stair rail as though seeking a broader span, something solid enough to out-pace the centuries; well cared for, the feeling of polished wood almost tangible beneath the phantom touch, a patina smoothed with the layers of patient waiting. Now her foot stretched forward, rubbing the edge of the top step as though pulled by an invisible string.

Ah, this again. This was what had happened on the attic steps in her cottage; this tense, acute awareness, the same stance; toe pointed, perfect balance for instant flowing descent down a big staircase – so where were these stairs? Who was reaching out, guiding her and whose form was she being moulded, oh so gently, into? A woman, for sure, and whoever she was, whoever she had been, she was used to waiting hour upon hour, for here was a dedicated patience that knew no pressure of time. Perhaps it was a night time vigil, for how else could she have waited so long, undetected? She was a listener too, listening for sounds from below. Sounds from a very long time ago.

Stella's head had tilted slightly, searching now for other voices, other vibrations, waiting, listening for whom or what? Poised like this, she could move downstairs at a second's warning and no one would ever have suspected her of spying, yet that's what she must have been doing – spying. Not in a vindictive way but her ears had strained as Stella's were doing now, for tiny sounds, perhaps whispered secrets drifting up a stairwell from the landings and cellars of a big house.

Stella frowned as the mind pictures flowed. Was it a guess or could it be a channelled memory? What would this woman have heard... What would she have been listening for, remembering, storing... connecting bits of information, keys to dangerous secrets? Secrets sealed behind lips that never betrayed...

'Oh, that was horrible, frightening.' Stella put a hand across her mouth, an instinctive gesture. At that time and in that place, life itself had relied on silence and economy of words. No slip of the tongue, information was security… should the time ever come again. 'What time? Why am I thinking this way?' Anxiety was back, fear was building about something not quite remembered.

'Calm yourself, calm yourself.' Stella breathed deeply while her mind combed for a key that could link the strange happenings of the last few days, then she noticed a lifting of her mood, a gentle acceptance that this girl had eventually found happiness.

Minutes ticked away, more possibilities teased and stretched her imagination, though logic was slowly entering the equation and when Josh called again, the link was finally broken.

Shaking her head, Stella blinked hard, confused for a moment. 'I'm coming. Give me two minutes and I will be down,' she replied with an edge of irritation.

With little hope of recapturing the magic, eyes closed, she groped for details but the more she concentrated the more vague they became. 'Could it be my past life? Have I lived here before in more dangerous times?' The unpleasant prospect found quiet voice once again. 'If I have had a past life, it wasn't spent at my cottage or here at Witetune. In these hills, yes, I'm sure of that.' She looked back at the landing window. 'The only other place it could be in this area is Sennington Manor.' She stood there trying to find connections as thoughts came and bounded away like a soft ball falling down stairs, one by one. 'I've never been inside Sennington Manor and I don't know anyone who has, so there's no way to compare. Wait a minute, the gardens will be open to the public on Open Day so Andrew, being the vicar, might be able to get us inside the house. It's worth a try. Cynthia mentioned something about an invitation. Maybe we could go along as his assistants.'

'Stella, are you coming down? We're eating in the kitchen, lunch is on the table, and the soufflé is going down for the third time. Even a drowning man gives up after that!'

Tuesday 13th August

After their long relaxing lunch with Miss Jenkins, Stella had left Witetune House feeling optimistic – and it wasn't the result of a gin and tonic and a large glass of white wine. In those few most extraordinary moments on the landing of the lovely old house, when times had changed places, she had become convinced that there had been a happy and positive outcome for the Myer sisters' terrifying ordeal. Later, tossing and turning in bed, unable to sleep, Stella had relived every detail of those precious moments, over and over, and it was not the wonder of seeing the garden change from summer to winter that was paramount – but relief in the conviction that Hannah had survived. She had been cared for, too. The sweet feeling of security and love that she had sensed all round in those delicate moments had been quite tangible.

She must have slept well because she woke light-hearted, keen to get on and help Andrew and Josh with the investigation. 'You've beaten me to it', she laughed, entering the vestry; papers were everywhere, both men busy sorting.

'Yes, come on you part-timer.' Josh tossed a note pad to her.

'OK. Now before I start I have something to tell you both. Forgive me, I didn't tell you yesterday, Josh, because I wanted to save it until we were all together. You remember I left you and Miss Jenkins and went upstairs to get the books Vera had mentioned. Well, something really strange happened when I was alone up there. It was quite wonderful; I'll even call it magical. It gave me a real lift and I came away feeling happy and optimistic.'

'I thought you looked happy when we left,' Josh said. 'I thought it was the effect of the gin. So, we're waiting: tell all.'

And she did, proceeding to describe the happening in the smallest detail. 'And I've written it all down,' she finished and, not inviting questions, picked up a batch of church records and started work.

It wasn't too long before they made their first find of the day and it was enough to sober Stella's mood. 'I think I've found it – yes, it fits.' Andrew put two torn pieces of paper together. 'This is it, the other part of that deed about the cottage.' He flashed back through the pages and putting both sections together laid them carefully on the table. 'Now give me a minute to see what this is all about.' He seemed to be taking a long time, reading slowly, looking back, checking and frowning, then, 'You had better sit down for this one,' he said warningly and began.

"The long house is to be built over the remains of the old hostelry where one Rachel Myer, daughter of the Miller at Syreford, and guardian to her young sister Hannah," his voice faltered *"was accused of bringing plague to the hamlet by sorcery and was burned as a witch in the August month, in the year of our Lord, 1623."*

Andrew paused, and then gasped, 'Dear God! Wait... there's more.'

"Her cottage was torched to cleanse all evil and was thereafter to be left in isolation, never visited and never to be spoken of again. This being the order of the parson.

The cottage stood on my land and I, Lawrence Roberts, Gent., believing that a great injustice was perpetrated against Rachel Myer, have no hesitation in revoking this order from the Church.

I hereby sign and affix my seal as testimony of my instructions. Signed by my hand, the first day of the New Year, 24th March, 1630"

The scrawled flamboyant signature of Lawrence Roberts followed.

'Bloody hell!' Josh looked at Stella with astonishment, her description of plague hitting the village going through his head like the re-run of a sound track. 'This is immense! can you believe it? And it's been lying here all these years. Cynthia will be on a high, all right. This will be massive; think of the publicity. It should make the local papers and it totally beats anything the rest of the village has dug up. We're on a winner here and it's well worthy of the centre fold in the Special Edition.' Josh rubbed his hands together, jubilant though Andrew looked apprehensive.

'What have we disturbed? This poor creature would have been ex-communicated without any trial. The permutations and implications are enormous. I don't think we should go down that path. It's too important to be used as public titillation. This is something to deal with later – for now though, there's enough material here to use without that, don't you think? Let's just use the rebuilding of the house; say it went in a fire, add a bit of romantic speculation and leave it at that.'

He lifted his head and his serious gaze was met by Stella's ashen face as, nodding in agreement, she sat down heavily on the pew.

'So you're saying that a woman was burned on our land, in our garden?' she said, separating the words as though to understand them.

'She was actually burned to death feet from where we live?' Voice barely above a whisper, she stared blankly. 'That is absolutely horrifying!'

'Yes, it seems so, poor creature and this wasn't an isolated case, it happened to many old crones,' Andrew said philosophically.

'She wasn't old, she was very young, wasn't she, so why did they pick on her?'

'I don't know Stella. It is an unpleasant thought.' His tone became measured. 'Please don't be too distressed.'

'Putting it into perspective, like the plague, it did happen over three-hundred years ago. We can't put the clock back; history is full of injustices, and that's why I think we should keep this to ourselves. From my point of view, I can see great tidal waves of questions and work that threaten to engulf me in everything from church politics to newspaper headlines. Let's let it go.'

'I know I should but somehow this feels… personal,' she retorted. 'Look, the hairs on my arms are standing up and my hands are shaking! I'll just sit here quietly for a while. You just carry on, please.'

Apart from the ticking of the clock, silence fell heavily on the vestry. Andrew and Josh started to tidy the papers away and mindful of Stella's distress, they didn't speak. Immersed in her own thoughts, watching shadows in a mist of memory, she seemed almost to have forgotten they were there.

Books were put away, files closed; carefully, quietly replaced. The shabby little room, hung heavy with dust and neglect and forgotten expectations, seemed suspended in time; the walls had heard it all before. Even the silence seemed muffled until, with the softest of groans, the vestry door started to open slowly, as if of its own accord, riveting their glaze.

'Oops, sorry,' Vera came in smiling. 'I weren't sure anyone was here.'

'God almighty, Vera, you nearly gave us a heart attack!' Josh whipped round, glaring at her. 'What are you doing here?'

'Thanks for the welcome,' she said tardily, not talking offence. They had known each other since school days. 'Cynthia gave me John's key. He was the verger here, Vicar.' She smiled at Andrew. 'She suggested I keep up my hours by polishing the brass and doing some cleaning and it needs it by the look of this room. Now you're obviously busy so I'll come back some other time.' She turned to go, then one hand on the door handle, said, 'Cynthia's taken a sudden interest in the place hasn't she? Wonder what brought that on?' The question was framed innocently enough; she smiled at the vicar who suddenly looked nervous, then transferring her attention to Stella, asked, 'You OK love? You don't look at all well. Want a cup of tea? I've got my thermos.'

As she closed the door behind her, Andrew heaved a sigh of relief. 'Now where were we? Oh yes, I kept this file out. It's something that should interest you both and it's not morbid,' he promised. 'It's some instructions to the work-men who built Brook Cottage, your place, for the said Lawrence Roberts. It seems that he had it erected directly over the ruins of the old one but that wasn't all. He was an educated man remember, who didn't believe that Rachel had practised witchcraft. If he had, he wouldn't have stipulated that use had to be made of several parts of her old home still in situ, such as the fire place, hearth stone and section of a wall. They are specifically mentioned here. If she had been a witch, these objects would have been thought of as cursed, and the peasant workers wouldn't have gone near them. That means there must have been a change of heart by some of the local people.'

'And they were used,' Josh confirmed, eager to strengthen the positive and cheer Stella up. 'I told you about it only a few days ago, didn't I? The fireplace with its side bread oven and the hearth are in the wall that divides Abby and John's place. They are on Abby's side so both cottages share the relics, if you see what I mean. It's Abby's place now – until she sells it,' he said.

'That's confirmation enough, so we can use that in the write up. I'll make a point of seeing it when I call on Abby. I'll tell her I'm calling on all my parishioners and that I'm interested in local history, which is true, of course. You know what beats me? It's why a wealthy landowner like this Roberts chap should use old and probably worn materials, when money was no object. There's no evidence that he was the penny pinching type, is there? So what if there's another explanation?

'What if he wasn't able to prevent the murder and looking after her sister was his way of keeping faith? Not that it matters now.' Andrew said, wanting to move on.

'Thinking once more of fund raising, wouldn't it make a more appealing story if we could hint at a little more than romance?' Josh offered. 'Everyone likes a happy ending. Come on Stella,' he cajoled. 'This calls for female thinking.'

Andrew called out and stopped him. 'There's more here and this is really enlightening. It seems that Rachel Myer stood accused of bringing plague by sorcery and the medicines she made from herbs. Ah, and that's the answer to your question, Stella. That is why they singled her out,' he said flatly. 'And if you look back…' he flicked through the pages, '…the date of Rachel's murder coincides with the sweep of Black Death and the break in the Parson's records.'

'She must have been a herbalist like me, and those wicked, ignorant, cruel people slaughtered her,' Stella caught a sob in her throat then covered her face. 'I wonder if we share some common ancestry?'

'Who knows? They were superstitious and ignorant and un-educated.' Andrew spoke softly. 'You have to feel sorry for them too. Their ignorance bred a most terrifying fear and in those circum-stances, would we have behaved differently? Would we have had the courage to stand up against the mob and defend her?'

'I know, I know, turn the other cheek and all that stuff but I'm not ready for this one yet. I feel emotionally involved so let's stop, please, I can't take any more. It's all too much.' She stood up. 'Perhaps it's because I'm tired I can't feel sorry for them.'

'Slow down, girl.' Josh moved behind her, massaging the back of her neck, feeling the stiffness ease beneath his probing fingers. 'I think we've done more than enough to-day. Perhaps there's nothing more to find. Shall we leave it for now?'

'Yes please, and do you mind if I leave you to tidy up?' She stood up. 'I'll wait outside.'

Sun on her face, she leaned against the porch, the comforting warmth of the stones penetrating her stiff shoulders. Small blobs of purple cloud were bruising a steel blue sky as crows, like ragged bits of burned paper tossed by a skittish wind, took off from the clump of high elms. Life was moving itself reassuringly across the day regardless of any trauma past or present and, refusing to be swept back into the black pit of speculation, her tension slowly evaporated for Fear, by its very nature, cannot live long in the examining light of reason.

It was a good ten minutes before the men joined her. The afternoon had moved well on, surprising them with the time and the lengthening shadows and it was in reflective mood that they walked back along the path together between the gravestones, enjoying the early evening cool and pre-occupied with private thought.

'I've been thinking.' Josh stopped. 'About Abby. We have to proceed with caution, to coin a phrase. She's in a very fragile state at the moment because of her loss. Stella and I have already talked about this recently and we both think she could be becoming agoraphobic. She has a routine you could set your clock by and never sets foot over the front step unless it's strictly necessary. Home is her one security now that she's lost her Uncle John. We really must not undermine that.'

'Tell her that a poor woman was brutally murdered virtually under her feet and that relics from that time are built into the walls around her – well, the shock could be one straw too many,' Stella added her concern. 'Why not keep this information to ourselves, as you suggested, Andrew. Just give Cynthia and everyone else for that matter, a sketchy outline, say we haven't found anything conclusive though we do have leads. That should keep Cynthia ticking over for a little longer.'

'Fine with me,' Andrew shrugged as his car purred into life. 'You two have a nice evening.' The car moved forward then stopped.

'Stella,' he called. 'There's no record of Rachel's sister, Hannah, dying, is there, and she is the one you feel an infinity with, right? If I were in your heightened state, and not knowing what might be presented next, I would keep a note pad and pen by the bed. Dreams can free the mind and the more you record them the more instructive they are.'

'Thanks Andrew,' she replied. 'I'm already doing that.'

'I'm not surprised, and I have a suggestion that you allow me to guide you back in time; regress you. You know that I am very qualified and I've had much experience helping ex-service men and women face difficult problems. I promise you that you will not find yourself in any situation that is unsafe or that I can't handle. I wouldn't suggest this if I were not utterly confident.'

'Hypnosis – for Stella? You're joking!' Josh looked aghast.

'I'll make the decision,' Stella came back instantly, leaving Josh open mouthed. 'Yes please, Andrew. When can we do it?'

'Good.' Andrew laughed. 'I'll come round tomorrow, just to discuss how we are going to handle it. See you both then?' and lifting a hand and drove away in the open-topped, navy blue Jaguar.

They walked slowly home across the field, Josh trying all he knew to dissuade her and finally, 'Stella, what if I can't get someone to look after the shop?'

She laughed out loud. 'You can always get the *Reserve Team* in.' (The *Reserve Team* were two retired school teachers who spent hours in his book shop, ostensibly conducting researching in the antiquarian section but who positively enjoyed acting as unpaid assistants. Free tea and coffee; economically they were a sound investment.)

Wednesday 14th August

Vera had finished the upstairs cleaning and, taking a last look out of the window, was amazed to see the Reverend Andrew open the latch on the front gate with very careful fingers then close it soundlessly and with a darting sideways glance towards Cynthia's window, sprint up the path to Stella's front door. Vera had thought that Cynthia must have rubbed Josh up the wrong way and that was why he had slammed out and gone into Stella's cottage earlier. Nothing unusual in that. Cynthia could rub anybody up the wrong way but now all three were huddled inside as though they were hiding! 'So, what is going on? Something they don't want Madam Cook to know about, that's obvious,' she smirked, 'and by the Vicar's actions, he hopes to keep it that way. What a turn up for the books. *Miss High and Mighty* downstairs has no idea that her brother and her intended are up to something right next door. Hmmm, so the love-match she assumes will take her to life in the vicarage mightn't be as cut and dried as she's encouraged us to think,' and putting the snippet into her mental file, Vera went downstairs for coffee.

Vera's assumption that she would get biscuits too always irritated Cynthia, plus the fact that, if the tin wasn't out, Vera would get it from the cupboard. Vera knew the effect it had on Cynthia and rubbed salt into the wound by helping herself unasked, deliberately picking out the chocolate ones. Secure in the position as cleaner to all four cottages she didn't care two hoots. Efficient and trustworthy cleaners were hard to come by. Someone with a car would charge more and Cynthia begrudged even the going rate, so turning to Cynthia with an overly-familiar smile, she said, 'I'll have to come here in the afternoon next week.

'I've got to take little Dennis to the school dentist. I'll come in after I've finished next door. Say about 12-30 to 1 o'clock. OK? It's your half day at the Post Office, you should be home by then. We'll find a place for Uncle John's brasses first. Somewhere where they won't get touched; keep the polishing down.'

It was not OK. Cynthia had thought about changing the day once

Uncle John's affairs were in order and now Vera was dictating it because of that wretched child. 'I suppose so, if it must be, though I might be delayed at the vicarage.'

'No problem. I'll use my key.'

Cynthia sucked in a tight breath. 'I hope you're not going to overtire yourself Vera, giving this place a good going through after doing a full morning's work for Stella.' Cynthia tried and failed to sound concerned, for what she was really saying, and they both knew it, was: Don't come here worn out and too tired to clean the place thoroughly. I won't be getting my money's worth and, being smack on lunchtime, I'll have to offer you a sandwich or something. Vera was one of the very few people who could manage to get one over on Miss Cynthia Cook, and she reached for another biscuit; the last of the chocolate ones.

* * * * * * *

Next door the atmosphere was a little tense. 'I tried not to let Cynthia see me sneaking up your path,' Andrew confessed, as Stella, with an understanding smile, handed him the file. 'I feel guilty because she doesn't know I'm here, though goodness knows why I should; I am perfectly free to visit my parishioners. Sorry Josh, no disrespect to your sister but now that she's organising my diary she knows my every move and I'm getting to the stage where I feel I should consult her before making appointments. I don't quite know how it happened, how I got myself into it,' he looking uncertain. 'Problem is, she's good at it – organising my diary that is.'

'Don't worry about upsetting me, I know how you feel,' Josh said. 'I've thought for years that Cynthia is wasted in this backwater. Running the Post Office just isn't challenging enough. She would be good in politics or even as the wife of an MP. She's first class in a crisis and needs to be at the cutting edge of things, to be stretched. If she had any suspicion we were here she would be in under any pretext, wanting to know the ins and outs of everything; convinced she could do it better. So, back to our business. I want to make it clear, Andrew that I think you should drop this whole idea; this 'regressive' investigation. However,' he sighed, 'I've been persuaded to moderate my stand after having my ear bent by Stella, on the 'phone last night. So now if we collate all the findings and get a clearer picture of what we have so far, we can then consider the next step yours!'

'Thank you,' Andrew looked relieved. 'Let's re-read Stella's notes,' he fanned the pages. 'What we have here should put more flesh on the bones of those seventeenth century records. All right, shall we make a start?'

The hands of the clock moved on and Stella was glad to have been so meticulous in the recording as, studying the text critically, Andrew passed the tightly-typed sheets to Josh, one by one. She wandered about quietly, aimlessly; the murder of Rachel, and her own empathy with the girl Hannah, occupying her mind and rather as if reading a gripping novel, she too wanted to know the outcome. Stuck fast in that suffocating tomb of an oven, the oven that was just two cottages away, Hannah had not died. So what had become of her, how had she survived and where did she grow up? Where had she spent the intervening years before going to the Manor House as housekeeper? It was concern for the child, the *not knowing* that was bothering Stella most. Typing up the report she had exaggerated nothing.

It might seem far-fetched to the uninitiated but nothing on God's Earth would make her change a word or convince her that she hadn't experienced all that she had written. How were they taking it? They weren't making many comments and it was unnerving to hear the scratch of pens as notes were made in the margins. Disagreeing, doubting? Stella kept quiet, prepared herself, longed for a cup of coffee, looked at the clock again for, with sensitivity heightened, time seemed to be slowing down. An atmosphere was building in the room, as though they were not alone, as though other ears were listening, waiting...

Vera passed the window pulling on a cardigan, ready for the cycle home. Everything out there so normal and the diminishing sound of her footsteps served only to increase Stella's isolation. Waiting,

waiting, waiting...

'How shall I put this?' Andrew said carefully, when at last the reading was done. 'It would be an amazing coincidence to have *happenings* as vivid as these, supported by church records, and as you know; I don't believe in so many coincidences. Now don't go off the deep end because I have to ask you Stella, are you sure it wasn't a sort of imaginative thinking sleep you were in, your subconscious regurgitating and elaborating on what we had read in the parish records?'

When Andrew finished the question, Josh didn't look up; tapping the papers into order and setting them carefully aside, he waited for the back-lash.

Stella knew Andrew hadn't meant to be undermining but with nerves already stretched she could have snapped at him. 'I was aware of my duality,' she said grindingly slowly. 'Aware of working on two levels, and it was not a dream or whatever else you might think.' her irritation was barely disguised. 'I have this...' she searched for the word, 'this gift; Clairvoyance. Various past members of my family have had it too. I'm the last. There will be no one to follow me. I'm the end of the line and,' her teeth clenched together, 'I did not imagine it!'

'All right, all right, please understand that I had to ask. When I start the regression, it will be strictly controlled; professional. I will be in charge at all times. Now, on to the commercial aspect. We already have an interesting story suitable for the church magazine. It will be our revised version. What we publish has to be understood by the general public so I must lay down a few ground rules first. I think we should make it a good old village ghost story. Sorry, Stella.' He held up a hand, palm towards her. 'No matter what my private views are, because of my position in the parish, it has to be this way. I'm in this village in an official capacity and for the time I hold this office, I've got to walk a tightrope. I'm not ducking the issue and I appreciate how important and personal this stuff is, so please try to understand my position. Based on selected facts and a bit of elaboration, we should be able to weave a story interesting enough to, as Cynthia so subtly puts it, encourage the punters to shell out for this money-making project. She has the right idea though. The whole village is going to all this trouble and expense of printing its history, for one reason: money.'

'And we can still rake it in if we are a bit creative and make it spooky enough,' Josh encouraged, taking up his pen. 'Now, to work.' Pen in hand, Josh started. 'Now, based on what we have so far, let us agree that Lawrence Roberts, as a mature man, had Brook Cottage built because he had a relationship with the murdered woman and therefore felt some responsibility for her young sister, Hannah? Stella seems to have received a request for help but her attention was directed to what on the surface would seem to be a casual meeting; a girl talking to a young man in the woods. I think it must be an important piece in jig-saw; a clue. Also, let's keep in mind that in those days the word Gentleman meant more than having good manners. It was a title and it was added to his name on that plaque in the church: *Lawrence Roberts, Gent.*'

'*Gent* in those days,' Andrew took over, 'equalled money, breeding, connections, education, and position in society. Friendship, however strong, couldn't have crossed that social gap, so his concern for Hannah's welfare would have to have been seen as philanthropy; the squire looking after his people.

'Let us go along with the idea that the girl was Hannah, the girl hidden in the oven in Abby's cottage, and the young man was the Lawrence Roberts who later inherited the manor here at Sennington. The girl survived and according to church records, Lawrence Roberts, now a man of means, had this place built specifically to house her. That must have been because he wanted her future to be secure, long term; whether he survived her or not. Now that really is a big commitment. Later, Hannah re-emerges as housekeeper at the manor. Stella, you described her as standing at the top of a broad staircase, listening to what was happening down stairs. It sounds as though she was used to standing there for a very long time. Now we have to ask ourselves, when and more intriguingly why, was she taken in by the Gentry in the first place? We don't really know, nor do we know what happened to her in the intervening years. For instance, who actually took care of the girl directly after the trauma?'

'Perhaps he did; this Lawrence fellah. Perhaps she was good looking,' Josh threw in. 'Perhaps, thinking of the future, he had an eye for the main chance?'

'Could be,' Andrew shrugged, 'but let's use our imagination. He could have inadvertently been instrumental in the crime in some way, or didn't help when he could have, and needed to ease his guilt. From your notes Stella, it seems he quite openly teased the girl and called her his *Little Witch of the Woods*. Damning words I fear if, as it reads from this account, the endearment became generally known and misinterpreted.

'You have a feeling of urgency, Stella. So have I.' Andrew turned to her, suddenly serious. 'So, are we going to do this regression?'

'Wait,' Josh was on his feet. 'Not so fast. Think carefully. This has already caused you a lot of stress, Stella. Are you even sure you want to go ahead with it? Why don't we go away for a few days, give you time to think it through. It's not too late to call the whole thing off, is it? Or, why not leave it until after Gardens Day, only a couple of weeks off, and see if it's necessary. Once everyone's attention is off the 17th century, the whole thing could just die.'

'I can't,' she said gently. 'I don't know why but I don't think we have much time. I've been thinking, though; perhaps I can do it myself by meditating or just by sitting quietly and clearing my mind. That's how it's happened before.'

'Yes, and you couldn't handle it,' Andrew reminded her sharply. 'That was because you became emotionally involved, took the happenings on as though they were your own experiences. With my guidance you won't be swept along by personal involvement. I will hold you in the present moment. Josh will be here so you're in safe hands.'

'Assuming I'm agreeable,' he grumbled.

'You wouldn't leave me alone.' She clutched his hand and he softened.

'I've just had an interesting thought,' Andrew interrupted. 'A variation of this said theme. You two have an especially close relationship and in your notes, Stella, you said that when you came here as a young woman, to live with your aunt, you knew that someone who would be important in your life would be waiting for you. I'm not surprised; early teens, that's often a spiritual time in a young person's life. Perhaps Josh was with you at the time when all this happened and he has chosen to reincarnate again, to help you; a sort of long-term protector.'

'I got you all wrong Andrew,' Josh said. 'I never had you down as such a free thinker. Are you saying this just to get me on board?'

'Could be; nothing seems impossible,' Andrew grinned.

'Why did you allow yourself to be manoeuvred into this back-water?' Josh asked.

'Perhaps I was meant to be here. Or perhaps it was the hand of Fate? Anyhow, it's temporary. Now, timing, what about tomorrow?'

Thursday 15th August

When Andrew arrived at Stella's cottage, he had already decided to use the method of relaxation that Stella was familiar with and when that level was reached, to follow his own judgement. Josh, pen in hand, was sitting close enough to hear Stella's every word but Andrew was hesitant.

'I want you both to feel totally confident in my ability to conduct this regression. Remember that I have a great deal of experience and have worked for the Military, officially,' he added with great emphasis. 'So, are you ready?'

Sure of Andrew's integrity and confident of his obvious ability, Stella relaxed and prepared for regression to a previous time, her own or that of someone else. It was an interesting prospect that didn't worry her, totally committed as she was to unravelling this mystery. With Andrew holding the reins and Josh at hand taking notes, she was confident that the experiment could be controlled. Nothing should go wrong.

Relaxation of mind and body came easily as she followed the familiar pattern; head, shoulders, trunk, hips, legs, feet; the energy ran down and into the earth like the flow of a river, finally washing away all physical sensation. Warm, comfortable, feeling removed from the world out there, she wondered in a detached way, if she had left her feet crossed or hands linked. They could be floating in the air for all she knew, for there was no sense of weight or contact pressure. Only her mind was holding its place – or was the mind also at rest and the subconscious taking over? She didn't know – it didn't matter. The world was at peace. Smells, fresh, warm, floating in from the fields drowsy with heat – summer heat; always high summer; soothing, smoothing, lazy. A heat haze out there, long hot days, one following the other. In here it is cooler, thick stone walls, deep shadows, like being in the dairy. Nice…

'Can you hear me, Stella?' Andrew spoke slowly, unemotionally, reminding her of a gramophone that was beginning to wind down.

'Can you hear me Stella?' She nodded. 'That's good. Whenever I speak...' He sounded a long way off. 'Whenever I speak...' he repeated, 'my words will not surprise or distract you, and you will be able to respond to any instruction and answer any question. Is that quite clear, do you understand, Stella?' She nodded again. 'That's excellent. Now stay where you are.'

To Stella's ears his voice was a monotone, every syllable lengthening. 'Where are you Stella? Are you still here on this land by the brook?'

'Yes, I am still here but the original cottage, the thatch, has long gone. I think. It is much, much later.' She was speaking slowly as though readjusting to the new situation.

'I am in Brook Cottage. It's not been divided yet. It is one long and quite substantial building and I – Hannah is mistress here...'

"Lawrence had it built for me and it is far, far too big a house for one person. Yet I am installed as mistress of this house and I dictate how it is be run.

"I choose to live alone, upstairs." Josh looked at Andrew, wide eyed as Stella carried on. *"I – I occupy this upper floor, so that I don't have to meet people."*

'Any persons in particular?'

"Oh, people I used to know and some of the travellers. The ford is still a meeting place, a spot to water the horses and for travellers to get refreshment. Lawrence said I could stop this practice if I found it an intrusion. It is of no concern to me, it has always been a place of rest and I am not bothered by the passing trade. There is no carousing. People are respectful of my privacy. My maids still make bread and beer to feed them. It keeps them occupied. I don't need them much. Days pass, I stay alone. I like it that way." Her words lacked animation. *"When I am at peace, those shapes, those shapes in the mist of some other time, don't plague my mind."*

Stella was silent for a while, her head turning as though viewing from different angles. 'How different it looks.' To her own ears, her words seemed to enfold themselves in veils, hearing her voice take on old country intonations when she empathised with

Hannah. 'I can see everywhere. It is as though the walls of the house are transparent.'

'You are doing well, Stella. Now describe the house to us.' Andrew's voice was very *matter of fact.*

'All right, I'm downstairs now. This area is divided mainly into three sections, three large rooms. It seems so much bigger of course, without the dividing walls and doors. There's not much furniture, no clutter either.

'The room on the side nearest the brook is the kitchen where food is being prepared at a square scrubbed table. The open fire is in the wall that divides the kitchen from the middle room. It's convenient because the maids can use the fire from either side and the oven, built in at the side of it, opens into this middle room. This is where the bread is taken out and cooled. There is a lot of bread-making needed for the house and the travellers, so there is much activity down there.'

"My maids sleep in a very small room at the back and washing and other domestic jobs are done at the end. There is a staircase winding up at the side of the fireplace in the middle room, leading up here. This is where I live. Alone. Silent. Yet I am never lonely. There is a great difference between loneliness which is forced upon one, and solitude, which is a state that I choose."

'Stella, let's get this clear. Are you saying that the kitchen area is now Abby's home and the room the other side of the fireplace was where John lived?'

'Yes, and as I said, it seems so much bigger without the dividing up. Those big downstairs rooms with cupboards, larders and brew houses, would have divided very easily into four small dwellings.'

'That is interesting. Now go and see what is outside.' Andrew directed but it was some silent minutes before Stella spoke.

'...now I am higher, above the trees. I can see over to the little church. Ah, the Parson is saddling his horse.'

"He's coming over to see me I think. We spent much time together when I lived at Witetune House as companion for the girls."

'Companion for the girls?' Josh nudged him, but Andrew waved him to silence.

'Describe the parson to me,' Andrew said quietly.

"*He is still tall, though bent now. Slender of frame, long fingers, silver grey hair. He has the refinement of scholarly learning and we share a love of books. He says I have a good mind and he values my opinion. Rare for a woman to be so honoured. He looks tired and old, so much more than his years.*

"*For as long as I can remember he has had a weariness of spirit about him that he will never talk of. He is a dear man and his burden distresses me so. He was handsome once.*" The delivery of her words was beginning to show an old formation and an economy of use.

"*As tutor to the girls, he educated me also. He visits regularly and tells me of what is happening out there in the world. I listen for hours though rarely express an opinion. He is so tolerant and doesn't seem to mind.*" She looked sad, far away, so Andrew changed direction.

'Where were you born? What is your name there?'

"*Parson told me that I was safe delivered in the Mill House, down where the two streams meet in Searford. Sadly my mother died soon after. The mill lies yonder between the fold of two hills where the drovers rest and water the sheep. Sheep are not watered here, at the ford, only horses.*

"*Lawrence tells me that my father was the miller, a free man, respected by all. Not that I remember any of this. For fear of plague or fever, Father kept the drovers separate, sleeping them in a barn down the lane. They understood, for it was for their own safety. They say my father was a good master. He's long since gone and I fear I have no family. No one left.*" The vacant look and sadness in her voice; she was drifting, so to bring Stella on track, Andrew repeated:

'What is your full name there and when were you born?'

"*I am Hannah Myer, born at Syreford Mill in the year of our Lord, 1610, in the rein of James the first. He was called the wisest fool in Christendom,*" she laughed brightly, reciting the facts as a sing-song, like a child at school. There followed a few minutes' silence, then…

"*It has become a very hot month.*" She waved a hand as though to cool herself. "*The corn is golden and being harvested into small ricks.*"

'August again, why is it always August?' Stella asked, and Andrew took the opportunity to keep the two-way contact strong.

'We don't know. That's one of the reasons you are there, Stella. Can you describe what you see around the house?'

"*The stream is sluggish, very little water. Farmers are drawing heavily from it and at such times there is always the fear of the lepers.*"

'Lepers? Tell me about them.'

"*There is a leper house nearby. They are supposed to drink from the lowest point of the stream, so we don't get infected, though who alive knows how this evil travels? We all fear it.*" Stella's voice was fluctuating, taking on an old country burr that made Josh dart a look of concern to Andrew.

'She is fine. Fear of water poisoning, that's why they drank cider and beer. Dark stuff for men, lighter brews for women and children.'

"*The monks who have leprosy are dropped into the lazareen, the pit.*" Stella talked over them, putting her hand to her throat. "*They have the last rites read over them and never come out. If the clergy who live good lives are not protected, how can we expect God to protect us?*" She turned her head sharply, something had caught her attention.

'What is it Stella? What can you see?'

"*I see a young man in my garden, digging close to the brook. There is an underground spring there, pure water. I have walked the ground with my sticks and have marked the exact spot. I have the gift of divining and have found water for the farmers in these hills in times of drought, like this summer, though the stream has never been this low. We have never needed to look for more water before.*"

Andrew whispered 'Make a record; she called divining a gift, not just an ability, as she does now.'

Josh went back to his notes, gold pen flying across the pages.

'And where are you now Stella?'

"*I am still in my day room, here upstairs. Up here there is solitude. Sometimes I go for days and don't utter a word. I don't know why I am so very reluctant to speak. I will not tolerate chatter or noise so the household moves around in whispers. Sometimes I want to talk but words thicken my tongue.*" A note of distress had crept in.

'Stella,' Andrew's voice was sharp. 'What are you wearing?'

"*Ah,*" she brightened and looked down. "*My shoes have fancy silver latchets. They were a gift from Lawrence.*"

'Latchets?' Josh lips formed the question.

'Buckles or any fastening,' Andrew reminded him.

"*My dress is a fine cotton, sort of grey and soft to the touch. I wear a white smock over it.*"

'Where do your clothes come from?'

"*From?*" She frowned. "*From here of course. The flax is grown and beaten here, then it is woven into linen cloth in the village. It is very strong quality and takes much wear. The maids cut and sew for us all. I am well-dressed but plainly so, as is the custom for women in my position, unmarried and living alone.*"

'Do you have a position in society?'

"*In society, no...*" The words trailed, examined. "*In this village I'm sort of in-between. They pay me great respect, more than I.... I'm not sure..... always been vague. It doesn't matter. Thinking deep makes my poor head hurt. Ah, Lawrence is home,*" her voice lifted. "*He shouldn't hurry so. He is no longer young.*" Affection flowed with the scolding.

'Who is Lawrence and when did you meet him?'

"*Lord of the Manor of course. Where did I meet him? I can't quite remember. He's always been with me. I think I have an early memory of him as a young man, riding in the woods, and when that comes back to me I see flowers and spring time. Strange, he doesn't like my stirring of old memories so I do as he says,*" she smiled indulgently. "*He has always taken care of me since – since before it all went misty. When I once asked, Lawrence did tell me about my childhood at the mill before I went to live at Witetune House. I can't recall any of it. I'm not stupid, so why can't I remember?*"

Irritation registered openly on Stella's face so Andrew side-stepped the subject. 'Is Lawrence Roberts your friend?'

"*Not just a friend, my protector. I moved to his home, the manor here in Sennington, as his housekeeper, after Ann and Apollina*

Cotton were wed and my duties to them were over. I could have stayed on at Witetune House, lived out my days there, but I wanted to move to the manor, earn my keep, and serve dear Lawrence. Parson had so well educated me, and with my being quick of learning, he had taught me how to keep numbered accounts. We read many books together, though I could already read and write," she added with satisfaction, her back stiffening straight.

'One of the things that frightened the villagers; they thought she was reading spells,' Josh confirmed the connection.

"Lawrence has love for me,' Stella said coyly. *'I know he always has had, I read it in his eyes and because of this knowing, I have waited long."*

A few moments' silence, a pained expression clouded her face then was gone, the rigidity in its place. *"I have always been reluctant to speak to him openly of this, afraid that if I did, the magic, our special unspoken bonding, might be broken. Perhaps I loved someone once, someone dear to me who went away. I can't remember who yet I have always had this feeling of having to hold back my words. It's a kind of safeguard I think, for myself or those I love..."* The voice had a distant, puzzled quality, as though she were thinking aloud. *"Yet I long for Lawrence to pull me to him and break through this barrier. So much yearning, so many years, if only we could say what is in our hearts,"* her voice ached.

'Why, oh why, doesn't she confront him?' Stella clenched her fists, her own voice now, edgy with impatience. 'She is a strong woman, intelligent, educated. Why is it difficult for Hannah to show emotion? I know why; in those days the men held all the power and women were supposed to be subservient.'

'Easy Stella,' Andrew soothed. 'Just relax.'

With a flick of the head she ignored him. 'Lawrence and Hannah are talking again, it's nothing important. Now I am out of that body, out of that room, drifting high above the trees.

'The Parson's coming; his horse is plodding down the bumpy gully. Both look hot and tired. What now? The old man is shielding his eyes, trying to see through the haze and focus on the source of the digging. Now he's shouting, shouting for the digging to be stopped. Why is he so agitated? He's at the gate, dropping from his horse in sheer panic, poor man. What's wrong? What's this? The man who was digging for the spring is screaming! He's thrown down the spade, sweating with fear and backing off, terror in his eyes. Now the maids are crying, clinging to each other. Something is very wrong.' Stella clenched and unclenched her fists.

'Relax. You are only an observer,' Andrew broke through. 'Tell me, where are you now?' No answer.

'Stella, tell me where you are.' Firmer, commanding.

'I am still above,' she snapped back.

'Where is the woman you have identified with?'

'Hannah? She's following Lawrence and he is rushing downstairs. She is close behind him, running into the garden. The young man has grabbed her arm, he's trying to hold her back, but she is struggling. Now the Parson is whispering to Lawrence.

'I would like you to keep well back, Stella. You are there as an observer, only. Now, what are they saying?' Andrew asked in a voice strong and deliberately relaxed.

'Quiet!' Stella almost snarled. 'It is Rachel.' That's what the Parson has just told Lawrence. Lawrence is looking back at him in disbelief. Now they are both looking into the hole, both as white as ghosts.'

"*Rachel? Is it Rachel? Tell me man.*" Lawrence is challenging the parson. The poor man is ashen, trembling, stressed beyond belief and he's nodding.'

Stella was stretching forward, craning her neck. The air in the cottage was electric and Andrew spread his hands, palms down, a warning to Josh; keep silent.

"*You left her here, in the garden?*" Stella's voice changed as she repeated the exchange of words.

"*Yes, I was alone,*" the parson is saying. "*I had no one to help me carry her away. I had no time, they might have returned and they were crazy with hate and terror.*"

"*And you let me build here!*" 'Lawrence is outraged.'

"I did not want the poor bones to be violated again but I have lived a life time with the dread of this find. That is why I never moved away."

"Then no more deceit, she has to know now. Time enough has passed. Let Hannah see."

'Lawrence is ordering the parson to let go of Hannah,' Stella whispered, at the same time shrugging her shoulders as though freeing herself from a grasp.

Josh and Andrew watched closely as Stella leaned over, then her expression altered to disbelief and her voice took on gruffness.

"Oh dear Lord. Bones! Human bones? The latchet on that charred shoe, let me see it. I remember those latchets," Stella's hands spread wide, then holding her head. *"They belong to – to my mother; our mother and she gave them to her first born; to my sister, Rachel. I had a sister! What happened to my sister?"* Silence. Stella said nothing, obviously no one was volunteering information, all shocked to silence as Hannah's memory rapidly unfolded, then, *"Oh no, is this her body, lying here these years? How? Why is she here – and why is the shoe burned? Wait – wait, I'm remembering, it's all locking together."*

Hands in hair now, eyes glazed, Stella's face showed clearly the shock waves as she demonstrated Hannah's awakening.

"They came for her didn't they? Oh dear God, I'm remembering it all – the sounds, the screams, the hammering on the door and my being pushed into the bread oven.

"So the pictures that haunted my dreams were real! I always tried to stifle them, now I know they were real. No more! Don't let them stop now. Don't let them stop," she cried to the sky. *"Let me be free!"* Stella began to rock backwards and forwards, arms crossed, fists clenched. *"How long have I walked over my sister's grave?"* she cried and Andrew gripped Josh's wrist just in time to stop him reaching out.

'Don't touch her,' he warned. 'The shock might be too much. We don't know Hannah's state of health at that time. Leave it to me. Relax, Stella.' He spoke a little more loudly but still a monotone. 'Relax, Stella,' more assertive, more authoritative now. 'There is no need to be upset. You are merely an observer of something that happened long ago. Breathe deeply, steadily and slow down your heart rate. Slowly now, slowly breathe in and slowly breathe out, you know what to do.'

'Bring her out,' Josh whispered fiercely. 'I insist you bring her out now. I'll have no more of this.'

Andrew nodded, lifting a reassuring hand. 'Yes, she's had enough.' then turned back. 'Remember Stella that you are operating on two levels and that you are quite safe here with us, Andrew and Josh. Now start to leave there and move on to this time. It is the month of August, and the year is 1963. You are in your own home. Josh is here for you. When I count to five you will open your eyes, know where you are and be perfectly relaxed. Concentrate on my voice. One, two,' he counted slowly. 'Remember that it is August 1963. You are coming back, Stella, three, four, almost here – five. Now open your eyes slowly and smile. Good. Hello,' Andrew planted a kiss on her cheek.

A deepening intake of breath, eyes brimming with tears, no words, she looked around the room as though trying to recapture the reality of it, then lifted her head and scrutinised their expressions. They didn't speak, giving her time.

'I don't think I can manage a smile,' she whispered eventually, reaching for a tissue to wipe her tears. 'Though it was worth it, wasn't it?' A small sob, intake of breath.

'Yes,' Andrew reassured. 'Do you remember everything?' She nodded. 'You were courageous, my dear. Josh experienced a nasty moment or two and he was only taking notes! Now, let's have tea to steady ourselves and then we will begin to assess the day.'

'Tea, you must be joking. We all deserve a stiff drink!' Josh corrected, going to the sideboard. 'Stella, brandy?'

'Yes please. I think I deserve one for medicinal purposes; my shattered nerves!'

'I'll join you and have a small whisky,' Andrew said, then smiled. 'We're moving on at a cracking rate aren't we? I hope you are both enjoying the spirit of adventure?'

'Adventure? That's pushing it a bit. I didn't exactly volunteer for it, did I? Matter of fact, I feel I've been hijacked, so cheers!' She raised her glass. Andrew and Josh sipped their drinks and went over the notes while Stella rested and gained composure.

'So we have names, dates and location of Hannah Myer, born in 1610 at the mill, here at Syreford,' Josh said. 'She was companion to Ann and Apollina Cotton, daughters, one would assume, of the owners of Witetune House at the time. We can check that easily enough by looking through the house records. The owner of the house, Miss Jenkins, is a friend and she will be intrigued and delighted to help. I know that a retired archivist took over the sorting of the historical records some years ago; there were boxes and boxes of them so he was in his element. I'll give Miss Jenkins, a call, she can ask him. He will assume it's for the history project for the magazine; no problem.'

'Then I'll leave that to you.' Andrew ticked it off the list. It shouldn't be difficult to trace the name Cotton, a wealthy local family, now that we have a date. This is fitting together very nicely,' Andrew smiled, well satisfied. 'I'm only sorry we couldn't go on, find what happened after that but, even with my guiding hand, you were becoming a bit too involved, Stella. Nevertheless, we have done well and it only remains for you to give the go-ahead for the next and I think final, session.

'We need to know what happened to Hannah after the revelation, and what happened to her sister's body. In there could be the answer, the reason to all this unrest. I firmly believe that we have a trapped soul here, one that cannot move on without help.'

Consent was a foregone conclusion though Josh wasn't at all happy. Andrew looked at his diary.

'I would like to do the next hypnosis without delay... Unfortunately tomorrow is booked and on Saturday I've an appointment at Sennington Manor. I'm looking forward to seeing inside. It should be quite interesting. You two can come with me if you like.' He looked at them enquiringly. 'Then Sunday is hectic of course,' he

turned the page, 'so I'll make it as early as possible for next week –
but I can't say exactly when. Sorry Stella, my diary is blocked – as
Cynthia can confirm.' The expression in his eyes spoke volumes.

'The *Reserve Team* will want hard cash for working on Saturday,'
Josh grumbled, knowing that there was no way that he would miss
the opportunity for anything.

Friday 16th August

There was no moon to be seen but it was a warm night and after sitting in the garden under the pear tree for the best part of an hour, Stella's night-vision, and awareness of every tiny creature rustling in the undergrowth, was so acute that she jumped at every sound. The problem was that despite a busy day, she couldn't sleep and to be out of doors smelling the sweet night air was infinitely preferable to tossing and turning in bed, worrying. Andrew was expecting her to undergo a second regression and she had misgivings. The first part of the regression had been a comfortable experience and she had felt in control; observing Hannah's early life, happy years before the plague struck. From then on, time had fast-forwarded of its own volition to show the shocking discovery of her sister Rachel's bones.

Neither she nor Andrew had had any control over what had been presented; the surge of energy had overtaken her and for that short time, theirs had not been the guiding hand. So, with the details of Rachel's brutal murder fresh in her mind, might a second hypnosis throw her back into the time when the murder was actually happening? 'That's really scary stuff,' she shivered. Refusal was an option, of course but would that guarantee an end to it; an end to her historical 'sight-seeing'?

And why can't I rid myself of a nagging sense of being needed, *urged on*, of time running out, of someone needing help before it's too late. Too late for what? We can't rewrite the past, and past evils cast long shadows.

Time, she mused. I always come back to time, so let me concetrate of this time factor, she frowned. Rachel's body was discovered in August 1663. It's August 1963, now, three-hundred years to this very month. So what do we actually know of what happened in this month in 1663?

Hannah was living here, so she had retired from the position of housekeeper at Sennington Manor. She was still close to Lawrence Roberts and the parson and they were here when Rachel's remains were discovered. Now what can I do about that? Nothing, so that can't be it. There has to be something more and it must have happened after the discovery, otherwise, what would be the point of my needing to carry on? 'And I really do have to carry on,' she decided nervously. 'And I'll tell Andrew that he has to concentrate on the end of the month, August, 1663.'

The decision was made; no more procrastinating, she would go through with the second hypnosis because it felt right. Time for bed; she yawned and stretched and smiled at the settled feeling in her heart.

* * * * * * *

Stella didn't have to wait for the hypnosis; it must have been around two in the morning when she floated free from her body, like a transparency peeling itself very slowly from her sleeping form. As always, the separation was serene, like this weightless state, floating some four feet above the bed and looking down on her sleeping body. No light from the moon and yet the room was bathed in a soft bluish glow giving it a rather surreal look with every object clearly, sharply defined, as though eager to display itself in its own right. The colours of a tiny enamelled dish gleamed like jewels as they had when she first held it as a child and she found herself viewing the objects as though through eyes not dimmed by familiarity. How wonderful to be so appreciative again. Maybe it is new, perhaps I've gone back to my early years – and with this prospect entering the equation, everything started to distance itself. Now outlines in the room were becoming vague, blurred, evaporating like straggled mist, and then she was outside; still in the hollow by the ford above the trees, and the cottage below was small and thatched.

Back to that time again?

Careful to give no energy to surprise, to create no ripples, she maintained neutrality, relaxing even more deeply, for the tension in the air had a knife-like edge.

There was activity from a small settlement high and to the right, on the hills. It must be Old Sennington before they deserted it, Stella decided. If so, Hannah was still a girl, the horror of her sister's death still to be faced before she could find refuge at Witetune House. Then many years would turn before she would go into service at the manor house, for it was the ruin of Old Sennington on the hill that she would view from her private room in the attic.

With feverish panic, people were milling round a coarse, heavy-jowled male who, loudly dictating condemnation, was whipping up their level of agitation to his. Stella didn't know what it was about yet in her altered state she could see that the bully was inhaling the crowd's energy, drawing it like smoke from their frantic mouths, converting their willpower to his, until, controlled by his magnetic force, they formed into a mob.

Who was this? A parson, young, fresh-faced and frightened. Unwilling, arguing for reason, he was shoved unceremoniously to the front by the loud-mouthed leader, determined that *The Church* should be at its head. The Parson was being harried at every step and they gave him no leeway. With a *Man of the Cloth* in the lead, they became an official party, doing God's bidding. Marching their thunderous steps down the Nut Walk, self-empowered, no time to think, they crossed the dirt track and went down the gully at a trot, to the thatched cottage by the brook, baying like dogs for blood. And on the hill a church bell tolled out another death from the plague! Stella watched aghast. This was a witch hunt and no amount of reasoning from the youthful church man was going to stop them. As far as these peasants were concerned, the sisters down there were witches.

Hadn't they heard the gentry call the young one his "*Little Witch of the Woods*" when they met while she was collecting special herbs; herbs that could kill? Proof enough if needed. Time for reckoning; was the Parson on the side of justice and God, or in the pay of the Devil and under the spell of the maiden and her sister with the golden curls, to whom he paid so much attention?

Attention redirected, Stella was seeing events through the Parson's eyes now. There was no higher authority within summoning distance. The manor house was deserted, his friends away. Fearing for his life, the young man had no choice but to maintain a degree of dignity as they hustled him on, hoping with every step he took to bring a degree of sanity to their superstitious madness; for madness it was!

Clouds moved fast across a wild sky, there was lots of noise, then everything went out of focus, and when the picture reformed, the parson had been pushed aside and Rachel Myer was already tied to a stake heaped round with hastily gathered twigs, dried branches and anything that would burn. Hate needed to be satiated and eager hands set the pile ablaze, and they screamed in rage when she slumped before the flames could roast her belly.

"She's cheated us. She's taken poison. She's dead!"

They did not know that Rachel's life was still in the balance as they dragged her across the glowing pyre, the smell of burning flesh pure scent to their animal nostrils. *"She has taken her life. The suicide of a witch, she's the Devil's worker,"* they screamed. *"Get the Preacher back; he knows what has to be done. It is written, she must be staked!"*

Staked? The Parson was a gentle man, a man of peace who had never lifted a hand in anger. He was horrified yet he dared not try to cheat the pack; they would have lynched him! A dagger of sharpened wood was thrust into his reluctant hand.

They had no thought for his feelings; as judge and jury they wanted blood and his title vindicated their primitive savage lust. Praying as he had never prayed before, for courage, escape, and forgiveness, the young man positioned it over the heart of one, Rachel Myer.

In complete and sudden silence the crowd waited as he mumbled some order of banishment not quite remembered, never really learned. He tried to think of more, holding their attention, putting off the dreaded moment, then, was it his imagination – a tremor from the body? Salvation, a way out?

A second's hesitation, and before he could pull the stake away the blacksmith's hammer smashed it down, bludgeoning the breast, cracking through the rib bones, forcing the last winded groan from the poor scorched throat and, hearing her last breath, the mob as a body reeled back in terror of Holy Judgement. She had been alive!

Rachel Myer had been alive. Silence. The ardour of the chase had been sucked dry and some started to back away as doubt trickled through the ranks. Then from the leader, hate regenerated, *"That was the Devil's last call. Finish the job!"* And desperate for justification, they did.

As was the order of things, Rachel's cat, screaming, and clawing was then nailed to the yew tree in front of the burning cottage. That yew tree – could it be the one still growing outside in the front garden at Brook Cottages? Stella watched in silent horror.

It was the young parson, no longer naive, suddenly a man of authority with anger in his belly, who finally drove them away, ordering silence, as, unsure and ashamed now, they slouched away. If it was a sin, it was a sin the whole village shared and he alone would bury the body. *"Not on church ground."* A few, trembling at the thought of judgement to come, still argued for justification.

"Here, on her own patch where she will rot forever."

"My decision, not yours. Leave me, away with you."

He stood up to them now, a man with authority, bolder and oh, so very much older, though even he wasn't sure, not absolutely sure, and in his heart he knew he would not risk the violation of consecrated ground...

'Dear God! So that was how it was.' Logic broke the trance and in an instant Stella was back in her body, back in her own bed, wide awake, shocked by the clarity of the experience. So she knew the order of things. Now she came to appreciate that while mayhem exploded, even when the cottage was set to the flaming torch, Rachel's sister Hannah was safely hidden in the big bread oven where she was falling into deep, drugged, shame-accepting surrender.

No one knew she was there and she knew nothing of what was happening outside. Shock must have wiped the trauma of those last frantic terrifying minutes from her memory, and that's why she was devastated when the well was dug and Rachel's remains were un-earthed. She had had no idea, yet the memory was still there like a scar, buried so deep that she had never been able to access it and grieve and so she never freed herself from the haunting past. No one knew where the Parson had laid Rachel to rest and he, poor man, had hoped to bury the record of the atrocity with her.

Staring into the dark, Stella now unequivocally accepted her vital role a catalyst to this mystery; the driving force, whatever it was, needing her attention. She wasn't quite sure why but time was of the essence and would not await her convenience; any idea of delaying the next hypnosis until she felt more settled was no longer an option. She looked at the clock: 6 am.

By 8.00 am, everything had been committed to paper and the neatly-typed carbon copies, one set for Andrew, the other for Josh, were in their envelopes on the seat beside her as she set off for Stratford-on-Avon.

Not far and with any luck she would beat the traffic and there shouldn't be any customers in the book shop. She could not delay the next hypnosis and did not intend to try. There was no choice. Everything was moving so fast; too fast. They must be heading for something crucial, some aspect that they had not, as yet, even considered. Josh and Andrew had to have time to consider everything she had written before her next regression and she would make it clear that she didn't want to discuss it until then. Anyhow, there was nothing to discuss and they had a busy weekend ahead: A visit to the manor and Sunday lunch with Cynthia.

Saturday 17th August

They had looked forward to his company, but unfortunately Andrew could not join them for lunch at the pub and it was just before two when Josh and Stella met him, as arranged, at the church gate. It was a sunny day but the wind was freshening and she was glad of the fine wool shawl across her shoulders as they walked up the hill to the manor.

'I've been saving this bit of information until we were together.' Stella stood still to deliver it. 'I had a call from Miss Jenkins. They have found the record of the Cotton family and not only do the dates fit, they also had two daughters, Ann and Apollina. Are we on the right track – or are we on the right track?' she laughed.

A little early for their appointment at the manor, they were using the time to take a leisurely stroll right around the walled garden, speculating on the cause of a fire that had long ago gutted a wing. Seen by moonlight, it still clung to the main house like a skeleton held in the grip of death yet now in the light of day, the empty window sockets, like hangings in a gallery, were making frames for passing clouds as they rippled into streamers and rags. It was a pure Salvador Dali creation.

'I do hope that whoever buys the place wants to live here and become an active member of the community.' Stella sighed, looking up beyond the boundary wall edging the road, to the Nut Walk on the hills opposite. 'Not just one of the smart set from London, weekenders, who just want to invite friends down to gawp at the cottages and play at country living. 'This big house should be the central part of village life,' she continued. 'It's been out of bounds for too many years and in a hamlet as small as this, we've no other meeting point. I know the church is there,' she answered the obvious alternative, 'But one Sunday in the month hardly pulls this scattered community together. We're glad to have you though, Andrew; new blood, new ideas.'

'Don't expect too much. I'm only temporary, I didn't volunteer, remember that, and I hope to have a replacement soon because I'm planning to travel for at least three or four months, get away for the winter, somewhere warm where I can catch up on a backlog of work. Then I will come back and settle down here.'

'Cynthia's not mentioned it.' Josh looked surprised.

'Cynthia doesn't know,' Andrew grinned. 'I don't want to waste time so before I go, I want to get started on these old parish records. There's enough to keep me occupied for years. I'll make a start on the ones stuffed into that old metal filing cabinet; a chuck out from someone's office I think. It's such a pity. They're deteriorating rapidly, the tops and corners fraying each time the drawers are opened.

'Rather you than me. Deciphering all that scrolled hand writing could send you blind,' Josh said sarcastically.

'The point I'm trying to make,' Stella cut back in, 'is the need for a heart for this area. The manor at Christmas time, people cutting holly and ivy and mistletoe to decorate it in the old way and everyone singing carols round the log fire in the hall.' She stopped, 'How... how do I know that?'

'What?'

'That there's a fireplace in the hall. I sort of pictured it, as though I was actually looking at it. How strange...'

'An easy guess I suppose, nearly every place of this age and size must have had one; sort of central-heating heat wafting up the stairs to the bedrooms.'

'Yes of course – though it seemed more real than that.'

Andrew had studied the details in the estate agent's brochure, *"The sale of a distinguished 17th century house, Sennington Manor"* and he had not been disappointed when they walked along the front aspect with its long attractive line and high imposing front porch. Broad lawns to the front were shaded by high trees and backed by dense, low shrubbery and to the rear the boundary wall edged the graveyard and small church of St Andrews.

Josh gave him the local history as they walked. It was a jungle that had afforded the local children cover when exploring the forbidden territory, with thoughts of the old man spotting them from some high up window, adding a knife edge of fear to bravado. The recluse, grotesque in imagination, had never actually been seen and dread now had given way to pity, for who would ever know what had kept the old man isolated from all outside human contact.

'Provisions were left at the door and the housekeeper did any business in Stratford-on-Avon.' Stella added detail. 'She never took any part in local affairs and rarely gave anyone more than nodding acknowledgement. Two of a kind, they must have suited each other.'

'How could this kind of existence not be investigated?' Andrew asked, looking at his watch. 'Those old folks obviously needed support. This is sheer neglect. Where was the vicar?'

'You replaced him. He lived in a world of his own too, just like the people here. He must have respected their wishes.'

When Andrew finally pulled the ancient bell in the porch they couldn't hear it ring. It must have sounded somewhere for almost at once the inner door rattled and the front one was flung wide by the agent, a slim young man, cord trousers and open-necked shirt, who welcomed them in effusively, glad of the company as he heeled away a lovely soft mouthed golden-haired retriever, holding a well-chewed ball.

'I'm Harry,' he shook hands. 'Come on through to the kitchen.'
They walked across the square hall, the men talking, getting acquainted, not noticing Stella's fascinated inspection of the place. The fireplace, tall and shallow, just as she had visualized, situated on the wall siding the ruin. Excessive heat building up in these internal beams, she mused, could have been quietly smouldering away over a long hard winter

It was a comfortable-sized hallway, the wood-blocked floor leading on to the main stairs 'That's an impressive staircase Harry, but it looks as though it hasn't been used for years. How sad.' Stella surveyed the neglect.

'They didn't have any staff, didn't want any and apparently the owner and the housekeeper didn't use this part of the building. I did hear talk of this staircase being haunted,' he laughed.

'You know, the usual stuff, a young woman dressed in grey, just standing up there on the top steps. Never seen her myself, my senses not fine enough I suppose. It's odd though,' he stood still, thoughtful for a moment, the smile gone from his lips, 'this one,' the sitting dog got an affectionate shove from his foot, 'follows me all over the place. Can't move an inch without him yet he won't go on that top landing. He will follow me up the back stairs and along the corridor up there, past the bedrooms, then the instant I step out onto this main staircase, he stops dead. Feet just on the edge of the carpet and no further. Funny isn't it?

'Coffee?' He dismissed the subject, striding ahead, a springy step mostly on the balls of his feet. 'Follow me. Not in any hurry are you? No need to rush off, I hope. It's a barn of a place, needs a family to live here and there isn't much for me to do. I show prospective buyers around and I'm cataloguing what's left but almost everything of interest has gone. I read the rest of the time or go through the records here. They're rather fragmented, so I fill in the days with a bit of weeding.'

The manor, stripped of most of its furnishings, had a hollow ring and the men's voices echoed on and away through empty rooms as subjects and explanations and laughter filled those first few minutes and they sought common ground. To Stella, dropping a few paces back, their effusive exchange seemed like an invasion of the peace and she experienced a slight embarrassment, as though she had brought in some noisy guests who, not sensing their host's need for moderation, were throwing their energy about.

But those hosts, the housekeeper and the old man, had long gone, and Josh and Andrew were hardly boisterous. Just a feeling – like a reminding finger pressing lightly on the shoulder.

'Oh, before we go through to have coffee, you might find this interesting' Harry doubled back, unlocked the cellar door beneath the main staircase, groped in the dark, flicked on a light just inside, and picked up a torch. 'This is the head of the cellar and part way down on the left is, I think, what they used to call a priest hole. Its position suggests an underground tunnel to the church at one time, though there's no sign of it now. When this place was built, the owner of the manor would have been responsible for the upkeep of the church and in this case, the family had direct access through a private gate in the garden wall. It's still there and you must know that, of course, being local. You must know more about this place than I do.'

The dim, uncovered light bulb did little to make the descent inviting as they carefully negotiated worn stone steps to the musty smelling cellars below. 'Here it is.' He stopped and flashed the torch into a large cavity in the wall on the left. They might have missed it, eyes fixed on the precarious descent, carefully positioning their feet. 'This is it, a Priest Hole, I think. If it's not, it must have been part of some escape route that would have been a God-send to poor blighters on the run. If you think about the history of this area in the 17th century, the odds are that more than a few Royalists would have hidden in there and hopefully made their escape through the tunnel. It gives me the creeps, I don't mind admitting.'

Josh gave Stella a meaningful look. She knew how he disliked confined spaces and she wasn't exactly relishing the experience.

'It's small and it would have been cramped but at a pinch several men could have hidden in here if their lives depended on it. When you look inside do take note of the height of the cell. This space is cleverly positioned between two floor levels so it wouldn't have been easy to detect as long as the bricks were replaced carefully. No one would push against that far wall. It's this one you hang on to. There might be others in a house this size. I haven't had time or inclination to tap all the walls yet, it's a big job. As you can see these steps are extremely narrow and you have to negotiate every one or risk breaking your neck. Think of it, with only a candle or a taper to light the way, searching eyes wouldn't have dwelled much on the walls would they? Anyhow, in my opinion there's little else this room could have been used for; the access was too difficult for storage. I think that's where the tunnel would have started don't you?' He pointed the torch at the back wall, then handed it to Andrew and moved down a step.

There was only room for one at a time and when Andrew stood back Josh took his place, leaned in, waved the torch into the dark space, inspected the ceiling, and then made way for Stella. He had assumed she would want to look too and she could not refuse, could not explain her lack of enthusiasm. Was it an unreasonable reaction, this reluctance to be left alone, staring into this eerie place? Yes – though it was more than that.

'Oh, do wait, I'll come with you,' she called to no use, the men having already disappeared rounding the tight steep bend that deadened their voices. They were as keen to investigate the cellars beneath as the searching Roundheads would have been.

It would have seemed childish to get them back.

It was just that their host's rather loud voice and cavalier attitude to the priest hole had caused an unpleasant tightening, a surge of anxiety in her chest as darkness chased the moving torchlight across the back wall. It was as though his speculation and easy reference to this secret room was putting them in danger and Stella wanted to put a stop to it, most urgently. Her heart started to race as she tried to rationalise then dismiss this groundless feeling of dread, but it would not be dismissed and, like accepting her fate, Stella turned full circle and embraced as fact that an event of importance had taken place in this little room.

Something most unpleasant and the distress, the anguish of people involved in that event, seemed to have coated every brick of the old walls. What she was tuning into was fear! Perhaps men had been trapped; perhaps they had been found, or betrayed? Was that it? Betrayed? She doubled over, clawing at the walls for support, struggling for breath, her heart racing. 'I don't know how; I just know I'm right,' she accepted with dismay. Flight or fight, instinct told her to get out of this place and into the garden, wind on her face, clear it all away, dismiss it, yet she couldn't. There was a *need* here. So accepting her fate she relaxed and then, guided by some force, soft as vapour and strong as the hand of a trusted friend, she let go fear and waited.

Harry headed Andrew and Josh up from the cellars, talking avidly, all three totally unaware of the subtle change in Stella's attitude. 'Do you want to have a look down there Stella? I'll go back with you,'

Andrew offered. She shook her head decisively and moved sideways
for them to pass. 'After you,' he waited, puzzled by the gesture, not
knowing that she was playing another role, one grounded in old
custom. Her instinct was to lean back, pull the folds of her skirts tight,
and let them pass, just as a person in a subservient position would
have done. Still they waited and she had no option but to go first.

Quite naturally they were including her in the discussion and, with
so much to talk about, they didn't notice her lack of response. Not
only did she not want to join in, but the person whose role she was
shadowing felt she didn't have the social right to that privilege. Stella
understood this now, this almost subservient desire to be unobtrusive,
invisible almost, as though it was not her place to have an opinion
and certainly not to give it. So many words, so much speculation and
why did these men have to be so vocal, so loud? 'Your voices are
echoing, the whole house can hear, why take such risks?' she wanted
to shout. The protest stayed in her throat and she bit back the caution.
Feigning indifference, Stella nevertheless, found herself listening
closely to subjects so casually explored, consciously committing
every one to memory, a storehouse to be sifted through at leisure and
in private.

Her mind flashed back to Witetune House when she had, for brief
moments, re-enacted the scene on the staircase and listened intently,
just as she was doing now. Linking these incidents gave her courage,
a more secure hold on events. A pattern was emerging and dove-
tailing, and now, as if she were a spy, every word, every emphasis
was registered. It was as though someone else was using her eyes,
directing her attention to what it wanted to see – or what it wanted
her to see...

The force had become tangible, wrapping itself around, steering
her clear of even the most casual physical contact with the men as
they cleared the cellars. Stella knew it had been an act of protection
but she was a strong woman. She had gone with the flow for that
limited period; she had not given permission for a take-over. Out in
the hall she shrugged, freeing herself of its influence, brushing hands
through her hair and across her face and arms, pretending to brush

away cobwebs and dust, as the cellar door was locked.

'I'm glad to be out of there!' Josh threw out his arms. 'Another half hour would have buckled my brain.

'Remember, The Count of Monte Cristo, and The Man in the Iron Mask, thrown into the dungeon, never to see the light of day again. Did you ever see the films, Andrew? I did and now I know how they felt!'

Following Harry, they turned right and moved into the panelled dining room. 'One of the few things left.' Their guide slapped an impressive refectory table, 'Too big for most houses, it fits in perfectly here and whoever buys this place is sure to want it left in situ.' He led them to the library along a stone flagged passage that ran the whole length of the house and windowed on to the back gardens. Stella let them go on and turned right and entered the kitchen, once the hub and heart of the place.

A table with a scrubbed top, a couple of stools, used coffee mugs in the sink. The kitchen was cool and lofty, with a pulley clothes line hoisted high for drying laundry on wet days, and big iron hooks in the ceiling near the fire, once used for hanging hams while they smoked and matured.

Harry had described it as a barn of a place and so it was, yet it was also bright and airy with a pleasant atmosphere. This would have been the hub, where cooking and domestic service for the same family was a lifetime's work. Given a good master, it would have been a secure life, regulated and uncomplicated, and Stella found herself smiling, as though sharing the moment; as though other people, going about their long ago duties, were milling around on the periphery of her vision. How had the old man and his housekeeper managed all alone in here, she pondered? And deep in the reverie, Harry's sudden appearance made her jump. 'You all right? Josh and Andrew are sorting through manorial records in there and wanted to know you were all right. Coffee?' he asked, filling the kettle. 'I'm making some.'

'No thanks,' she hesitated at the door. 'Harry, is it possible to come again? I really would like to spend some time just looking over the place. I might never have the opportunity, once it's sold.'

'Of course, I'll be glad of the company.

'I'm not here tomorrow. Any day after that will suit me. I'm sure Josh and Andrew want to come back too; they've got to keep at it, make the most of the time left. Why not suggest it to them?'

Sunday 18th August

The wood seemed to wrap itself, cool and loose, around them, padding the silence with greenery, softening the harsh high sun they had left stretched across the fields behind. The dog had wandered on, sniffing his way towards the mill and the clear cool water, confident they would catch up eventually.

Preoccupied, Stella was walking slowly along the narrow track a little way behind Josh, when the drone of a small plane, unseen above the leafy canopy, called across the years from her youth. She couldn't breathe; an aching misery twisting in her chest as, eyes narrowed, she searched frantically the small spaces of azure blue sky, begging the hint of breeze to part the broad fans of beech leaves, but, apart from the occasional call of a bird, all was silent, still and waiting; shadows in the undergrowth listening with her.

Ears straining, Stella did not know if she wanted to grasp at these delicate strands from the past or run and leave them far behind. Rooted to the ground, she prayed that Josh wouldn't turn and that if he did, he would not call out; desperately anxious to be alone, to give this private moment all of her attention, as the sound of the engine thinned into the broad sky, fainter and fainter, like someone calling a last goodbye.

Twisting the worn engagement ring that now only fitted her little finger, tear-filled eyes slightly blurring everything around, she looked at Josh, almost out of sight on the twisting path, and was shocked by her desire for him! What was happening? His dark outline was the only thing in focus, everything else was hazy, almost surreal. She had felt this intensity once before, here, the first time Josh had made love to her.

She looked at the engagement ring remembering back, before that, recalling her first love, her first lover, the War, the missing plane, the letter: *Missing, presumed killed in action.*

Months had passed and she hadn't cried, hadn't talked about it, not even to Josh. Outwardly strong, always controlled, a very private person, Stella had hidden her pain from public speculation, seeing it as a weakness, fearing that the sharing would feed it. This was too private for public airing. She would get through it alone and with dignity. It had been a day like this, this time of year too, walking here with Josh, when the droning of a small mono-plane unseen above the trees had split the thin veneer encasing her heart, as cleanly as a sharp axe through soft wood. She remembered how he had once flown low, circling the cottages and, like lovers having their own song, the sound of that plane brought back the memory of that sunny, joy-filled last day. Then she had faced the truth. He would not come back; this young man, barely out of boyhood, brave, in love, planning for their future, was now dead.

And now as then, the unseen and the unreachable, linked by a sound. Strange really, how anything so common in war time as the droning of a small aircraft could have had such an effect, but heard in the silence of the wood, it was like a call, his last goodbye, a last reaching out to her, and the hurt that burst forth had been like the breaking of a great dam.

No surprise, no words; that day Josh had pulled her into his arms and held her there as though he had been expecting it, as though he had been watching and waiting patiently for her to leave the aching path of dead days. He had led her off the track then, down towards the stream, grassy, hidden, private and lying them both down he had cradled her head on his chest until there were no tears left to cry. Empty inside, needing his strength, she had clung to him as he stroked and kissed her hair with great tenderness. No words were needed as the caresses slowly lengthened and the last breath of a sob gave way to a sweet, light hypnotic trance.

Mind asleep, senses totally focussing on his touch, her body and long-suppressed needs had begun to waken with tingling throbs. Kisses were mere brushes across her forehead, closed lids and lips, as his hands massaged the stiffness from her neck and shoulders. At peace and totally secure, she had not protested. Her physical longings had not died with the death of her fiancé and, as Josh held her close and adjusted his position, she had been aware of his longing, too.

He had laid her on her back and leaning over, said, *'Say now if you want me to stop.'* The words, breathed into her hair were electric. He had waited, then he had made love to her, bringing tears of joy and relief, followed by the deepest, most peaceful sleep for months. The sun had been low when she had finally opened her eyes, waking slowly, stretching, smiling at his uncertain gaze. 'Are you all right, Stella? No regrets?' And when they had left this wood he was smiling and so was she. It was the start of the long climb back.

Hers was a slow recovery and Josh had been patient. Respect was the measure of his love and never, by even a glance in those following weeks, did he refer to their intimacy or try to press her more. It was established however, this new dimension, a stimulating and passionate bond that was finally acknowledged; one that had fulfilled their needs, both physical and emotional. A total commitment and joy in giving and receiving, never taking; it was called love – and love has many faces.

'Let it go, let it go.' Stella rubbed her face and hands but it was easier said than done. Eyes brimming with tears, she blinked hard – then blinked again, peering deeper now into the shimmering translucence of fresh green foliage – for spring had replaced the tired summer woodland – and Hannah was here!

The most powerful emotion; lost love, hearts broken, tears shed in this ancient woodland, had joined them across the years. Parallel dimensions held together for a moment in this gentle woodland and Stella was desperate to ease Hannah's hurt. 'Hannah,' she called softly into deep shadow under the arm of a great old oak, the leaves small and pale green with the freshness of new growth. The passion of young love, first love, filled the air yet it was not Stella's memory.

'Hannah, were you here, are you here, can you hear me?' Now Stella's tears were real, happy, spilling over. 'Caution my dear, caution with your hopes.' Anxious to protect one so young, so vulnerable, she spoke again, 'I must tell you that it is not spring. Not the spring you seek to relive. This is a tired summer, the year is 1963, and already the leaves are falling.'

It was as though in a haze, a collage was forming: through the trees, soft colours like polished autumn leaves, dappled light on the neck of a well brushed chestnut mare, the flash of brass on a bridle, shades of rich green on a velvet gown – and thick flowing auburn hair. Then, like a zephyr disturbing the surface of a still pond, Josh was by her side and the collage fragmented into woodland.

'What is it Stella?' Looking into her eyes, the expression in his changed, anything now but casual. 'Stella?' Slow question in the name, seduction in the tone until she held up a hand. 'Tell me. What's happening? What is it?' he persisted, more gently now.

'I was remembering, here, our first love making.'

'Wonderful. Is it our anniversary?' A hopeful smile.

'No darling, though I've just been through a fast rewind of my past. It was rather emotional and now I'm getting something more – from further back.' Her voice had dropped. 'Let's sit awhile.' Josh sat down beside her, knowing he could be in for a long wait.

'I think I'm picking up on Hannah Myer's life again,' she said eventually. 'She was here in this wood Josh, many times, with a man she was deeply in love with. Think of it, if you wanted to be alone with someone, it's a secluded and obvious way to walk from the manor at Sennington, across the meadows, through this wood and on to the mill or to Witetune House. It's longer than following the lane and it would give you more time together.'

'Were they lovers?' he asked with interest.

'Well, I feel she loved him desperately and he loved her too, but no, they were not lovers, I feel sure of that. I think it was an unrequited love. An all-consuming, all-forgiving, true, one and only love that will wait forever as long as there is a glimmer of hope. Like waiting for someone to come back from the war...'

'I wonder, why weren't they lovers?' Josh quickly glossed over the reference to the past. 'If it wasn't the done thing in those days, though I'm sure it was, I'm sure it always has been, why didn't they get married?'

'Remember what Andrew said? No matter what the relationship, the great barrier of class couldn't be crossed. I'm not getting that much detail, just a strong sense of their being here together, very much together. I think Hannah, because of pride or perhaps of being not quite sure of her ground, kept things light, waiting for the man to make the first move. In those days the woman couldn't make the first approach.' Then, pleading with him as he groaned, 'Do take this seriously Josh, you know how tenuous these feelings are and they're all I've got to build on. I'm trying to put a picture together and I want to be clear in my mind what messages I'm receiving.'

Eyes closed, she was quiet again, searching the spaces between the trees for movement; Josh watched as sunlight skimmed off her hair.

'There was an unspoken barrier between the couple,' she spoke at last. 'On his side I think. Remember his name for her, Little Witch? Whatever it was, it stopped him admitting the depth of his feeling, though he too wanted to consummate their love. They both wanted that.'

'Do you?' Josh asked hopefully. 'I'm asking because of the way you were looking at me just now. That misty faraway look in your eyes was quite encouraging.'

'Josh, you're spoiling my concentration! Here is an innocent passion I'm privy to, and if my feelings for you intermingle with Hannah's, I might get a distorted picture.' She didn't speak again for some minutes, then, with an exasperated sigh, 'Nothing, it's all gone.'

'Then let's get out of here.' Josh put his hand out. 'The strain is beginning to tell.'

Monday 19th August

Stella didn't know she was dreaming as she became enmeshed into the drama of what she was witnessing:

Down by the brook there was frenzied activity as the child Hannah, shaking with fear, hunted and tore at the hedges for glossy purple black berries. Hurry, hurry, must hurry. What have I said, who did I speak to? Rachel had warned her not to be so trusting but youth, fresh to human pain and senile suspicion, had wanted only to share the joyous gifts of healing and learning.

At last she had collected enough and running into the cottage, slid a wooden block across the door and secured the shutters as Rachel handed her a bowl. Unhesitatingly, Hannah drank, spilling liquid down her front, while in the half light her sister mixed the fresh berries of deadly nightshade into a thick paste for herself. Now the *vengeful* were heading for the gully and with a quick kiss, Hannah, already falling fast into drugged sleep, was being bundled into a round hole at the back of the fireplace, the iron door not quite latched, a gap for air.

'It's the bread oven, the one in Uncle John's cottage,' Stella whispered and another detail slipped into place as, grey faced and trembling, Rachel lifted a bowl to desperate lips, greedily scooping death into her mouth.

The mob had arrived and like dogs cornering the prey they bayed for the kill; vicious screams and words of hate demanding blood and flesh, convinced that death would cleanse at once the scourge of plague. Two relentless axes splintered the sturdy door as wood was heaped into a hastily erected pyre and Rachel was dragged out to burn. "*Look at her mouth, she's taken poison. Quick, light the fire; don't let her spirit escape to haunt us!*"

The silver buckle on one of Rachel's shoes scored the earth floor, fell off and was trampled unnoticed underfoot as she was hoisted up and bound to a stake as the flames began to curl.

Appalled at what she was witnessing, Stella was finding difficulty breathing. Rachel's terror and the hate from the crowd, was all-consuming. Still she held on, determined to follow through, determined not to abandon this woman, and it was this strength of commitment, a refusal to let go, that mentally locked her into the illusion of blind burning terror.

'Fire, fire, it's all around, I'm in it! No, I can't be, it's an illusion, don't go there, it's an illusion.' Stella struggled, trying to maintain the duality but it was like falling down a well. 'It's becoming real – it's happening to me. Help me!' she demanded.

'Relax, it is in the past.' Andrew's tone was flat; uncaring?

'It's really frightening me, don't you understand? I'm living this, it is actually happening to me and it's not illusion, I've somehow transferred and I can feel it, I can see it, it is real and I am in real danger. Stop this bloody nonsense and get me out!'

And the instant she believed that she was a victim; that what she was witnessing was reality, it became her reality, and the fire roared and flashed its heat, splitting dry twigs and flicking vicious red hot sparks at her eyes. Now came a smell of burning cloth and leather, and the nerves on her body, twitched as though in a remembered pain – and she could not break free of it.

'I've lost it, I can't keep the two levels apart,' she screamed, then realized that it was a silent scream, locked up in her throat, locked up in some long dead past. 'Andrew, Andrew, help me.' Calm indifference was his response, he didn't believe her! Rearing back, turning to one side, she tried to save her face to no avail, the pull of bonds tying her to the stake were firm, and the prospect of being burned alive, so over-whelming that Stella felt her heart would give out.

'I'm in the fire,' she sobbed. 'The fire is burning my feet, my shoes are alight. I can't clear it, I can't escape. You must take me out. Please Andrew, take me out now or I will surely perish!'

And her conviction that she could burn to death if she didn't escape, bound her instantly, as Rachel Myer, to the stake.

The next surge of heat was suffocating as hot smoke dried her throat and scorched sucking lungs greedy for air, yet even as the blessed poison began to numb and the cottage was put to the torch, her last prayers were for the child. The pain, the struggle was over.

'I can't break free of her,' she groaned.

"*Then die with her.*" Andrew's voice, silent within her thinking was without emotion. "*Your mind. Your choice. Your imagination. Your concept of what is real. What you believe is real to you and you are living it.*"

'Andrew, how can you do this? You can't abandon me. Andrew,' she called his name again as he continued to move away further and further away, leaving her to her fate. Wait – my fate, this is my fate? Who said so? Suddenly, enraged at his callous indifference but more by her own acceptance of victim status, one alien to all her beliefs, Stella felt the power of righteous anger. He bloody well had to come back and finish the job, she would make him, and taking control of her destiny sent her spinning back to the night!

'Oh, dear God, it was a nightmare,' she gasped.' A dream – and I'm not even in bed!' Sitting back in the chair, she hugged a cushion tight. It was dusk and all was silent in the cottage. Nothing had disturbed the air, no one was at the open window, and she had made no sound, given no cry for help. 'Oh I'm free of it, thank God,' she whispered taking great gulps of the cool evening air then she began to laugh hysterically, suppressing the sound with the cushion, 'and poor Andrew had been cast as the Devil incarnate!'

Later, as she made notes she began to understand the psychology behind Hannah's acceptance of her fate. To her childish reasoning, Hannah had blamed herself for the catastrophe. What did it matter if a mouth that had spoken so unguardedly was sealed forever? This was the punishment. What need had she of words? She must not cry out, this was the clearing of the debt and this sleep was so, so welcome. How much did this affect her in later life, Stella wondered? Then, work finished, she closed the curtains on the beauty of the night and went most gratefully to her bed.

Tuesday 20th August

As fate would have it. Andrew had been called to a Diocese meeting and wouldn't be back until late evening and Josh had sighed with relief, glad to have the pressure eased off. He had been away from the shop so much that the paperwork was, as he so descriptively put it, crawling out of the door. So, with unexpected time on her hands, Stella was in the back garden helping Abby tidy up Uncle John's vegetable plot. The joy of working with her hands, not having to think about anything in particular, doing normal everyday jobs, was therapeutic. There had been a short, heavy downpour in the early hours. Everything looked sharp-edged, the air washed clear of dusty pollen. Weeds gave up their hold with satisfying ease, so did the slugs as she slid them off the lettuces and threw them over the fence to a couple of waiting thrushes. Gardening put everything into perspective; even the sagging lines of the runner bean canes looked beautiful.

I could make a painting of them; Stella squared her hands to frame a picture. Even Abby seemed happier, perhaps because she was at home and had company though the autumn school term was looming on the horizon and going back to work and relating to people was never easy for her.

Hannah and Rachel must have lived here so simply, Stella mused, so happily; a roof overhead, food grown in the garden and water from the stream. Whole communities lived this way in these hills for hundreds of years, maybe thousands. She had stopped working and was looking up to the ridge of hills, just savouring the moment.

'I'll go and make a pot of tea, then we must lay the table. Cynthia will be home for lunch,' Abby broke into the reverie and Stella bent her back once again to slug throwing.

It was Pension day and also Market day and Cynthia, having bustled off early to collect the bread from the bakers next door, was back at the Post Office, dealing with the queues, ignoring the mumbled complaints about slow service.

The bread was still hot from the oven and the tantalising smell coming from her basket in the corner was making her feel hungry and irritable as she banged the official stamp from ink pad to counter-foil and back, before begrudgingly handing over the money as though it were her own. Market day was the only day Cynthia went home for lunch; madness in the village, the tea shop would be full of strangers and her seat would be taken. A bit of a rush to get home and back, though the very thought of fresh baked bread, cheese, some home-made apple and cider chutney and a decent cup of tea, made it all worthwhile.

'The sun is drying things up so we will eat in the garden, under the pear tree,' Stella called as she went into the kitchen to put a jug of iced lemon water in the fridge as Abby appeared with a tray. 'Tea and a slice of my lemon drizzle cake?'

'Don't mind if I do, I love your cakes.' Bertie came round the corner, beaming smile, carrying a ladder. 'I knows how to time things don't I? 'Morning Abby dear, morning Stella.'

'Oh, life is good,' Stella smiled a welcome as they sat down on the rustic bench Uncle John had built years before

Just after one o'clock, Cynthia arrived, starving. 'Everything ready, kettle on? Oh,' noticing Bertie, her voice dropping a fraction. An extra one for lunch, she hadn't planned for this and she didn't like surprises.

'Don't worry about me, I've got my sandwiches,' he smiled, reading her like a book. 'Made them myself first thing this morning, corned beef with my own tomatoes but I'll sit with you and have another piece of cake.' Without hurrying he put a paint brush into the turpentine and turned to Abby. 'Mind if I wash my hands in your kitchen, love?' and she went in with him to give him a clean towel.

Cynthia was busy attacking the bread, tearing the bun off the top of the cottage loaf and putting it on her plate. It was a bit burned; she liked the burned bits and had been relishing the thought of sinking her teeth through the cheese and butter to get at it, all morning. Get it before Bertie got a look-in. He might have sandwiches but men could always put a piece of crusty bread and cheese away.

So busy was she that only Stella saw the faint flush on Abby's cheeks and the smile she and Bertie exchanged as they went indoors. 'Oh, that could explain a lot. How nice!'

It happened just after lunch. Bertie had gone back to painting Uncle John's bedroom window and Cynthia had hurried off, leaving Stella and Abby to clear away, when Bertie came down the ladder in his unhurried way. 'Will you go in and open that bedroom window Abby, so I can paint just inside. It will look smarter when it comes to selling.'

Abby's face drained, not to white, rather as though something had sucked the colour from a canvas and with it, the vitality. Stella later likened it to a colourwash she sometimes laid on a too-bright sky. She had sort of stopped; eyes fixed on the table, milk jug half way as if listening or waiting for something else. The greatest shock for Stella was to see that frightened *little girl* look again, just as at the funeral. ' I'll – I'll give you the key. You can do it yourself. I'm busy, you can see I'm washing up,' she snapped and hurried away leaving Stella and Bertie staring after her.

'What's that all about?' he asked.

'I haven't the foggiest idea.'

'She's not frightened to go in, is she?'

'Why should she be?' Stella shrugged. 'They were close, good friends as well as family. Come to think of it, I've not seen her actually go in since the funeral. Cynthia, Josh, Vera and I have shared the decisions about what to do with his things just to make life easier for her. Abby had been either too busy to help – or she had a headache or was waiting for a phone call or had to write a letter – trivial things like that. Once or twice she sort of hovered outside, taking bits from us to put in the bin, making tea and that's all. Considering it's her inheritance, she's not shown any real interest.

'Vera said that the only place we've not to touch is the attic and that's because we need Abby there to instruct us, and she's right. We need Abby to make decisions and give us some instructions as to what to do with all the stuff. Some of it could be personal; family letters, photographs, business-related documents.

'We've told her we can't possibly do it without her help but she hasn't committed herself to a time yet and there's no real hurry, I suppose.'

'If there is a problem, what's to be done?' Bertie followed in his measured way.

'I don't know and I think I'll go out and leave it to you,' Stella didn't wait for agreement. 'It could be too much pressure if both of us start on her. Abby's not strong, her confidence is paper thin. No, you talk to her alone Bertie. You can have the whole afternoon to yourselves, you won't be interrupted.'

* * * * * * *

The scent of lavender and roses warm in the sun encouraged Abby and Bertie along the back path. Key in hand, they stood at the locked door, Bertie at her shoulder, a large hand on her back discouraging any idea of retreat. 'I know it's silly,' she was trembling, 'but going in, seeing it empty, well it will be the end, won't it? Final. Finished.'

'Now remember what John said? *"That's life. It is the way of things."* I'm your friend Abby, always have been and I'm here to support you. You can rely on me; always could. So, in you go and I'll just step inside the door. Now take your time.' And Bertie sat himself down on a stool and waited as Abby wandered about studying marks on the walls where paintings had hung, sliding a hand across empty shelves, touching stains on the old table.

Finally, though she had been avoiding it, she stood in front of the piano, hesitatingly she lifted the lid, hovered a hand, then recalling his words, "Make it sound beautiful, Abby and send it on its way." she pressed a single key. 'This is for you, Uncle John. Thank you,' and so doing, she carefully closed the lid. Around her the shades hovered, spreading the soft unbroken note across the still air until it became the sound of silence and, with sweet sadness, Abby let go of her Uncle John.

Thursday 22nd August

'Oh, in Heaven's name, why am I going back to the manor?' This was Stella's first thought as she woke feeling uneasy. 'It's a waste of time. Josh and Andrew don't need me. They'll enjoy picking Harry's brains and showing them around will give him something to do.' In truth, it was the prospect of going back to the house that was making her uneasy 'So why go?' she asked the empty room. 'Feminine intuition?'

They all arrived at the manor at the same time and Josh and Andrew, eager to get to the library, immediately headed off down the corridor leaving Stella at the kitchen door. 'Give me a few minutes and I'll and make the coffee,' Harry called back to her. 'You can put the water on if you like,' and he hurried off to join the men. 'Surely coffee can wait.' Stella said crossly. 'We're not here to socialise.' No one heard her and with a resigned sigh she filled the kettle. The water boiled, she put coffee in the mugs, and the minutes ticked away as it went cold, and there was still no sign of Harry.

Bored with waiting, Stella wandered back into the dining room. It was dim in there, light from the garden filtering in through small squares of thick glass, distorted and scratched, bound in iron frames, held as they had been for over three hundred years. Utter silence, complete stillness, she became aware of something – a smell.

It was as though someone had burned apple logs here, bathing the oak panels and wooden floor in sweet dusty smoke but the hearth was empty, not used for many a year – and there was something more. Sensitive to change, Stella relaxed and stilled herself, then looking through the haze of half-closed eyes, beyond the hard lines of the furniture, beyond what was obvious and solid...

Blurred edges, vague at first, just shapes moving around each other, slowly clearing, taking on the outline of people, seemingly unaware of her presence in their past. Undisturbed, they went about their daily tasks as, like a phantom, she walked out of the dining room and back to the square entrance hall with its shallow ceiling and high fire place.

It was easy to imagine it ablaze with logs, the fire dancing warm colours over the wood, welcoming travellers in from the cold on bitter winter nights, or in spring with doors flung wide, jugs of flowers and the harmony and the sweet smell of a well-ordered house, run by a small army of servants.

The moment Stella turned to the imposing staircase her heart leapt with happiness. It was back – the Presence, soft as an apology and closing in like an old friend, drawing her up, inviting her to a place that she knew would be warm and familiar. Still she was hesitant and when she finally reached for the banister rail, it was her heart that lurched with joyous recognition, a seeming age before her brain could evaluate what had happened.

Oh, this was it! The handrail, broad as her outstretched hand, was the one she had felt beneath her fingers when time had warped at Brook Cottage and at Witetune House; déjà vu? Or memories, folding in on each other again, overlapping, and pulling things in from a past that she needed to remember? Whose past?' Then she gave a little startled cry, her very skin giving warning of sudden change as the words flew from her lips.

"Oh, I'm back my dearest love. I'm back!"

Where did that come from? Shocked, clamping a hand to her mouth, she looked around. Yes, she had said the words, set them free but they were someone else's words; the yearning to say them aloud, held in check for too, too long. Whose words were they, who was calling and who was listening?

Don't question, just flow with it.

No apprehension now. As though pulled by an invisible cord she began the ascent of the stairs, her body stiffly erect as though held in a tight corset, moving its measured way on and up the broad steps with exaggerated dignity. It knew the way, every step exactly placed; each turn of the staircase was anticipated.

Keep calm, keep calm. Don't lose this precious hold.

Reaching the first floor, prepared for any encounter, she walked the length of the corridor to the right, doors opening on to lofty, well-proportioned rooms. Just as in the dining room and the kitchen below, she felt the energies of the people who had used them. They were still here and there was no unease at the overlapping of time or dimension. No feeling of intrusion or of undue familiarity from either party. Rather it was an unspoken, courteous and mutual acknowledgement, each of the other's existence. No need for more – no intimate exchange.

Back at the main staircase she turned suddenly, surprised to hear voices. The voices of children, running indoors from the fields, excited and tired from a long-ago summer day and still chasing each other. Oh, here they came; the dear children! Stella couldn't see them though she felt them all around now, smell and excitement, breath on the back of her hand. Then even as her heart rose with a great song, logic asked coldly:

'Whose children are they?'

Stella dismissed it, she was happy, then something tugged at her skirt, once, twice: Look at me, can't catch me. Not actual words but she knew their games as they ran higher and she followed them joyfully, bunching up her skirt as though it swept the floor – only to stop abruptly, for bewilderingly, the flight had come to a sudden end. Nothing!

'So, where are the stairs, the final flight to the attic?' she demanded out loud, returning to the present and agitatedly pacing the landing as the children went higher.

'Where is the way up? There has to be a way up,' she persisted, eyes examining the immaculately plastered ceiling. 'An immaculate ceiling in a house this old – this doesn't make sense.' Back down the stairs she flew, feet confident as they paced the flanks of oak, hand on banister, strong and familiar; down, down, round, round. 'I must find the way up to the attics. I must find the children.'

Nothing else mattered. Across the hall she went, through the dining room, past the kitchen, feet tapping on the stone flags, stopping at the open Library door. The men were there, laughing and surrounded by books.

'Harry, Harry, where has the top flight of stairs gone? Is there a way up to the attic rooms?' Puzzled by her irritation and impatience,

Josh, Andrew and Harry laid down the books. This just wasn't like her. 'What happened to the stairs? Tell me Harry, how I get up to the top?' she demanded.

'Er – I think the fire that destroyed the wing of the house, burned the staircase too,' he said. 'I suppose they never replaced it. To get up there now you go along this corridor,' he pointed. 'Second door, there is a back staircase. It was used by the servants at one time I would think. Want me to show you?'

Stella had already gone, 'Down the hall, second door,' she gasped his instructions. 'Yes! Here it is.' Climbing what was little more than a strong rough ladder she flung open the door at the top – and she could hear them again! Of course! The children's nursery and play room would be up here. Living on the same level as the maids made sense. They could make as much noise as they liked up here.

She stopped suddenly, ears straining for something had changed – and the children had gone. All was silent and now the attic was pocketed by deepening fast moving shadows, as though the day was running to its end, fading, and the long-ago children had faded with it. 'I won't let go. I mustn't,' she groaned.

Then she saw it; a door at the far end that opened onto a large square area with a big window that looked onto the ruined wing. This must be directly above the place where the stairs ran out, she judged. This must have been the top landing and within a foot or two this must have been where Hannah Myer must have stood, waiting out her long nights for Lawrence.

'Poor girl,' she whispered, subdued by sadness as thoughts, or were they indeed her memories, came tumbling in one after the other. Too fragile for Stella to analyse, yet she felt there was an overwhelming sense of being needed, of someone trying to attract her attention. 'It has to be you, Hannah,' Stella whispered. 'I want to help. Just tell me how to reach you. You have to show me how.' And to show that trust, once more Stella cleared her mind and waited.

Slipping back into that 17th century household was, for Stella, as simple as turning a page. There it was; the drift of their wild flowers again. The children had gone, though the pungent smell of wilting flowers dropped from hot little hands was still here, sweet to the memory, caught like the rest in this in-between state. Drawn from the past, the children had tried but could not quite access the present moment. 'And why should they want to?' Shocked by the bubble of savage resentment that swelled instantly in her throat, Stella let Hannah's words flow. *"Why should they reach out and why should I open my heart? They are my master's children, not mine. Never mine, never ours. I have no rights, no claim to anything, just this unspoken understanding between us that one day...!*

"Oh, dear Lord, surely there is going to be a one day?"
Stella shuddered; her empathy with Hannah's situation was becoming much too personal. As a gifted clairvoyant, it was critical that she distance herself if there was to be any value in her interpretation of what was happening so, sitting down heavily on an old packing case, she went over what she knew.

Hannah had been frustrated by more than her situation in this household. She was too well-connected and educated to be in the servant class but not quite part of the Gentry, either. She had no definite place in either stratum of society. Her life had been a balancing act. Social boundaries dictated what was, and what was not, acceptable in those times, yet she must have had a very close relationship with her master to even think of having his children. She had wanted children; I felt her need and it was like a physical ache. She couldn't allow herself to get too fond of his children either. Always the barrier, always guarding herself emotionally. She would never have roared with laughter at their funny ways or scooped them up to be kissed and hugged. She was never that relaxed.

'Why? Why?' Silent minutes ticked by then, 'Oh yes, that's it!' Stella's stillness had paid off and the details were becoming clearer. 'Oh my goodness, now I understand,' she whispered on the verge of tears. 'Hannah just couldn't face the total impossibility of her dreams. No children and no Lawrence! It would have meant the end of hope. Hannah couldn't have spoken the truth even to herself; she could not have made herself that vulnerable!

'How sad, how very sad,' she said to the walls, for those children never knew of her longing to love them like a mother, or of the words of devotion bitten back behind lips that might have been sealed, for all the freedom they had. As the years passed, Hannah had stifled her emotions until nothing, virtually nothing was spontaneous.

So, when had it ended? When did she finally accept as a fact that her dreams would never come true? Did she dream at night, revisiting times in youth when her hopes were high and her laughter free? Perhaps not. Stella shook her head, understanding and reliving again the raw pain of lost love.

Distressed and emotionally drained, elbows on knees, Stella cradled her head in her hands and silently wept. She must have slept, perhaps only for a few minutes but on waking, limp from crying, all resistance gone – she had moved back again to another long-ago seventeenth century summer...

Now the stairs reached right up to the attics and polished floors gleamed and stretched away to the nursery wing. Servants were busy downstairs, much preparation, great excitement, visitors, titled gentry were arriving from the Royal Court in London, and the attics, free now of their bustle, were ready for Hannah's inspection. Grasping the possibilities of this altered state Stella was instantly alert.

So where does Hannah live? Not in the attic with the domestics. Being able to read and write, she would have had to distance herself from them to keep authority. She looked up, this was the top of the house there was nothing above and yet, and yet a sixth sense said she was missing something. This time she looked at the walls, slowly retracing her steps, then 'Yes, I knew it!'

The door was set back in a dim recess and opening it, Stella mounted the four steps to a small landing, a room on either side. The one on the left hand with no window held a narrow bed with good quality linen and a camphor chest for holding clothes safe from moths, a small bedside table with a pewter candlestick and a prayer book. Three small embroidered samplers decorated the walls and there was rush matting on the floor. It was well ordered and comfortable. She crossed the landing to what must have been

Hannah's sitting room. Flowers in a white bowl on the window-sill, rush matting on the floor. A well-used leather arm chair that had probably been down stairs at one time, a ladder-backed upright chair set at a small table that also served as a desk and held several books, a quill pen, ink stand and a few squares of parchment paper with linen ties, neatly lined, to bind the scrolls.

Through the low window across the room, Stella saw the old Nut Walk, leading to what looked like the remains of an abandoned village! She had no doubt that, as legend had it, this was Old Sennington, set to the torch when the plague struck.

'And that's where the mob came from when I saw them charging down the gully to commit bloody murder. Am I that far back?' her eyes widened. 'Yes I am! I mustn't anticipate,' she cautioned, trying to suppress tiny flurries of nervous excitement. 'Don't go any further back; there's no need to relive the horror. Leave it. That's not why I am here.'

Returning to the landing, preparing to leave, Stella smiled understandingly, as with an involuntary movement, her foot stretched out again. 'It is that strong a connection!' she sighed, head on one side, taking notice of vague images. 'Hannah was sort of on guard up here – always prepared, though I'm not sure for what. Undisturbed, she could probably have stood quite motionless up here, listening to gossip of the household below, detecting any hint of disloyalty, intrigue or resentment. No one would have been aware of the deep-rooted, unspoken fears that dictated this obsession. How could they? Hannah herself did not know.

Still in deep thought, Stella didn't react when a girl appeared from the nursery, met her eyes, bobbed a respectful, disinterested curtsey before hurrying down to a bedroom below and, with that brief encounter, Stella knew that, like a shadow, she was indeed sharing another woman's life. This blending of two dimensions had happened only once before in Stella's psychic experience and confident now that she was being guided, she waited to see what would happen. This was the17th century and these people could see her just as well as she could see them. So who were they seeing? Not a stranger.

They were seeing someone they knew. Was it Hannah? And what did Hannah want? Questions, questions with no real answers. Frustrated, tired and ready to give up, Stella spoke softly again: 'I know you need me, Hannah, and I'll do my best to help you regain peace of mind, so you have to tell me how. What do you want of me? I believe that you are still living the pain of something that happened over three hundred years ago and your distress is affecting me. I don't think you want that, and so my dearest, it is time to let go. Do you recall what I said when I spoke to you, in the wood? We are in the month of August and it is now the year of our Lord 1963.'

Stella made the date come up big and bold in her mind's eye and projected the numbers on to the wall. 'Your people have long since departed and you should be at rest. How can I help you fulfil your destiny? I'm at the end of my tether. I don't know what to do next. Please, please help me.'

As if in answer, tightness came to Stella's throat, she felt again the bubbling up of Hannah's fury and then it came to her – clarity: The accusation and the shame of witchcraft that had stained her sister's character and had shamed the family, had to be cleared – yet there was more.

There was a personal grievance.

In all their time together, her friend and protector, Lawrence Roberts had never seemed to appreciate Hannah's own sacrifice: the sacrifice of her own life as she waited out her childbearing years, for him to claim her. The sacrifice of her own, *"...sucked dry by the bloody hour, unlived life!"* and realizing this, Stella had to stifle a scream of rage that ripped silently through her chest...

'At last!' she gasped. 'It is Hannah's unquiet spirit that links my cottage to both manor houses. She lived in all three places and never knew peace of mind in any of them. It's her unquiet spirit that can't find rest and is it any bloody wonder?'

Again the tears spilled over unchecked as detailed mind pictures, came flooding into Stella's consciousness, painting a broader canvas, pushing wide the door of memory:

Oh dear Lord, how many years did she spend waiting, keeping

watch? Hannah had waited at the top of the old staircase, night upon night, fingering the rail, the patina burnished with the layers of patient waiting while her ears strained for any creak on the stairs below that would herald the arrival of her love. Though that wasn't the only reason for her vigil; unable to sleep, fearful to sleep, she was guarding the children, checking the maids, and always, always listening. She was obsessed with listening, not only for the longed-for tread of the man she loved but for any sign of danger from below. Now was the time of the Civil War and this was a Royalist household. Panic was rising in Stella's throat but she didn't halt the pictures as they came faster and faster. The opening of a hidden chamber, rooms between floors, religious persecution, Royalists hunted by Cromwell's Round-heads. Urgent whispers in quiet corners had drifted up to these rafters, tiny laughs caught in the throat, a footstep creaking on a lower stair, hurried steps, frightened steps.

Other ears straining for warnings, sounds trapped in old timbers, layers of lifetimes and always, always, *the Visitors*.

Hannah knew them by face, by name, by intent, and in their intent they posed a mortal threat! Political loyalties traded behind locked doors, a bolt drawn in the night, clandestine meetings, fleeting shadows across the lawn, urgent, running. All were warnings in time of danger. So she had been patient over the years, vigilant, gleaning much, telling nothing, knowing their strengths and, more important, their weaknesses.

She knew them better than they knew each other, better than they knew themselves and all this kept inside her head, the power of knowledge not to be dissipated by the telling.

Knowledge was a bargaining tool against accusation when boastful young men, tongues loose in drink, departed with the clink of chain in the middle of the night from the place in the cellar. Not her betrayal. No! Burning makes for a tight tongue. Burning can seal a tongue – forever!

Dark shadows of dread haunted Hannah's mind, and that's why the outgoing confident child of the miller became reclusive; reluctant to speak, economical with words. Stella touched her lips, remembering; Rachel being put to the torch and the child in the bread oven accepting punishment, accepting it as her fate.

No one had ever explained to the grown woman that she had not been to blame, that she had misjudged herself. Why should they? She had lost her memory and that was for the good, wasn't it? Let sleeping dogs lie, they nodded sagely, *"It's all for the best."* But it was for their *"best"* not for Hannah's and no one knew of her dread of sinking into deep sleep, when, freed briefly by unguarded slumber, screams and the smell of burning flesh would surface from the past. Wide-eyed, sweating and fighting to wake up, she would struggle from her bed, the incident instantly blocked: An oven door slamming on a memory too appalling to be examined in the cold light of day. Her instinct to suppress was so powerful that she promptly forgot the horror.

It was just another dream. And what did she need of sleep? Snatching little naps in the day, that was enough sleep. The bad dreams never came in the light...

'All so long ago, all so deeply buried; let it go,' Stella sighed wearily. 'I've had enough,' but there was to be no let up.

Now, like a speeded-up film, deepening nights swallowed up flashing days that thrust away summer mornings and raced on to winter. Candles flickered everywhere, the smell of logs burning in the hall below, snow, white against the small, square mullioned panes. New Year's Day; they were preparing for a party and the wild flowers were already out. Wait, a New Year and wild flowers? Little bowls of yellow coltsfoot were everywhere. Yes, the coltsfoots, Stella's favourite wild flower, a March flower. Then she recalled Andrew saying that New Year still began on the 25th of March, until the date was changed in 1750. So this would have been the time that Hannah would have gathered baskets of coltsfoot for her sister. Rachel would have made infusions with them to ease the hacking coughs that often heralded the plague.

It all fits. Another confirmation that the child Hannah and the woman who came to this manor here as house keeper, were definitely one and the same person, the line was that clear.

'Oh, enough, enough,' Stella felt on 'overload' as she massaged her temples, trying to ignore the start of a tension headache. She wanted to stop, take stock and rest yet still the channelled energy, like an excited child wanting to explain more, wasn't considering the host's weakening state.

Muddying pictures now, clarity sacrificed from concentrating too hard and too long, Stella was trying to clear them from her mind's eye when, like a sound from hell, a bell began to toll – and it was then that she screamed!

A single bell, the church of Old Sennington, when the inhabitants were fleeing and the place was being set to the torch. The bell that was tolling to tell of a death – and another – and another, and it was happening, now!

Time had run back; the plague had struck, the mob was on the march, Rachel Myer was about to burn and Stella had been here before. Stella had felt her own shoes on fire!

"No, no! Not her fault, not my fault." Appalled, horrified. *"Stop the bell. Stop it. In the bowels of Christ, stop the bell!"* she screamed, out of control and with hands pressed against ears. This was how Andrew found her, grieving savagely, having crashed back through the barrier from that horrific time.

'Oh Andrew,' she sobbed as, holding her tightly, he finally got through to her. 'I've got to free myself from this haunting duality. I'm crying Hannah's tears. This is her anguish, and the pain is so, so pitiful. I have to release myself and Rachel and poor Hannah if I can.' She gasped for breath; deep, jagged sucks of air, struggling to gain control again.

Back in the kitchen, with her hands wrapped around a mug of hot tea and the reassurance of good companions, Stella finally calmed down. Harry, all agog as he refilled the mugs, just kept quiet and listened.

'I've got to help her, Andrew,' Stella said. 'I can't walk away from her now, can I?'

'No, and with your gifts, you know you can't,' he replied. 'After what's just happened, I think you're coming round to my way of thinking. You must not on any account, try to go it alone. It is too great a risk. And we have to accept that there is something more. We haven't found what is really at the heart of all this; the kernel. We know why Hannah cursed Brook Cottage but there has to be more, some vital detail that is still eating away at her peace of mind. So, are we going to do it my way?' he challenged.

'You mean hypnosis, of course. All right, I'll go ahead with it.' She was steadier now and nodded. 'I trust you Andrew, and I really don't have any choice, do I? I can't go on like this. If I don't clear these ghosts they might torment me to my dying day, and if that happens I will surely go mad.'

Andrew knelt down by her. 'Then let's tackle it. Let's make it tomorrow, while the memory and the emotions are sharp.'

This time, Josh raised no objections.

Friday 23rd August

'Almost 2 o'clock, they will be here soon.' Stella checked her watch. She had refused to answer the door or telephone. The isolation had been therapeutic and, composed now, she was prepared for the hypnosis. Josh arrived minutes later, pen and pad at the ready, quickly followed by Andrew, both keen to get started. Getting down to business, Josh gave them a rapid recap, emphasising key points, making their progress so far absolutely clear.

'Now that we know exactly how Rachel died and more or less where in the garden she was buried, I think we are concentrating on Hannah this time. Find the key; that is, if you can manage to locate her again.'

'She will, with my help,' Andrew was confident. 'Let's start.'

Stella began the relaxation and soon there was no sound apart from her soft, regulated breathing and the muffled tick, once every second, from the big clock in the hall. This regression was different; new sensations, she noted without concern, as the surface of her skin became desensitised, then numb. It was her hands that reacted first, lying limp and heavy on her lap, then inside, like butterflies in a chrysalis stretching to be free, invisible fingers began to expand and push against the physical glove. It was a kneading sensation, palpating, massaging, growing stronger, until the fingers eased themselves through, flowing out, then back a little, gaining strength until she felt them curled above her lap and into the air, pulling her out with them. Totally conscious, knowing that a flicker of alarm would instantly put her back, Stella allowed herself to experience once again the delight of weightlessness and, secure in the knowledge that her earth-bound body was safe and protected, she let go the present to search the past for Hannah Myer.

As Andrew had predicted, finding her wasn't difficult.

The time was the same, high summer, and there was great change in the cottage. Angry words had replaced Hannah's resigned silence. Here was a woman with a cause, ready to make demands instead of gratefully accepting what she had taken as favour, and her questions raged as old memories surfaced. Stella tried to stay neutral but as she took on the cloak of Hannah, her replies to Andrew became edged with irritation and contempt for men and their right to authority. Like a child asked questions at a difficult time, she wanted to be free of the need to reply, Andrew, however, was skilled and knew how to handle the situation.

'Stella will remember all the finer points when she is back with us,' he whispered to Josh. 'In the meantime I'll work on main events. I don't want her to become antagonistic.' Then, to their surprise, Stella spoke out calmly again, her delivery clear.

'I am upstairs in Hannah's private sitting room. I am listening to Lawrence Roberts and the Parson as they talk to Hannah. I am also beginning to pick up pictures from her mind; the restructuring of memories as they surface, nasty shocks of the remembered past. It is difficult to keep myself separated from her reactions. I am, I feel, deeply bound, deeply involved. I cannot seem to resist this empathy. Hannah has taken to her day bed.

'It is high summer, still she feels a terrible cold. I, too, shiver each time she does and this concerns me.' Then, with a note of anxiety, 'I must try to stay outside this body. It is not strong – not at all strong! The men are not aware of the activity behind Hannah's dulled eyes. I hear them say that Rachel's remains have been reburied in the churchyard with an unmarked headstone. The villagers have been told it is the body of a murdered drover and that Lawrence has paid for the burial. No one thinks this strange, it has happened before and the servants have been ordered to remain silent.

The Parson and the Lord of the Manor have enormous power and no one will go against their wishes if they want to remain in their service. The arm of their influence sweeps wide so there would be no welcome elsewhere.

Hannah is not satisfied with what they have told her. They think they are protecting her but she is an intelligent woman and is demanding more information. After my time with her at the manor, I know well how she feels. She is tired of living in a twilight world and needs to know what is real, before it is too late.' Josh and

Andrew kept quiet through what was obviously a pause.

"*You have to tell me all.*" Stella was obviously speaking Hannah's words now. "*I now recall my sister giving me a potion. She was greatly distressed as she pushed me into the big bread oven to hide me. I was warned not to come out until dark and everyone had left, then I was to go home to our father at the mill. There must have been a fire for I felt the heat coming in through the walls, though I was too drugged to move as the bricks – as the bricks became hotter and scorched my lips,*" she said faltering, as though making a discovery. "*Fire! Fire can seal lips forever,*" she cried out violently. "*My lips or my sister's? Tell me what happened to make me afraid to speak? How could I have forgotten about the very existence of my sister and of our cottage here, a home where we lived so happily?*"

Stella detached briefly. 'Hannah is struggling to get up.' Then resuming. "*Why did you not talk to me of it, Lawrence? Why did you not talk to me of other things? There were countless opportunities when we walked alone in the grounds of Witetune House, or through the deep wood past the mill to Sennington Manor? We seemed to be so close, yet all that time there was this dark secret in you, one that kept you from me when we each knew well the heart and the needs of the other. You say you did not harm Rachel, so what was it? Why did you not speak?*"

Andrew and Josh waited in silent anticipation, then Stella continued – deeper in now – the story unfolding like scenes from a film…

"*Guilt.*" Lawrence formed the word, face buried in his hands.

"*Guilt – yours?*" She frowned.

"*And mine, for my sins,*" from the parson.

"*Do you remember what I began to call you that summer, my special name for you?*" Lawrence asked.

"*Yes, I do now. You would call me your* Little Witch of the Woods, *for whenever we met I was collecting plants for my sister. You always wanted to know what they were for, what they did and how long they lasted, and how you laughed when I pointed to the herbs that had to be mixed by moonlight. Rachel had warned me not to gossip but I felt free to talk to you, the Gentry. You were my closest friend, I shared my growing knowledge with you, and that's why you called me a witch. Yet you meant it most kindly and we made much merriment of it."*

"That's right, all innocent jest," his voice lifted eagerly. *"Then drinking too much with my cousins at the tavern in the village, I told them about you and your special name. We laughed, so did the men around."* Another pause. *"So, through the foolish talk of drunken young men, the seed was probably sown and when plague came to the village soon after, you and your sister were obvious targets for blame."*

A long pause, then Hannah's voice came through slowly. *"But – at the start – the very start, it was my loose tongue that did the chattering. I suggested cures, when I should not have. I felt important; I wanted to be like Rachel. She had warned me not to gossip about her work.... So her murder, the sin of it, is on my hands? Dear God, no!"* she whispered in disbelief. *"My Rachel was innocent, yet it was the words of her own flesh and blood, my words, that destroyed her,"* she moaned in horror.

"No, no, you were a child, it was just cruel timing. Plague struck when I was away and not there to defend you. Do you remember how your sister used to treat sick drovers and their stock, with herbs and compresses and paste from the pool bed behind your father's mill? She also had amazing powers of divining and knew the practical use of nature's gifts. She was a wise and gifted woman who had always practised her craft in solitude, preferring her own company to that of folks around here. So you see, the rumour was a mixture of fact and fancy. Looking back it is possible that a drover carried the plague and it could just as easily have been a traveller passing through and staying over at the Inn in the village.

The night I came back, the cottage was still smouldering. There was no one around, no one to question. I was devastated and had been standing there alone in the dark for some time when I heard you start to whimper. Being in that bread oven saved your life. The side of your face was blistered and I thanked God that you were not badly scarred, not marked for life."

"Not on the outside maybe." Hannah's voice was bitter. *"Tell me, how old was I then?"*

"You were only 13, still a child, dainty and delicately boned. By taking off your outer garments, Rachel managed to get you in the bread oven. It was August, 1623."

"And now it is 1663 and I have had 40 years in the shadows." She clutched at the cloth of her dress, crying pitifully.

"Under cover of dark, I got you out of the oven and took you back to your family at the mill, but they had heard and were in fear of their own lives, so I delivered you instead to my cousin at Witetune House. My cousin shared the guilt too; we often drank together, so the family took you in. The mob wouldn't have dared to invade the great house or cross the parish boundary. As it happened the new dawn brought many a doubt as memories of your sister helping the poor, for no payment, were whispered abroad. Though the villagers were numb with shock, life had to go on and the plague still spread. We had isolated the manor and grounds, then the disease was stopped when the old village on the hill was abandoned and fired.

It was then that the few who had been spared moved down here to the valley, but further up stream to be away from this accursed spot. With so many trees around, this area was avoided and for fear of ghosts, or old spells, it was left alone. No one spoke of it to you because all dreaded the return of your memory. Mercifully, the shock had blanked everything out for you. You remembered nothing and so you became a companion for my little cousins, Ann and Apollina, at Witetune House. You fitted in well; you had natural breeding and a most beautiful home to grow up in. You learned ladies' skills and even now your quilling passes your hours peacefully. I was able to visit often and walk and talk to you in private. No one minded us being alone together; it had been ever thus from the time I delivered you into their keeping.

That meant much to me and I watched you grow in great dignity and beauty as your womanhood flowered. You were intelligent, noble in countenance, and fine in principle and character, higher somehow than your goodly miller breeding, with your glorious golden hair and elegant stature, so tall and straight of bearing. You were always different. It is said that you were sired by a nobleman who stayed at Sudeley Castle to hunt deer in the park and that was another reason that folks left you alone."

"We were all weighed down with a deep shame," the parson took up the story. *"I, because my attentions to your sister were misread and also, being so young and inexperienced at the time, I could not control my parishioners and was forced, for fear of my life, to head the mob."* He broke down and began to cry but Hannah felt no compassion; spared him nothing.

"Go on," she said coldly. *"I've cried enough inside to cripple us all."*

Haltingly, as though interpreting, Stella's voice surfaced again.

'The Parson is telling her about the murder and the way Rachel died. He is saying that when everyone had left, he buried the body in the garden so only he knew where it actually lay, so he forbade anybody to go near or talk of it ever again. The parson was a tutor for Lawrence Roberts' young cousins, Ann and Apollina, at Witetune House. With Hannah's removal there, he made a specific effort to educate her alongside the girls, an education that would enable Hannah to earn her living. This was his way of easing her situation, and by easing her lot in life he eased the burden of his guilt.

'He must have tried to hold her hand.' They watched Stella pull her hand away as if stung...

"It was torment for me; daily torment. I loved and wanted you so. When the girls married it was a joy and a relief to be able to take you to my household here in Sennington. As my housekeeper you had a position, could earn coin and I could take care of your welfare and protect you under my roof."

"Where I continued my twilight life," Hannah snapped. *"I had no friends, for I trusted no one. I was always afraid, afraid to sleep, afraid of fire, afraid of something unseen, unknown, unidentified."* She waved the air as though in search. *"I had no idea what it was, so I suppressed my emotions, all of them and they lay in my breast like lumps of black rock, rising enough to choke me when anything stirred that unknown terror. I was constantly on my guard, never, never at peace, afraid to speak of it even to you, and now I know why,"* She

pointed an accusing finger.

"*I thought you had found a haven with me,*" Lawrence lowering his head in sorrow. "*Yet you were afraid to sleep. I didn't know.*"

"*How could you?*" she whipped back. "*You never shared my bed, though I waited moon to moon. I have no offspring. All that youth, all that longing, all those flowing juices, dried and gone forever. They took two lives. Mine along with Rachel's and because of your cowardice and for no sin of mine – I shall die a maiden!*"

Razor-edged in the meaning, they looked at each other openly for the first time, as man and woman, both totally spent, both grieving for what might have been.

"*We were God fearing daughters of the Miller. We had a right to expect a full life. Why did you bring me back to the scene of the crime; for crime it was? Why did you build here?*"

"*To try and give you some feeling of belonging, perhaps to lay a ghost. Perhaps – my own ghost.*" His voice shook.

"*And has it been laid? Tell me true, were the villagers responsible brought to justice? The mob leaders and the blacksmith who dealt the killing blow?*"

The parson and Lawrence shook their heads. "*No.*"

"*No? So no one paid for my sister's murder and she died* Unshriven, *without cleansing or blessing from the church? Your church,*" she pointed at the parson.

"*I did pray for her soul.*"

"*But it was unofficial. So to this very day she is still marked as a heretic in these hills. My own flesh and blood lying outside holy ground all that time and still the truth is not acknowledged. The shame is still on my family name.*" Nothing to add, they did not answer. "*How was it recorded?*"

"*At the time? Oh, that she died from plague.*" Barely above a whisper he waited for the backlash.

"*What mean you by, 'at the time'?*"

"*When I decided to build on this land, to give you a secure home for your advancing years, legal documents had to be signed, under oath. There were those who remembered. I had no choice. I had to have it recorded that she died as a witch. Please, let me finish, I beg you,*" he raised his voice above her screams of protest. "*There was also a second reason. You see, she tried to commit suicide before she was killed. That was a double sin, witchcraft and suicide, too strong a case to fight – and what reason was there to fight when so many years had passed and scars were healing? I just wanted to give you your home back. I was doing that for you and for poor Rachel. Leaving it that she had been accused was easier on your family,*" he finished lamely.

"*What clever talk is this?*" Hannah was incandescent with rage. "*She was innocent and forced to take poison or be burned to death! So, what is on her headstone now she has been moved to the church? And will you now spread the truth and accuse the murderers?*" The voice, shrill and on the point of hysteria was releasing frustrations stifled over a life time.

"*It cannot be done.*" The parson pleaded for understanding. "*There are a few still alive who believe she was a witch and, as a witch, should have been buried at cross roads. I risked much by laying her poor body here to rest. Now that she is in the churchyard, I cannot put her name on the stone. These are simple people who cannot accept their part in the murder of an innocent. The thought of the consequences when they go to meet their Maker, well, they might riot, perhaps violate the grave. Let's have an end to this, please Hannah. It is done and what is done cannot be undone. Let them sleep peacefully for their few remaining years. It is over.*"

"*Let them lie in their beds asleep and in peace at night, while I toss and turn here in mine, smelling the dead in my dreams? Is that what you ask?*" she asked incredulously, the delivery becoming scornful. "*Then you have no understanding of my rage. So let me tell you this, Parson, and you Lawrence Roberts, and hear me well,*" she hissed; the hate in Hannah's eyes contorting Stella's face as through bared teeth, she said "*My time of passing is close but I will not rest in my grave or give a tidy end to this injustice, until my sister is once more taken back by the Church, officially,*" she thundered. "*With my passing I will leave the misery, the desperation, and the bitterness of two souls in torment, impregnated in the very stone of this tomb you built for me. And you will not be free of me when I die. I will not let you go, Lawrence. I swear that until the truth is told and the shame lifted from our family name, I will haunt the stairs of your manor house where lie my wasted, child-bearing years and until the world knows of my sister's innocence, the ground here that is stained with her blood, will never know true peace. It will be like an invisible mist that chills the bones and makes stones in the heart every time the moon returns this date. Whoever follows me here will have cause to remember the turn of this month and the 63rd year. It was the day my whole life was laid forfeit.*

Now I lay a curse of dread on Brook Cottage, and on the last day of the August month of the 63rd year, which will fester until the wrong be righted.

The wrong must be righted, the wrong must be righted, the wrong must be righted." Stella began to chant hysterically, tears streaming down her cheeks, layers of pain peeling across her face, exposing Hannah's soul-wrenching hopelessness and Andrew tensed. Stella was taking this on as her own reality just as she had when witnessing the burning of the witch, then before he could move Stella had stiffened, pulling herself upright as though waking to the danger. She was trying to move out of Hannah's body but the empathy was too strong…

"*With my passing I will leave the misery, the desperation, and the bitterness of two souls in torment, impregnated in the very stone of this tomb you built for me*". Hannah was getting weaker, the heart dying under the burden of total acceptance.

Now the poor creature knew why, throughout all those years of longing, Lawrence had never spoken of love. Now he never would, never could. Marriage to a kindly woman, grown children and their inheritance, held him tight in the social mould. It was all too late.

'Hannah is giving up on life,' Stella hissed the warning. 'She has nothing left to live for. I must be free of this body before she dies in it!'

Her head snapped back and Josh stood up in alarm. 'She's going into shock. Bring her back Andrew. Now!' he ordered.

Andrew was already one step ahead. 'Quiet, it must be done slowly.' He held up a restraining hand. 'Stella, Stella, can you hear me?' Andrew sounded as calm as ever. 'Do not distress yourself. The date is Friday the 23rd of August, 1963. What you have witnessed is all in the past, so view it as you would an old film in a cinema. It is time to turn the lights on. Listen to me. Pay attention to me. The date is 23rd August,1963. It is 1963,' he emphasised. 'It is Friday and Josh is here with you in your home, Brook Cottages. Like actors on stage, the ones you have witnessed playing their part cannot hurt you. You are in control. I am in control. Now, I want you to remember everything but you must leave the emotion behind as you come back. Slowly, slowly, breathe yourself through it; deeply, regularly. Follow my voice; it is becoming clearer, louder as you return to the present. We are here waiting for you and you are safe. It is 1963 and you are in your own home in the village of Sennington.' Not doubting his ability for a moment he began to count, lifting Stella to the surface, instructing, assuring, welcoming as her lids flickered and comprehension dawned in her eyes. 'Slowly now. Open your eyes. Remain in a relaxed state. Take as much time as you need. You have done so well my dear, so very, very well.' His voice eased to a comforting whisper.

No one moved, no one spoke, as in the silence of the house they each recalled Hannah's last day and registered the full implication of her vow – a vow made with such passion that it had held Hannah bound for three hundred years. But hate is like an internal fire; self-consuming, demanding constant attention. Now, striving to be free of it, Hannah was reaching across the centuries. There was another aspect to consider; to their knowledge, Rachel had never been taken back into the Church.

'If Rachel had received the Last Rites, would that have been enough for Hannah? Would she have let go and moved on? Or – or is there something else, some finer point we are missing?' Stella spoke with deliberation; something nagging uneasily at the back of her mind.

'What does it matter? We finally have our answer.' Rubbing his hands together, Andrew went to the window.

'Thank God for that!' Josh snapped.

'OK. Take it easy, Josh; it's over. We have the date and we have the reason for this whole amazing story. Poor Hannah.' Andrew raised an eyebrow. 'Hey, I wonder if anything unpleasant happened here in 1763 and 1863. It could be interesting. We could carry on with the search when all this is over. Plenty of records still to go through. It could take years,' he said with lightening voice.

'I don't give a damn if you devote the rest of your life to it. I do not want Stella to do any more delving into anybody's past.' Josh got to his feet. 'I don't remember being so scared in my whole life. Don't you ever take a risk like that again, I thought I was going to lose you Stella,' he choked, brushing her hair with his lips.

'Then be a love and make some very strong coffee, will you?' She smiled weakly up at him. 'While I walk in the garden. I need a little boring normality.'

A summing up was out of the question. Andrew didn't even suggest it. Stella was exhausted. It could wait until the morning.

Saturday 24th August

An early morning start: Josh had stayed the night, Andrew had just arrived, and Stella was in the kitchen. 'Sorry Andrew, I couldn't face the summing up, yesterday. I was totally drained, emotionally and physically.' She came in carrying a tray with three mugs and a large pot of coffee. 'So whether you believe it or not, and Cynthia doesn't, she thinks it's all coincidence, Hannah's words have come true haven't they?' She handed the mugs out. 'Throughout this whole month there has been no peace here. Now, the thought of Hannah's restless spirit, trapped in time, still waiting in the manor for her lover, will invade my sleep. Despite her fury, in her heart of hearts she never gave up hope of their eventual union. She loved him truly, deeply. Rather touching – or it would be if it weren't so tragic.'

'Waiting a lifetime for one man,' Josh said approvingly, 'that's what I call devotion, but as for unrequited love; some say it's the best kind, though I can't say I go much on it myself.'

'You wouldn't!' She gave him an affectionate sideways glance. 'At least we have the actual dates for the parish magazine, which will give it credibility. Hannah was 13 when her sister Rachel was murdered. Shock blocked all memory of the atrocity for 40 years, so that made her 53 when it came back. That brought it to August 1663. It is now August 1963, that just happens to coincide with a very special village history project! Is that coincidence or is that coincidence?'

'Sounds like material for a good novel. Anyone for a refill?' He topped his mug up. 'A bit unnerving if you live here though, eh Stella? Raking up the past, anything could have happened. I might have been done to death in my bed,' he did a melodramatic self-strangling.

'I doubt it,' Stella said dryly. 'You're as sensitive as a block of wood in that direction. However, you do have a point. Hannah's rage swept me along with it, I understood how she felt and I was no longer neutral; I was emotionally bound. It was as though I had been taken over – brainwashed. It wasn't my personal hate but it felt justified and I would have acted on that conviction if I had been in her place, at that time. Oh dear, if we believe something, even if it's wrong, we still believe it,' she added sagely. 'Imagine dying with a mistake of that magnitude hanging over you.'

'That's why some religions still hold the Last Rites, a service to clear the spirit of the departed.' Andrew looked serious. 'Christ and his disciples removed troubled spirits as a matter of course. Read your Bible. Not believing in something doesn't mean it doesn't exist – doesn't make it not true. If Hannah's spirit is still bound to this place, she must be attracted to Stella like a magnet; a clairvoyant occupying the cottage where she died.'

There was so much to take in and refilling the coffee pot gave all three time to adjust and think.

'So, Hannah is unable to move on until the truth is told and the wrong is righted.' Stella repeated the words of the curse solemnly. 'And the truth will be told and writ large, in the centre pages of the Commemorative Edition. But think. Surely what she really wanted above all else, *above all else*,' she emphasised looking at Andrew, 'was for her sister to be blessed by an ordained clergyman; as would probably have happened if she had died a normal death. You understand, Andrew.'

Andrew nodded in agreement. 'Yes, I understand Hannah's fears more than you think. Dying in sin, condemned as a witch would have meant eternity in Hell or at least the equally terrifying state of limbo; a place between Heaven and Hell, forever. That's what dying un-shriven really meant in those days so I'll get round to the blessing soon, I promise.'

'Good,' Stella said firmly. 'Three-hundred years have ticked away and the poor creature has no idea of the progression of time, no idea that all those connected with the crime are long gone.

Time stopped for her when she died of the body and left her spirit bound in bitterness to this place. It's like a nagging worry that goes over and over in your mind. You live it time and again in your imagination until it makes a mental groove so deep it's hard to get on another track. Nothing can frighten or depress us more than our own, out of control, imagination. What I think I need to do is revisit the places where she spent her youth, her most vibrant time of life and that is Witetune House. I need to contact her again – alone this time,' she said warningly.

'Now I know there is more to find, but now we have enough for the magazine, why don't I get on and finish the write-up, let you check it over and get that final version to the printers? Then, and not until then, will I be free to bring this drama full circle.'

'Oh, yes, we have to keep to the deadline. Can you do it, Stella? It's asking a lot; Josh and I are willing to help.'

'No thanks, I've done most of it. I would have liked more time, so being alone and getting the summary on paper while it's still fresh in my mind, will make it easier.'

'Stella,' Andrew said, peeping out on Cynthia watch. 'Remember our agreement; a lot of people are touchy about anything that links the Church to the supernatural, so the light touch, please.'

'I'll be diplomatic. We don't want to upset them with challenging ideas like 'life after death', do we?' she replied sardonically.

'Sorry,' he shrugged, 'but we don't want to offend the paying customers. Curb your creative talent a bit, will you please, and try to keep a happy balance. Make it understandable to the average unimaginative mind.' Grinning, he bent an arm as though to ward off Stella's blows.

'You mean make it bland; take the drama out of it? Come to think about it, I could write the unabridged version later, couldn't I? It would sell like hot cakes to the visitors and be compulsive reading for the locals. I could make a fortune.'

'Yes, and you could keep me in the way I wish to become accustomed.' Josh lounged back in the chair. 'You could start with buying me a Jag.'

'Aren't you late for work?' she gave him a blanked out look.

Sunday 25th August

Early afternoon; they were in the lofty sitting room in the vicarage, nice and cool with the windows open, 'It will be almost impossible to heat in the winter, though. With any luck, by then I'll be on my way to warmer climes. My replacement can deal with that ancient boiler,' Andrew said wryly.

They hadn't bothered with supper, resisting the temptation of cheese on toast, because Stella was impatient to hear Andrew's opinion of what was, in fact, their joint contribution to the Commemorative Edition of the parish magazine. Andrew read aloud and Josh followed from the carbon copy:

Commemorative Issue of the Parish Magazine
The Village of Sennington, Gloucestershire
1663 to 1963

Until the early sixteen hundreds the hamlet of Sennington was situated on the hills above the manor house. After a particularly vicious outbreak of Bubonic Plague in 1623, the much reduced population moved itself to the 'bottom' of the hills to be near running water and, as was common practice, they then set their old thatched dwellings on fire, as they left. (They did this to kill the plague, little realising that this was indeed a most effective remedy because it actually burned the plague-carrying rats.)

A new community grew amongst the trees, straddling the brook. Some of the cottages were built of stone, hacked from the small quarry in the nearby wood. A few of those original dwellings are still inhabited to this day, by our parishioners.

In 1610, in the reign of King James the First, (and only seven years after the death of Elizabeth I), a daughter, who was christened Hannah, was born to the wife of the Miller Myer, in Syreford, situated on the border between Sennington and Witetune.

Perhaps the mother died in childbirth and that's why Hannah's care was given to her much older sister, Rachel, who had moved to an isolated cottage here, by the ford; a shallow passing place for horses and men.

Here Rachel and Hannah made a living by providing refreshment such as beer, bread and cheese (the flour would have been supplied by her father) and by the making and selling of what we call herbal medicines. From Rachel, Hannah learned the art of healing and it would have been her task to gather the herbs, flowers and berries that made up the potions. Commonly used was the coltsfoot, taken as an infusion to help ease a cough when the lungs were attacked in damp winters. The little weed, looking like a poor relation of the dandelion, favours the soil in these parts and huge clumps of it grow along the hedgerows in early spring. Observation of the outcome of a treatment, or just trial and error, was the judge of most remedies. (For instance, pulling a man through a strong sapling to push back a hernia must have helped someone or the practice wouldn't have been continued.)

For many other ailments such as boils, bites and breaks, on both man and beast, Fuller's Earth poultices (much favoured by the Romans) were a favourite cure-all. This has various other uses and was (and still is) taken as a paste from the pond bed at the back of the mill. If left to harden, it shrank and became a very hard protective casing, protecting broken bones and giving them time to heal.

Fuller's Earth was also used to clean the oil from sheep's fleece. This was an added benefit as the mill, where the girls were born, was a stopping-over place for the drovers.

The track they used to get down to the mill can still be walked – along the high ridge, above the village. Down at the mill they could rest, eat, water the cattle, put the sheep through the sheep dip and tar and sand the feet of the geese before their long and final march to the barges at Lechlade, that would transport them to the City of London. (Lechlade being the highest navigable part of the Thames.)

Outbreaks of the plague, commonly known as Black Death, were dreaded by all.

In the year 1623, when Sennington suffered a devastating episode, Rachel Myer, spinster daughter of the Myers of Syreford (the house and the water wheel are still to be viewed, lying between Sennington *and Witetune) was accused of bringing the disease to the village by witchcraft. Before you judge the situation, remember that this was a time of sweeping terror and superstition. Rachel was what we call a herbalist. She did make up potions, an activity that could have been labelled as sorcery by the ignorant. So, without trial by the judiciary, she was most cruelly and unjustly put to death by the terrified peasants. Then her home and workplace, a small thatched cottage isolated then by dense trees, was put to the torch even as she died.*

At around 1630, a long low house was built on the same site. This house was later divided into four homes known now as, Brook Cottages.

The above information is fact and can be found in Sennington church records, but there are always ghost stories clinging to these places and visitors to our village who have an imaginative turn of mind might also like to read a more detailed and interesting account of Rachel and Hannah Myer's story, gleaned from, shall we say, unusual sources...

* * * * * * *

When Rachel Myer was murdered by the mob, her cottage was fired and virtually razed to the ground. Rachel's young sister Hannah, who had been hidden in the big bread oven at the side of the inglenook fireplace, was rescued by Lawrence Roberts, son of the owner of Sennington manor, and taken over the parish boundary to his cousin's beautiful home, Witetune House. Hannah was 13 years old and shock had made her lose all memory of what had happened. She became a companion for the small daughters of Witetune House, treated as one of the family and educated by the parson, alongside the girls, Ann and Apollina Cotton.

Educated people would have distanced themselves from the witch hunts that swept through England, at its height in the first half of the 17th century, during the reign of James I. In those times disease was thought to be punishment from Heaven. Matthew Hopkins, the "Witch Finder," must have brought nightmares to many an old, unprotected crone. It was right out of Pagan times; a human sacrifice was thought to appease an angry God, so the killing of a witch would stop the plague. Superstition was so strong that in 1677, a new law was passed: All rainmakers and weather seers would be burned.

Farmers must have been frightened to look at the sky before harvesting!

Around 1630, Lawrence Roberts, Gent., owner by inheritance of the manor house here at Sennington, had a dwelling built on the site once owned by the unfortunate sisters. The fact that he incorporated a piece of wall, the fireplace with its bread oven, and the hearthstone (all relics from the old cottage) into the new building, was probably a mark of respect to the dead woman. He signed a document, giving this new house to Hannah when she retired from service as his house-keeper. It was an unusually generous act, so we have reason to believe that he was more than a little fond of Hannah and that throughout her life he took responsibility for her welfare. Hannah Myer lived in the cottage by the brook until she died, though there was no happy ending to her days. Towards the end of her life Hannah regained her memory and must have lived the rest of her time in grief, tormented by the injustice of the act and the wickedness of the people involved, still living in the surrounding area. She would have grieved too for the loss of a sister who had died without the blessing from the Church and for her own wasted, twilight years.

There is reason to believe that, having regained her memory so late in life, Hannah Myer became obsessed with the idea of clearing her sister's name and of freeing the family from the shame of the accusation but there were no official records of the murder. In those days it would have been virtually impossible for a woman, with little money and no firm place in society, to argue such a case in the courts.

We have only recently unearthed this miscarriage of justice that once rocked the foundations of our little community and so, to help put the records straight and do a little to right that wrong, the Reverend Andrew has conducted a service dedicated to the dead girl. Attempting to correct a great injustice, he has officially taken Rachel Myer back into the bosom of the Church, and has directed all souls tied to this earth by this grief or shame, to leave this place and be taken into Heaven where they shall know peace.

For those of you who like to walk, the outline of the old village, once know as Old Sennington on the Hill, is situated on the slope of hills above the Manor. The outline can still be traced during particularly dry summers, when the earth is inclined to shrink.

The long dwelling, built by Lawrence Roberts, is situated by the ford and is called Brook Cottages. The owners have kindly opened the garden to the public and you are asked to respect their privacy.

THE END

'Well, what can I say?' Andrew beamed. 'Congratulations Stella. It's well balanced and cleverly worded. A professional job, very professional indeed.'

'Bloody brilliant, I call it,' Josh was bold in his praise.

Stella gave a sigh of relief. 'So you think it reads well enough to go ahead with publication?'

'Yes I do. It's interesting and diplomatic. Thank you for that. Why don't you leave this with me and I'll take it to the printers tomorrow morning first thing. It will save you the bother. Ah, wait. What's this about my having already conducted a special service for the departed?'

'Is that all right? I thought it a nice idea, sort of tidy things up and if it's done before Open Day, there won't be hordes of the curious waiting for flashes of light from the sky and a few choruses from the Heavenly Hosts. I thought just the three of us actually. It wouldn't take long, would it?' she encouraged. 'Not if we get on with it.'

'It's a lovely idea of course and now we are committing the story to paper, it means that by tomorrow Hannah's wish will have been granted, so there's no rush. Let's ease off a bit, take a breather.' Andrew slapped his hands on the table. 'I feel quite euphoric about our success. We could go out to dinner to celebrate – fancy it?'

Josh nodded enthusiastically. Stella hesitated, reluctant to put a dampener on their obvious relief but she felt she had no choice.

'Sorry Andrew, I don't think it's over and done with. Not yet.' She cringed at their look of disbelief, but there was no other way to say it. 'You see, the ambience in the cottages is the same, it's not changed. It could be that the writing of Hannah's story isn't enough; it's still a secret, isn't it – between us? Maybe – maybe the details have literally to go out to the public before the hold is broken.' She floundered, not quite putting a finger on the exact reason yet knowing for sure that there was something more.

'Something is eluding me. I know this isn't finished yet. Her family had been shamed in front of all the neighbourhood. Hannah wanted that put right, so maybe that's what's missing. Why not find Rachel's grave and do a blessing there, as I suggested? It's just tidying another loose end; after all, she was the one who suffered the most.'

Bewildered, Josh looked up. 'This is getting ridiculous. How many places do we have to clear? If you really want to cover every possibility, what about her first resting place, virtually outside our door? Doesn't that need some clearing too? The murder was committed on our land and the body left there for about forty years.

'Why not wave those divining rods about – and while you're about it, find the underground spring where she was left. We might need it if there's another drought,' he said sarcastically, glaring at Stella. He was fed-up and fractious. 'Then Andrew can say the necessary words and then, only when that's done, should we think of going to the churchyard if, and only if, it's necessary. I just want an end to it all.' Stella put an arm across his shoulders. 'Don't be cross. Actually my love, it's a good idea; finish it completely. Please help me.' She gave him a soft nuzzle and with a sigh he shrugged.

'OK, Andrew?'

'Well, yes. I'll be happy to go along with it.'

'Then what about tomorrow, say mid-morning? Cynthia will be at work. There's a chance that Abby might have gone into school to prepare for the new term but if she does appear, and asks why are walking round her end of the cottage waving divining rods, well, we're sure to think of something.'

Josh did not look at all happy.

Monday 26th August

Stella had completed a full hour of yoga and meditation before Josh and Andrew arrived and she felt calm and centred as she opened the door.

'Seriously, Stella,' Andrew put down his coffee cup, 'Do you really believe you can find the source of an underground spring that has never had the strength to break through the top soil, with those things?' Andrew looked doubtfully at the two pieces of bent wire coat hanger.

'Oh, she's multi-talented,' Josh waved a hand airily.

'Of course I can. I've helped farmers locate water in these hills for years. These rods also give yes or no answers to simple questions.' She raised an eyebrow and held them out straight 'Intriguing isn't it? Remember it's an ancient skill and not witchcraft. You ready? Let's go.'

'Wait a minute, wait a minute,' Andrew sighed and put out a restraining hand. 'I hate to curb your enthusiasm, but if Abby is around, we can hardly troop around out there, following two sticks, without arousing her curiosity. What do we say? Casually mention we're looking for a grave in the garden? She's not read the write-up yet. Let's have a back up story.'

'Good point.' Stella thought for a moment. 'Oh yes, if someone once tried to dig a well, then there must have been water here. So, if we're interrupted I'll say I'm trying to locate an underground spring that we read about.'

'I think we are heading for trouble,' Josh said unhappily. 'If we do find it, let's hope it's not going to be another catastrophe.'

'Catastrophe – what do you mean?'

'You just think for a moment; if the preacher who buried her had known about the spring, or if he hadn't been unfortunate enough to dig the grave there, then Rachel's skeleton would never have been unearthed; Hannah would never have gained her memory, the curse would never have been laid on this place and we wouldn't be going through all of this barmy stuff!

'Sobering, isn't it? So, all I'm suggesting, Stella, is that we proceed with caution. I want to enjoy the rest of my life, with you, my love.'

They were half way down the lawn when Bertie's van came down the bumpy track so they did a quick turn and went towards the gate.

'Morning, Bertie. Want some help?'

'Morning! Yes please. It's a good drying day for the paint.' He clambered out wearing white overalls, opened the back door and started to unload. 'You can give me a hand with these,' he pointed to the ladders and Josh and Andrew pulled them out of the van and ferried them up to the house. 'It's guttering and down-pipes today.' He looked at them curiously. 'What you all up to? Not working, that's for sure.'

'Oh, we have been. It's all last minute preparation for Open Day …and er,' Andrew's mind went on overdrive. 'I was just asking Josh if he had any idea how old this yew tree is.' He pointed to the corner. 'I think I read somewhere that they can live up to a thousand years.'

Good thinking! Josh and Stella were impressed and swung immediate interest in the tree's direction.

'Two thousand, more like.' Bertie stood and looked at it. 'Believe it or not, some could have a direct line back to the time of the dinosaurs. What happens is,' Bertie took a deep breath and Josh smiled. It was a phrase guaranteed to glaze Cynthia's vision as she anticipated boredom and, *not being able to get a word in edgeways.* Bertie was a chain-talker but he knew his stuff. 'What happens with some yew trees is that when it's dying it throws a circle of sapling up round it, so the direct line continues.'

'Didn't they plant them near churches to keep evil away?'

'The other way round, Stella,' he said knowingly. 'Because of the longevity of these trees they became land marks and places where the heads of the tribes would gather. These circles also became known as mystical places. What they didn't know, as they sat for hours talking and probably drinking mead wine, was that in hot weather the trees gave off a vapour that made the people in the confined circle below, hallucinate. They thought they were having mystical experiences, so the places became Holy.

'The Druids held their ceremonies in and around them and that's where the earliest churches were established.'

'Gosh Bertie, you're a mine of information. That's really interesting; I'll rope you in to give a talk in the village hall. We need something to breathe life into the place again.'

'I'll say no, if you don't mind, Vicar. Oh, one other thing. The black seeds are highly poisonous and were known for killing stock when cattle roamed free. Now, before I start I'll go and see if Abby is in. Don't want her sitting indoors on a day like this.' They held their breath as he rounded the corner of the end cottage and knocked on the door.

When he came back, shaking his head, there was a silent, collective sigh of relief. 'She's not at home and I'm glad about that. She must have been on the bus going to the village. I passed it on the way here. See you later.' He picked up a paint can and they heard him whistling and scraping as he put the ladder up at the back of Cynthia's cottage.

The brook gurgled and a few bees courted the scented flower heads, but apart from these gentle natural sounds, the garden held its breath. Stella stood on a spot close to the water where, under hypnosis, she had watched the ground being dug then, telling Josh and Andrew what she was going to say, she stretched out and held the rods to the horizontal; silently putting the question: Where is the underground spring in this garden?

In an instant the rods swung and pointed just feet away. Andrew gave a low whistle as he witnessed for the first time the positive way the rods responded. Josh, who had seen it many times before, just followed.

'It's here.' She stopped and holding the rods out again asked how deep the water was. Counting slowly the rods crossed once, at the count of four. 'The water is four feet down. This woman was buried in a very *shallow* grave.'

'Makes sense,' Josh stepped forward. 'The Parson would have dug the grave using whatever he could find, so he wouldn't have made it very deep would he; also time was not on his side. All he wanted, I'm sure, was to get the hell out of here. It was pure luck that he didn't go deep enough to release the water because he wouldn't have known about the spring, would he, being new to the area.'

Stella raised the rods again and asked if there had ever been a body buried on the spot. The rods swung in to the affirmative. 'Is the body still here?' she asked aloud this time and the rods swung away from each other. 'No, it's been removed. That confirms what we know.'

She took a deep breath then asked, 'Are there any traumatic energies tied to the spot that need to be released?' and the rods swung to negative. 'I don't understand,' she turned to them, 'There is no spirit to be freed from here. I can find no trace of Rachel's presence. Isn't that odd, given the unfinished feeling I have?'

'Well I'm satisfied because you've checked this out first. Now you can have your way and do the churchyard, see if she actually was reburied there. See if the Lawrence chap and his pal the Parson, thought it necessary or if they just kidded Hannah, to keep the peace. I know what option I would have taken.'

'So do I,' Stella glared at him. 'All right, let's go. It's only a small area so it shouldn't take long. All the old stones are covered with lichen and ivy; not easy to read, so my rods will have to point the way,' and, misinterpreting Andrew's look of concern, added 'Don't worry, you're not getting involved in anything untoward.

Where do you think I get my direction from? I always call on the Light of Truth and Love, for guidance. I believe that love is the most powerful of all energies, so pure love and pure intelligence must be the driving force of the Universal God energy. It's so logical.' Andrew didn't disagree.

They strolled through the meadow past cows munching good grass near the stream, and crossed over to the church No one was around and, once inside the lych gate, Stella again lifted the rods, centred her thinking and asked, 'Is Rachel Myer's grave here?' The answer was yes. 'Where is it?' The movement, instantaneous, swung both rods towards the left hand corner of the church, in the direction of the manor house.

No hesitation now, they followed her confident stride across the grass to a line of three small and very old stones, two of them still readable and dated from the 17th century; the third they had to scrape clean of moss and ivy. Underneath, the stone showed a clear band of decoration – but there was not and had never been, a name.

'What do you expect?' Josh said. 'The drover who is supposed to be lying there was said to be unknown. You said there would be an unmarked grave and you have found it.'

'Wow, this quite blows my mind.' Andrew squatted down and traced the carved edge with a stick. 'OK. Now that we have found her, let's make a time for that ceremony Stella. Do you have your diaries?'

'Diaries – why wait? What's the point, why not conduct it now and get it over with?' Stella asked anxiously. 'Hannah wanted the shame lifted from her family name; to become respectable again and let the neighbours know it, so to speak. Well, the very fact that you, an ordained clergyman, are standing at her grave in broad daylight and willing to say prayers – well that's almost it!

'We're all keen to draw a double line under this drama.'

So agreeing, Josh and Stella stood on each side of the little plot and positioning himself at the head of Rachel's grave, Andrew explained why he was there.'I want your help with the next part.' He looked from Stella to Josh. 'I am going to ask Rachel to forgive all those who have sinned against her, and then I'm going to pay attention to any spirit, good, bad, or indifferent, tied to this place or to this crime. I don't believe in just trying to banish a ghost or a spirit with force or argument; where do they go? Just because they haven't, for whatever reason, completed their death process, doesn't mean they are evil or a danger to us. They may have been badly used in life or they could have died in an accident. It could apply to any of us if we died in tragic or confused circumstances, needing guidance, so this next part must be done firmly, with love and respect.'

He stood with his eyes closed and they waited. 'Right, I want you to imagine the brightest of lights – say like the sun. Use this as a symbol of God's pure light and when I direct Rachel and all other entities to it, you should visualise them going towards and into that Divine Light and receiving a loving welcome. Comfort and reassure them, particularly Rachel, that this is the best thing that can happen, so be clear with your visualisations and strong in your direction. Ready? Now listen and concentrate.' First he gave the present date, pointing out that three-hundred years had passed, that Rachel's family and friends had long gone and were waiting to receive her in Heaven. Then he spoke of the tragic and terrifying circumstances that had brought about her end and he asked Rachel to understand and forgive. Then he spoke of God's unconditional love and said that anyone else connected with the crime should repent their sins and move with Rachel, towards the Light.

It was a powerful little service, an uplifting experience for all three and it left them in deep silence.

'Now, that's a proper end to it and I sincerely thank God, that that's over,' Andrew said with feeling as he closed the little prayer book with a bang. 'Now let's get on with our lives again. Are you ready to go?'

Josh was but Stella waved them off and sat on the grass by the little headstone to think. There was a lot to think about and no one to disturb her reverie. She was unaware of time passing; it was the sun, hidden by a dark cloud, and a slight chilling breeze moving through the trees that stirred her and cleared her mind.

'Do you know why I am here, Rachel?' Stella directed thoughts through to the spirit of the woman whose grave she now sat by. 'Do you know that we have cleared your family name of disgrace, publicly – and does it matter to you? Did it ever? I'm beginning to think not. You must have been a very balanced person for there is no trace of your anguish around your first grave – or here. Let me tell you that your shameful end has been written down and that the whole village will soon know of the wicked miscarriage of justice.

'Was this what you wanted – or was it what your sister Hannah, wanted?' It was an afterthought and surprise had made her speak out loud. 'Old grievances can become all-consuming. Could it possibly be that Hannah was the one who was not at rest; the only one? Perhaps we should have conducted this ceremony at the manor.' She tugged at the long grass edging the stone, then her eyes widened. 'Of course – Sennington Manor and Witetune House, how stupid of me.' She shook her head, annoyed at the wasted time. 'I'm fast becoming convinced that Rachel never was the one who needed help,' she talked softly, agitatedly. 'But if I'm wrong, if I'm wrong, dear God, where do I go from here? Only four days before Open Day and the turn of the month. If I miss it, will Hannah be bound here for another hundred years? I really don't know whether I'm up to this.'

She had slipped her shoes off and now groped for them, was anxious to be gone. 'This is not good. I'm getting nervous and negative thoughts will weaken me. I must stay relaxed and focused.' Shivering slightly, she stood up.

The breeze, drifting scent from flowers wilting on a new grave was an unpleasant, ever-present reminder of death and the shortening of time. Quickening her step, she left the graveyard.

Tuesday 27th August

At seven o'clock Stella opened her eyes and stretched lazily into the morning. Happy, relaxed and at peace after several hours of deep therapeutic sleep, she felt ten years younger and it took a while for her to realize why.

Sure that she was still missing the point, she had meditated before going to sleep, asking for guidance as always, from The Highest Possible Source: Was there something vital that she had overlooked? And, subconsciously dwelling on Hannah's plight, Stella had woken in the night with the answer on her lips, *The Unlived Life*! That was where the real hurt lay, and at once, everything had fallen into place. What you believe, right or wrong is your reality and, "*My life has been totally wasted*" had been Hannah's concept of her reality and the words on her lips as she had died.

It wasn't true, but in the short time between learning of her sister's fate, and her own death, Hannah's attention had fixed so completely on this warped interpretation, that it had totally obliterated all memory of the friendships and happy times that had filled those young years at Witetune House. Neither had she given thought nor thanks for the education received from the Parson, and because of this lack of balance, had she died in victim mode, bitter and blaming. In that moment of night-time waking and with the words, Unlived Life, uppermost, Stella had searched beyond the seemingly obvious interpretation of Hannah's damning last words – and then it came to her; Hannah's anger with Lawrence wasn't totally about her sister's tragic end, although pride had made her lash out and give that impression.

Hannah was an intelligent woman and she must have known deep down that Lawrence too, had been an innocent pawn in the tragedy, just as she herself had been.

No, the swell of Hannah's fury, when she talked about her wasted life, had been the years spent *waiting* for Lawrence to claim her and this frustration had, in the final reckoning, been compounded by humiliation and – and embarrassment!

'Dear God,' Stella shook her head as the truth expanded. For this man whom Hannah had idolized and whom she had made the very core of her existence, must have known of her secret night-time yearnings, her natural womanly needs. Yet in all those long years, he had never said outright why he could never, would never, come to her bed. If she had known, her life might have been very different; a home of her own, a family and grandchildren, instead of finishing her days alone, in a comfortable prison. For that was the sum of her retirement at Brook Cottage and what had fuelled her bitterness and three-hundred years of grief. She was still grieving. Grieving also for the way they had parted and her last cruel words...

'Lawrence was her Bright Star in the Sky; he was her Knight in Shining Armour – but he was only human. I know what it is like to love and lose,' Stella sighed. 'Though I never doubted he loved me because he always told me.'

Opening the window wide, she turned her face to the morning

sun, breathing in the good air, knowing what she had to do and which way to go. No confusion. No doubts now. To free Hannah Myer from this all-consuming black hell hole, all Stella had to do was to bring her back to, and remind her of, a time and place where she had been happy. Let her relive a glorious morning like this, Stella thought. A time when her days were full of hope and the future was limitless with possibilities; when the smile on her face had gone right through to her young soul. A time before that *delicate grip of doubt* had begun to primly suck the optimism of her youth.

Stella frowned then moved on. Reassure her too, that Lawrence had always loved her; that their devotion to each other was never in doubt and that he acted as he did from the highest possible motive; pure love.

She needs to relive the memory of those joyous times together, make them paramount in her thinking, and flood her mind with them. If she can do that, and I know she wants to, she can move her attention away from old grievances and free herself from this miserable earthly bondage.

Witetune House was the obvious place, the beautiful old building where Hannah had been given refuge and where she had grown up. That was the place, the loving home where the child Hannah, re-membering nothing of her early trauma, had been cared for, nurtured, and educated. Lawrence had been a frequent visitor, interested in her progress, enchanted by her fine features and glorious red hair, and young as she was, sensing his attraction, she came to see him as her protector; her champion. Witetune House was where she fell in love and that was a time in her life, filled with the most wonderful possibilities. 'And that's where I'm going.' Stella sprang out of bed. 'To do what I'm meant to do – help Hannah leave this earth with a blaze of glory – and I am going to do this alone. I'll tell Josh and Andrew later.'

'I feel sixteen again,' Stella laughed aloud, hurrying through the wood, apologising as she crunched an empty snail shell under foot, blessing everyone and everything. Razor strop; she touched it in passing, the broad hard fan of fungus bringing new life from dead wood. Hannah would have collected this for sharpening and cleaning those rusty iron knives. In nature everything has a use, everything is connected, everything has balance and we are part of that, *everything*. Stella felt quite light-headed!

Hannah had been happy in these woods, walking alongside her dear friend Lawrence, talking as equals, knowing deep down that the feelings she had for him, though unspoken, were returned.

'Oh Hannah, remember those times. Focus your attention on them. Relive the exhilaration you must have felt, just spending time alone with the man you loved. Did he ever kiss you, lightly, tenderly on the cheek perhaps, a touch that made you giddy with happiness? Oh, for your sake I so want you to relive those times. Listen to me,' she laughed,

I'm talking to myself – but maybe not...

Arms wide, turning from time to time in big circles, gathering some invisible energy to aid her task, Stella hurried on, powered along by a joy that ran through her veins like a sparkling river.

When Stella reached Witetune House, the doors and windows were wide open, letting in the lovely day. Calling as she went, sure of a welcome, she followed the smell of fresh brewed breakfast coffee permeating along the stone-floored hall and found Miss Jenkins in the little side kitchen. Delighted to see her, the old lady filled a second cup and without interrupting, listened to Stella's story as they drank coffee seated at the long table in the dining room; a fat china bowl, filled with white roses, arum lilies and green fern its centre piece, the perfume, intoxicating. 'So you see it is appropriate that we are sitting here in grand, isolated splendour,' Stella came to the end of her tale, 'because to-day is going to be a celebration!'

'What an amazing story, Stella. Now what can I do to help.'

'Absolutely nothing. Just be your lovely accepting self and let me have the run of the house as you have always so generously allowed, Oh, and if it's not asking too much, another cup of this excellent coffee, please?'

While Miss Jenkins was in the kitchen Stella sat enjoying the delights of the stately room, its window sills sporting tall white daisies in shiny brass jugs, their big heads swaying slightly in the gentle morning breeze; the smell of damp earth as the sprinkler swirled across the grass, wetting the bottom of a window pane, leaving droplets, tiny impressions pressing on the glass. Each one seemed to be saying, 'I am here, this is me, look, before I go for ever.' Stella didn't wait for the coffee.

Climbing the old stairs steadily now, calming her mind, relaxing her body, Stella entered the comfortable sitting room at peace and totally confident in her ability to contact Hannah and restore her joy; the Energies were strong and she knew it wouldn't take long. Eyes closed, arms out, fingers stretched, she concentrated on the things that never change; the hum of bees, the smells of a country summer. Then she spoke the words in from her heart:

'Share this with me, dearest Hannah. Come here; let me help you shed the weight of hurt and disappointment. Your call has spanned three-hundred years and I am answering your cry for help. This is why I am here in Witetune House, calling you back to the rooms that are filled with the happy memories of your growing years.' Then Stella settled herself on a big comfortable chair and began to breathe deeply, counting backwards, ten to one, gradually slowing her heartbeat until, eyes closed, she became distanced in time and space. The only link to the room was the sound of her breathing. It was like being underwater – enclosed in a liquid pool of consciousness and in that altered state, Stella's call to Hannah seemed to echo and vibrate in her head.

Concentrating, concentrating, silently she repeated the call, the plea, to Hannah Myer.

She didn't see, though she had felt the vibration of the room change like a ripple of tight waves as a shape, flimsy as vapour, spiralled invisibly around her. On the drift of a summer morning, the air like spun gold, the spirit of Hannah spoke clearly in Stella's thinking, as two souls bonded across the centuries.

Trust was the bond. Both were ready and the time was now.

Careful to follow Andrew's instruction, Stella first told Hannah the date and that the people that she loved and who loved her, had long gone and were patiently waiting for her to join them.

She then visualised the sun flashing through a canopy of leaves and branches and with a burst of sheer joy, Stella directed Hannah's young soul up and through the lush greenery, into the freedom beyond. Just for a moment, light seemed to fill Stella's whole body, then the power of love shone light into the darkness – and Hannah Myer moved on.

Standing by the window on the little back landing, looking out on to the flowering shrubs and bushes decorating the side lawns, tears of happiness ran down Stella's face. She felt like a piece of elastic that had been stretched too much and for too long.

'Is there anything else I have to do, anything I've overlooked?' she searched the rafters of her mind. 'No, nothing,' then more loudly, 'Nothing, nothing, please God.'

She laughed through the tears and turning, tripped lightly down the stairs like a teenager, really looking forward to the weekend and Open Day. Just three days to go, masses to do, and the thought of total involvement with all the trivia surrounding Open Day, and Cynthia in charge, bossing everyone around – sounded like Paradise.

Saturday 31st August

The last of the visitors had long gone and tired and happy with the numbers through the gate, and the interest and compliments they had received about both the terrace and their lovely garden, Stella, Abby and Cynthia were sitting out, enjoying the cool of the evening and a well-deserved rest. As the first stars appeared above the darkening line of hills, conversation became reflective, little pockets of silence falling about them as the fading light folded itself into the gathering dark, easing the need to speak, and allowed personal thoughts to drift unseen across their faces.

In the privacy of twilight, Stella's mind turned back to Hannah and their emotional farewell. She was glad that it was all over and yet, and yet there was a certain void, like having a relative go to live in a far off country and never hearing, never knowing if all had turned out well for them.

'I don't have any idea of how the Universe works, only theories, and I can't help wondering if Hannah found her Lawrence, her shining star.' The questions had repeated themselves at odd moments throughout the day and there could of course be no certain answer, and yet...

Trying to stop the thoughts going round and round, Stella turned her mind to the lovely early morning start, to what had been a hugely successful Gardens Open Day. Anticipating the arrival of the visitors she had been up early, looking unseeing at the garden when Josh had walked in. Stella hadn't turned, didn't need to, often sensing his approach long before he appeared; intuition – Zen?

'Get today over, then let's get the hell out of here, Kid,' he had said with a drawl, standing behind, wrapping arms tightly around her.

'Oh, very Trans-Atlantic,' she had snuggled closer. 'And, I would love to but unlike you, I don't work for myself.'

I've spoken to the *Reserve Team*. With extra help they can manage without me for a couple of weeks at the shop; they've had enough experience over this last month.'

'Josh, how can I? Start of term is in a week's time, I've done hardly any preparation, and I've got lectures to deliver.'

'Reschedule. Your student groups are small, they are young adults and they come to you by appointment. That's one benefit of working in the private education sector,' he smiled. 'The autumn term is the longest and we usually manage a break half way through – just make it earlier. With all that's gone on we both need a change of scene and we haven't been alone, really alone, for ages. Stella, darling, I want your company. Couples lose that special closeness, the magic, because they don't make time for each other. We mustn't let that happen to us.'

She had half turned and kissed the side of his face, holding back unexpected tears. 'Sounds nice, where?'

'Don't know, only thought about it yesterday when I was talking to Andrew. He suggested the South of France. It's the end of the summer holiday and all the tourists will be heading home. Think of it: a bit of glamour in Nice and Monte Carlo, empty beaches in September, warm seas, then into the hills of Provence, offering the best in country cooking. Leisurely alfresco meals, sun and soft breezes. Have I sold you the idea?'

'You haven't mentioned the wine,' she moved closer.

'I haven't mentioned the big feather beds either!' His hold tightened, his cheek by hers. 'Think of those remote country hotels with beds you need a ladder to get up to; thick cotton sheets and the smell of good coffee and fresh croissants to wake you after a night of deep contented sleep. Is Madam impressed?' For an answer she turned to him, arms up around his neck.

'Keep talking,' she prolonged the kiss.

'OK. Two other bits of information.' He narrowed his eyes conspiratorially as he came up for air. 'Andrew said we can swap cars; borrow his Jaguar for the holiday. I kept that under my hat in case you needed persuading.

'He's already making plans for this extended trip to distant lands. This winter, the Jag will be garaged while he's away, so we must make the most of this offer of luxury, while we can.'

'Fantastic! We can take turns; I really fancy driving a Jaguar on those curving coastal roads. The views are beautiful sweeping down to Monte Carlo; warm sparkling sea and luxurious yachts on one side, mountains topped with blue sky on the other. Very glam! You've talked me into it. Now what's your other news, something nice I hope?'

'Ah, yes, a bit of gossip. Someone is coming to look at John's cottage. Not for a few weeks though, so we should be back in time to give her the once over.'

'Her? It's a woman?'

'Yes, according to the agent.'

'Another female! Cynthia won't be very pleased,' she grimaced. 'She was hoping that a man might move in who could do a few jobs around the place. Hang on though; it's not on the market yet. It could

be months before the legal side is sorted out and then it's got to be
decorated and brought up to date; kitchen and bathroom, mainly.
Bertie will do that of course though it could be nearer Christmas
before anyone could move in. Anyhow, as I said, it's not officially
on the market yet.'

'That's no barrier, you know what the jungle telegraph is like in
the village. Word gets around. The estate agent came up to me when
I was in the paper shop and said he had an enquiry from a woman
who wants to live in these parts, wants a quieter life.'

'Does this buyer know that it's small, the smallest one in the
terrace in fact?'

'She must do, but that shouldn't be a problem. Apparently she's
on her own and it's quite adequate for one. Oh, and another thing,
she's an actress, in the West End at one time, I believe. How about
that for a change of company? If she moves in, 1964 will be an
interesting time in this place.'

'An actress? Well at least she should be a bit lively. I think we
will get on very well together.'

'You get on well with most people,' Josh waved and left.

Stella was deep in thought, working out ways of modernising
John's cottage when Cynthia's voice pulled her back to the evening;
she was startled to see how dark it had got.

'You can help me pick those beans for tomorrow.' Abby's
agreement was a foregone conclusion. 'It's a bit late but if we can
find enough they will go well with lamb. We can have fresh mint
sauce and the last of John's potatoes.' Uncle John's bean sticks,
holding up fading shadowy rows of leaves had made Cynthia think
of the Sunday roast, then it went back to finance. 'We took a lot of
money today.' Her smile of glee went unnoticed. A steady stream of
visitors had kept them busy, encouraged to come this far out by the
centre spread in the magazine. All had admired the garden and for
the most part, talked sensibly about the history of Brook Cottages.
Anyone asking daft questions about spiritual matters, she had handed
over to Stella. Looking along the terrace now though, she allowed
herself to marvel, just a little. Could be true, I suppose.

'Now, what shall we do with the takings?' Cynthia's mind turned back most energetically to business. She could look forward to private meetings with Andrew, long detailed discussions on how to spend the cash, but she knew the needs of the villagers better than he did.

'I'll let him suggest things then steer him in the right direction,' she smiled. The Alms Houses were in need of repair and the old people there needed the job done soon, with the winter coming on. They could have some much needed help with coal bills, too. It was nice to be able to do something practical for them, and the prospect of organising the distribution of the money where it was most needed, made Cynthia very happy indeed.

So it was all over for another year. Abby sighed and folded her arms. Open Day, the magazine, the research, summer and the school holidays.... 'It's been a life changing month for me; losing Uncle John and then my going away from home for the first time in years. I was quite brave, wasn't I?'

She complimented herself, forgetting that it hadn't been her decision. 'I've been terrified of losing Uncle John for years. Perhaps that's why I would never go away; in case he died when I wasn't here. And he did, didn't he? The doctor said it's quite common for people to die when they are left alone, even for a few minutes. It's as though they need that space. Anyhow, I've been frightening myself for years and what I imagined, was far worse than the real thing. What a waste of life. It was all in my mind of course though I believed it so it was real to me. I'll have to watch my thoughts. I don't want to go there again. Now I haven't really got any family left apart from my cousins, so in many ways, I'm on my own. I will have to make my own decisions!' Abby's eyes opened wide; a little surge of nervous confidence, she gave a little gasp.

'What's that for, dear?' Cynthia asked kindly, turning her thoughts from spending money.

'Oh, just thinking about the three of us and of time and life moving on, and how for the first time ever, I'm sort of looking forward to the autumn term. I like being secretary at the school. It's a very involved job and I'm good at it.'

'You're looking forward to the new term? Jolly good, I'm glad to hear it,' Stella's voice smiled, because apart from a patch of light on each face, their features had dissolved into the night.

White daisies gleamed untidily in a cast of early moonlight down by the fence and the sweet peas and tall hollyhocks stood proud against the cottage walls, ready to reseed themselves as they did year on year. Their warm perfume was quite intoxicating.

More stars appeared but no one moved, reluctant to break the spell, then for no apparent reason a blackbird flew past them out of the pear tree, fast and low, shrieking in alarm and all eyes turned back to where blackness had settled deepest in the branches.

'I wonder what disturbed him.' Abby murmured and as silence fell again, Stella found herself searching the shadows intently. Hannah, Hannah, are you here, she called from her heart. Did you find your heart's love? Did you finally understand how fine and noble was his conduct; that he was the best of champions, honourable, caring, and so protective of you? Do you know that now – and is his Star shining bright again?

The moon had drifted high above the hills; in a few days it would be a full blown harvest moon. Then, from the east and as though acknowledging Stella's call, a magnificent shooting star arced high and wide as though bidding its last farewell to earth, and in the gentle darkness, Stella, her heart bursting with pure joy, turned a radiant face to the sky:

'Goodbye dearest Hannah. Goodbye.' she whispered.

PART TWO

Fiction Becomes Fact
–
A Change of Reality

Going on Leave

Relieved that the daily demands of writing my novel, *Unshriven*, were at an end, I put the completed manuscript in a drawer and headed for the airport for a much needed holiday in England.

Interweaving two plots spanning three hundred years had been very demanding. The storyline and characters in my 1963 novel had been developing well but increasing distraction in the form of dialogue (silent but clear within my thinking) and animated mind-pictures, from the 17th century drama, had finally dictated their order of importance.

Now however, I was free to do and think of other things; perhaps write something completely different, I had a number of ideas but first, armed with a synopsis of *Unshriven* I intended to look for a friendly publisher...

Little did I realize that the story was less than half over and I was about to start a most amazing adventure; one that would change my '*Concept of Reality*' for life!

Finding Brook Cottage

I had had no luck in finding a 'friendly publisher' and it was time to go back to the Middle East where I lived with my husband. The weeks spent in England had been very pleasurable though hectic; visiting friends and family, catching up with post, paying bills, organizing things to run smoothly as we prepared to be away for a few months. My husband's re-entry visa to Saudi Arabia arrived and for the very first time, mine was delayed.

This had never happened before and there was no obvious reason why it had happened now, though I would come to accept that the delay had been 'pre-ordained,' leaving me, as it did, in a perfect position for what happened next. (I must emphasise that to the best of my ability and memory recall, everything that follows, is a truthful account of how the fiction I had written in Saudi Arabia became provable traceable fact.) I have since wondered, just *when, how far back*, those little *coincidences*, like guiding lines of a small tug boat gently manoeuvring a liner into position, actually began.

* * * * * * *

It was almost the end of the day and I was sitting at the bottom of my garden, watching the slow, hypnotic flow of the river, when the ring of the telephone sent me hurrying up to the house. It was a friend.

'I'm coming back from London earlier than intended. I've joined the Reflexology Society and there's a meeting tomorrow evening in a private house, in the Cotswold Hills.'

I was not a member, but after lots of pleading, the next evening found me, feet up, surrounded by about a dozen very nice women whom I had never met, having my tootsies massaged.

About half way through the evening a late-comer entered the room; grey haired, a lovely smile and eyes bright with energy and interest. Her name was Beryl G. and I felt a deep connection with this woman from the moment I set eyes on her; as though she was someone I had known well, long ago – though from where or when, I just could not recall. (Strange, although I was to see Beryl quite frequently over the following years, every single time that I saw her, I felt a faint shock: She was never the person I expected to see. I always anticipated someone shorter, rather slight in build with dark hair and a more retiring personality. Beryl later confessed to having the same reaction; I was not the person she expected to see. It was as though we had known each other in a different guise.)

That evening, Beryl, a member of the British Association of Dowsers (Water-Diviners) held our attention with stories of her experiences and successes, and then she proceeded to demonstrate the intriguing way that a crystal bead, suspended by a thread, would swing in circles, either to the left or the right, to answer simple 'yes or no,' questions. For example: Is there water here?

Testing the technique, I held the suspended bead above my knee and watched in amazement as it began to spin vigorously, almost horizontally like a Catherine wheel, as it apparently responding to my personal energy field.

As I was leaving, Beryl said, 'You seem intrigued by water-divining. I think you could do it quite easily. Would you like to come to my cottage and give it a try? There's another benefit in being able to use this ancient skill. When we bought our cottage, my husband John began to have severe headaches and by using the rods, I found what is called a negative, or black energy line, running through the house, right under his desk. It's a well-recognised phenomenon, a natural Earth energy, just like ley-lines. We stopped it quite simply by putting a piece of untreated iron in the garden to stop the flow. It must have moved, probably when I was vacuum cleaning, because John's headaches have returned. Why not come over and see if you can locate it? It will have to be tomorrow or early the following morning because we are going to Wales for a month.' She handed me a hand-drawn map and, studying the complicated directions, I could see why she always carried one with her; it looked like spaghetti! The hamlet, called Sennington, was very remote.

I went home and spent the next day pondering the previous

evening's events. I had heard of water-divining: a way of using something like a twig from the hazel bush, to locate water not visible from ground level. I had also seen it used in Saudi Arabia: a massive multimillion dollar piece of machinery laying new drainage for a city water supply, inching its way along the side of the highway, and walking in front, a Filipino with two twigs, slowly guiding the laying of the pipes along the source of water beneath. (Oh, the wonders of modern science! A sight like that, warms the heart!)

My dilemma was this; should I accept this intriguing and flattering invitation from a person I hardly knew? I wasn't totally convinced that I should follow it up. Water divining was unknown territory to me; I felt unsure of my ground. If I accepted, what direction might it take; might we both be embarrassed if I didn't come up to her expectations – didn't pass the test, and if I did, what then? I needed advice and using the teachings of The Silva Method, I directed my consciousness 'within' and silently said:

'I've met this lady, her name is Beryl, and of course you know that. She is a water-diviner. She seems to think that I am too, and has asked me to her cottage to try. The point is this; I have every confidence in her as a person but I don't want to get out of my depth, so should I go?'

The reply was instant, clear and silent within my thinking:

Go, because not only will it be great fun but it is important for the stage of life you are now moving in to.

Did I have a choice? (come on!) I picked up the telephone…

All of my life, I have had an 'awareness' of another Dimension. I am not religious, but if you have any religious faith, then a life after this one is a belief you all share. I call it a Dimension and scientists now claim to have calculated 22 others.

Often, to close my eyes at night means the start of a picture show! It's like watching a travel film shot from a low flying craft as I skim over countryside, seeing every blade of grass and every tiny stone at the bottom of a stream, trees, cattle, birds etc. Other times I will be presented with buildings as detailed as the Notre-Dame, or the fully furnished interiors of houses I had never visited. To me it is normal, although my husband, a physician, thinks it is something to do with my dyslexia. So, this clear instruction to go to Beryl's cottage was just another unexplainable twist, and it felt 'Right' and for my good. (Given all this clear guidance, I wish I could say that as the journey started and the pieces began to fall into place, I was becoming aware of an emerging pattern – but I wasn't.)

The next morning dawned bright and clear. I felt confident and not a little excited about my visit, particularly because of the definite way I had been encouraged to go. Just over an hour's drive, mostly past farm land, then through a medieval village of Cotswold stone with narrow streets, overhanging gables and punishment stocks, all seemingly held in a time-lock (the film companies would love it). The route led me out of the village where I crossed the stream by the tiny stone bridge that preceded the steep twisting drive up into the hills.

Concentrate! There was no way of predicting what might be around the next twisting bend in the narrow track of a road that snaked on for mile after high and low dipping mile. I followed the hand-drawn map, staring ahead, ready to slam on the brakes should I encounter another form of life coming in the opposite direction. 'I hope this is worth it,' I muttered.

The countryside was now high on my right and sweeping low to my left, undulating its intricate way, the grassy slopes like waves of green cloth carelessly spread then sprinkled with sheep and early spring lambs. Still no sign of civilisation; on through deep dark woods, a spill of trees as though a copse had slid across to the other side of the road, then out into the sunshine. Convinced that I had lost the way I decided to pull over and check the map.

Stepping out of the car I lifted my face to the sun, luxuriating in the first signs of spring and promise of warmer days. After a couple of minutes I opened my eyes and saw it: A huge clump of coltsfoot, a mass of bright yellow flowers on the grass verge almost at my feet. Yet the feeling of delight at seeing my favourite wild flower was mixed with a moment of uncertainty. (A sign that I would come to recognise – like opening a gate to a secret world, one that I felt I should remember yet couldn't quite recall.) Coltsfoot is a simple weed. It looks like a poor relation of the dandelion though it is a favourite of mine because as a child, on the way to school and crossing heath land, it was always the first wild flower of spring; confirmation that sunny days would soon be with us again. The coltsfoot flowers in March.

Then I recalled that as far back as I could remember, every New Year's morning I would pull back the curtains and say, quite spontaneously, 'But where are the flowers?' Think on this: January 1st was in those days, the start of a miserable month; muddy, grey, cold, and worse was to follow in February. Only in the last 20 years, have these months become noticeably milder.

The shock of being presented with a lifeless garden and actually hearing myself saying these words aloud, caught me unawares every single time, every single New Year's day. Why had I said it? Yet, not seeing the flowers was a momentary puzzle to be forgotten until it sprang from my lips again at the start of another New Year. 'For goodness sake,' I would say to myself, 'what flowers do you expect to see in mid-winter?'

Then some time in the middle eighties, going through historical records in the Bodleian Library, Oxford, I read that New Year's Day used to be celebrated on the 25th March, until it was changed to January 1st in 1750. This explained how the coltsfoot, would have been the first wild flower of spring in the Midland area. It would have been such a welcome sight, thriving along every hedgerow, thick bright cheerful yellow clumps, hardy and able to withstand a late snow fall. Coming to life at a time when the dear earth was waking from a winter sleep.

I also learned that it was a herbal cure and used as an infusion during the plague. They had precious little else in those days, so anything that gave hope was worth a try.

From then on, I never again flung open the curtains on New Year's Day and asked, 'But where are the flowers..?' It seemed that some deep unresolved need, an explanation of something missing, had been satisfied; put to rest. The *laying of a ghost*? Perhaps. For before the morning was out, I was to recall with a start that in the 17th century,

New Year's day was still celebrated on the 25th March....

I got back into the car with a smile on my face. There had been no sign of life anywhere and it was a relief when I eventually found a wooden sign post with the right name on it; Sennington. I rechecked the instructions: Go past the Manor House and past the lane down the side that leads to the church. Go on and take the next turn on the left. On a few yards, sharp left down a steep short track, high hedges either side, a few stone cottages glimpsed through big trees on the rise of hills beyond. I waited as a tractor forded the shallow stream at the bottom, surely the place to cross since ancient times, I put the gear into neutral and sat back; it shouldn't take long and I was in no hurry.

A little knot of anxiety was beginning to register and I was again pondering on the wisdom of my decision, when I heard a call; Beryl was standing outside her cottage waving to me. I had made it – yet seeing her again, gave me a mild shock. We had met only forty-eight hours before and it's hard to explain: the person I expected to open the door should have been slightly shorter and more slight – and with short black hair! Time and again this was to happen and the momentary feeling of surprise was never to leave me.

Beryl's cottage was not enchanting or eye-catching and I would have driven right past it. Long and low, two floors plus an attic; no window at the front to break the line of the roof's thick hand-split tiles; it was not a picture card presentation, rather a functional and comfortable home that had served generations. I pulled the car over and parked on an area in front of the door, Beryl ushering me into her warm comfortable sitting room; a small window looking on to some fields at the rear, white-washed walls, pictures of cows and rural scenes painted by her very talented artist husband, John. There was a nice cosy feel about the place. First impressions on entering a house are rarely wrong though. Time was short for both of us so coffee could wait as we were both keen to get down to business.

Beryl produced two angled pieces of wire (old coat-hangers) and popping each one into an empty biro holder so that I couldn't manipulate the rods manually, handed them to me.

I must confess that I had expected something more ethereal or theatrical, perhaps witch hazel twigs or something else organic. It took only a short time to understand that Beryl's attitude to things supernatural was very 'matter of fact'.

'Just to remind you,' she said, 'that when we first came here, my husband John started to have bad headaches. I used the rods and located a negative energy line, in other words a line of earth energy that is detrimental to health, going directly through the cottage. If you learn of a house where there is a lot of illness, where the people who live there seem to have had more than their fair share of it, it's well worth checking for a naturally occurring negative line of energy. It is so easy to stop it with either a lump of natural crystal or a piece of untreated iron, thrust into the ground, outside. The earth is criss-crossed with energy lines and the good ones, the really interesting ones, are ley-lines. Now first I want you to establish your polarity again to confirm which way the rods will swing for yes or no, questions. As you can see, I have placed a piece of rock crystal on the floor under the desk as a temporary measure, to stop the flow of that energy. Now, I will move the crystal and you can mentally think the question: Is there a black energy line here?'

Raising the rods, concentrating, slightly anxious in case nothing happened and not knowing what on earth to do if they did, I asked the question and was literally stunned by the surge of energy as they swung unhesitatingly across each other! This it seemed was my polarity for, "Yes." I was convinced that there was no way that I could have manipulated those rods – and why would I even try? Who would I fool? I was still coming to terms with it all when Beryl started on the next stage.

'Good. Now I will replace the crystal across the line, and you can ask again.' She put the chunk of rough crystal rock, back in place.

Shaken out of my scepticism, paying close attention now, I did as I was told and pointing the rods at the spot, asked the question again. Although I had absolutely no physical contact with those pieces of bent wire, I was amazed to witness the force of those rods as they swung unhesitatingly away from each other, like opening gates. No!

I now had to accept that some extraordinary power was responding directly to my questions and that I could not provide any logical explanation. The experiment was over, so where did that leave me? Was this the reason I had been directed to come here, to become a water-diviner and if so, why? It just didn't feel right, it was a sort of anti-climax.

It hadn't taken long; Beryl had finished her instruction and there seemed nothing more to discuss. She said I could keep the rods; she also gave me a coloured crystal bead on a longish thread, explaining that this was a pendulum that would respond in the same way to simple yes and no questions by swinging in opposite circles. Also, it was easier to carry about than rods. 'What did you think of all that?' she asked brightly. I could only mumble a reply. I didn't know what to think. I didn't understand it so I just had to accept that it had happened.

'Now, would you like coffee before you go?' she asked. And that was it – or so I thought…

About an hour later, having been fascinated by Beryl's stories and her success in locating water for doubtful farmers, but not knowing each other well enough to have much else to talk about, I asked quite casually when had the cottages been built?' I had no idea that this was a defining moment and her answer was to change my *concept of reality,* for life!

'We don't really know,' she answered. 'We haven't investigated it in any depth but we think it must have been around 1630.'

Hearing those words, I can only say that I felt as though I had plugged into a surge of energy so powerful that my whole body began to shake, though not with fear, I must emphasise.

"Accept it, flow with it. This is right and good. This is how it should be."

This was my instinctive decision as I recalled the words, silent and clear within my thinking; words that had lead me to visit Beryl's cottage:

"Go, because not only will it be great fun but it is important for the stage of life you are now going into."

Beryl looked concerned as I reached for my warm jacket. 'What's the matter – is something wrong?'

'Oh no, it's nothing,' I said airily, which was patently untrue as my body was still trembling even through the cottage was warm. 'I don't know why I'm shaking, Beryl. I just feel – odd.' (That sensation again, apprehension, as though a door had been pushed open, revealing a place unknown to me, yet one with which I should be somehow familiar. Try to remember, try to remember) How could I tell this virtual stranger, what I had just experienced? With a shrug I decided to take the plunge.

'This will sound most extraordinary, Beryl. You see, I have written a novel that is in my desk at home in Saudi Arabia. The story is based on events that happened in a cottage like this, in the seventeenth century. Something that you just said must have reminded me of it. Silly really, and it can't be this one.' My laugh sounded strangled. 'If it were, there would be a curve of stairs in that corner and that wall would be taken up by a huge fireplace with a bread oven.' I pointed.

'It's still there.' Beryl said quietly. 'It's behind that wall separating our cottage from next door This must once have been one long building and the fire, used for cooking, would have been accessed from both sides, and if you look up there,' she pointed to a corner of the ceiling, 'you can see the underneath edge of stairs that lead up to the bedrooms next door. They would have formed part of this room before the dividing wall went up.'

I sat down heavily and gazed up in disbelief at the under edge of a stair case jutting out from the old plaster. Shock waves and jumbled mind pictures swamped my thinking.

'Beryl, tell me,' I almost whispered. 'are there two steps in front of a blank wall, situated at the back of the attic stairs?'

She answered immediately. 'Yes, they are there, and we are knocking through to access a space beyond, that was probably used as a barn. Is there anything else you want to know?'

She didn't seem in the least surprised, though I was totally bewildered as to how this could possibly be.

Beryl in Brook Cottage showing the stairs in the corner of the ceiling.

I didn't know how to proceed. 'Yes there is, but before I do,' I said hesitantly, 'I think I should give you the outline of this story I'm talking about. I don't know why but it's suddenly important to me that you believe what I'm saying. Should there be any more *coincidences*, I want you to know that I am not making it up as we go.'

She didn't speak, leaving me to compose myself, regroup my thoughts. I was in a quandary, not only of how much to tell her, without risking my credibility. If this section of my novel; the fireplace, staircase and steps in the attic, was physically traceable, then I had to face the possibility that the rest was going to be true too. If that were the case, I had to accept that there was a *Guiding Intelligence* directing my attention.

Dear God! Have I really been writing about real people? (Until that very moment it had just been an intriguing mystery. Now though, the enormity of what I was getting into began to hit home.) Was it possible that I had unconsciously *channelled* this deeply emotionally-charged story about life in a past century – that it had not emanated from my fertile imagination and that I had been writing at someone else's dictate? Crazy! But not being able to prove the truth – doesn't make the truth untrue, does it?

Beryl moved and I became aware of my surroundings again. I was trying to claw back the order of events that lay on the pages of my novel thousands of miles away. With eyes half closed, I began to recall and condense the scenes as accurately as possible...

'Beryl let me tell you how this started.' She had been so patient. 'Living in Saudi Arabia with time on my hands I had begun to write again. I was well into the plot; set in a hamlet, near Stratford-on-Avon, and written on a daily basis, rather like a diary, it was to cover just the month of August, 1963. The building was roughly the size and shape of this one, nestled in the foot of hills by a brook, so I called it Brook Cottage.

'All was going well until the date August 1663 began to super-impose itself on my thinking. No matter how I tried, it would not be dismissed and once it had captured my attention, my fingers, flying across the keyboard, could hardly keep up with the changing events that raced across my mind's eye.

'It was August 1663. My story described the lives of two sisters, Rachel and Hannah, living on this spot in a small thatched cottage. Rachel, a herbalist, was accused of bringing plague to the area by witchcraft. The villagers, as a frenzied mob, murdered Rachel, torched her cottage, and virtually razed it to the ground. Only the fireplace, the large bread oven (where Rachel's little sister, Hannah, lay hidden, limp in a drug induced sleep) and its hearth stone, were solid enough to withstand the intense heat.

'Much later, these remains were incorporated in the new Brook Cottage, that was built over the old foundations – and I'm beginning to believe I'm standing in it now!

'Hannah was rescued by Lawrence, at that time the son of the Lord of the Manor, and taken to a large country house close by.'

'Close by? That will be Witetune House,' Beryl said. 'Most likely they were relatives; the Gentry would have closed ranks. They would have helped each other.'

'Well Hannah, who was virtually unharmed physically, had suffered complete loss of memory, which in the circumstances was a blessing. Hannah became companion to and was educated alongside the two girls, daughters of the owner of that house, and years later when they married, Hannah moved to the Manor as housekeeper to the man who had saved her life; he was now the owner and the man she loved.

'Theirs was an unrequited love and Lawrence had this cottage built over the foundations of the original one, out of
respect for Rachel.' I was watching for Beryl's reactions and she was still listening closely. 'Hannah eventually retired here, still with no idea of the history attached to the spot, and as I saw it, this area was heavily wooded and there was a yew tree in the garden, too.' I rubbed my arms and held my coat tight.

'Well, it's still there; so badly pruned you can hardly recognise it as such. Yes I can assure you that tree in front of the house is a yew. It's been hacked down many times over the centuries but they live for hundreds and hundreds of years. And another thing, this area was thick with trees when I first came here. A lot of them were felled only a few years back.' (I was feeling ever so slightly hysterical by this time as detail after tiny detail was being confirmed. It was like playing tennis; the balls kept coming back and I wanted to stop the delivery. I was getting out of my depth. I didn't want confirmation, I wanted it all to be a huge, easily-explained coincidence. I wanted to walk away, having had a logical explanation, and thinking only of the amazing coincidences, my new friend, and of our mutual interest in water divining. That surely was enough for anyone to be going on with – yet I couldn't leave it there.)

'Beryl, when it first began, my 'mind pictures' were muddled crowd scenes, then I began to make out individual shapes of peasants, mostly men, a rough angry mob of Lowry-style stick figures. Not in black and white exactly; rather, just figures without colour. These people were in panic, fear driven. as they headed down the gully, pushing a young reluctant Parson to the front. A gully like the one

I've just driven down. They had come from their village on the hills above the manor; it looked like the one that I just drove past, though I didn't see any buildings or any signs of life on those hills.'

'It was just a small community above Sennington Manor,' Beryl explained, 'more of a settlement than a village. There was a drought a couple of years back, the earth shrank and the outline was photographed by the pilot of a small plane.'

It was a couple of minutes before I could go on.

'The mob wanted to get their hands on the girls who lived here, murder in their hearts. Rachel and Hannah were daughters of the miller. Being a herbalist and living in so isolated a spot, Rachel was an obvious target for an accusation of witchcraft.'

'The mill is still there, about half a mile away; derelict of course. Let me take you to see it,' Beryl encouraged.

'OK, I would like that but that's going too far ahead. To make it brief, I think that Rachel must have had some indication of what was about to happen.

She had drugged her little sister and barely had time to push her in the oven at the side of the fireplace, before the crowd broke in. The oven was bigger than one used by the average family because the girls also cooked bread for travellers as they rested and watered their horses, before crossing the ford, the shallow stream out there. Beryl, if you have difficulty believing all this, I promise you that I have written all of this down as a theme of metaphysical fiction, running through a 1963 story of village life, mystery, and detection. You can't, in your wildest dreams imagine how I feel, standing in the cottage where all this apparently happened.' We sat in silence for a while, finishing the coffee, and then a quote came to mind:

> *"There is a destiny that shapes our ends,*
> *rough hew them though we may."*

'Shall we go up to the attic?' Beryl stopped my thoughts of flight. Climbing the rough staircase, I at once *knew* this attic.
The features were precisely as I had seen and recorded them; the style of the old window in the back of the sloping roof that had been

recently replaced by a more modern one and to the rear of the house, the stream, willows, high curve of hills cradling the hollow, and at the back of the stairwell, there they were – the two steps in front of a blank wall, confirming again the accuracy of something seemingly unimportant that I had viewed on my *mental screen*, thousands of miles away!

'Let's go next door.' Beryl said, leading the way down.

Meeting Grace

After all that I had seen in Brook Cottage, I should have welcomed Beryl's suggestion that we go to visit her neighbour to see this fireplace, bread oven and hearthstone, in situ from the original cottage for myself. In truth, I followed her with some trepidation. What would the woman next door make of it? She didn't know me from Adam and 'Excuse my calling, it's just that I think someone was hidden in your bread oven three-hundred years ago while a murder was committed in your garden,' was hardly likely to engender confidence!

When Beryl had attracted my attention and called me to park outside her door, I really hadn't had time to take notice of the outside of the building or that it was now two cottages. The conversion could have been done a couple of hundred years earlier. Either way, I knew, (I had written) that there would be a second entrance at the side. A sturdy buttress supported the wall, erected as a precaution, I assumed, by those familiar with local conditions. Snow and rain would have flooded over the banks of the stream many a year, and could gradually have undermined the foundations. Winters were of course, much harder in those times.

This cottage garden was a mass of plants and flowers and with bird song and the trickle of the brook running alongside the only sounds in this hidden place, it was a delight, but as we walked along the little path, my senses were acutely drawn to a spot close to the hedge. It was strange that I could detect nothing unusual with my physical eye and yet I couldn't easily move my gaze away from it.

The door opened and Grace, a softly spoken, short, rounded lady with white hair, had come out to meet us and after being introduced, I stepped back, feeling a little awkward as Beryl outlined the strange facts in my story, confirming what we had already found, and why I now had an interest in this second part of the building.

I don't know what I expected, certainly not the lack of reaction from Grace, who, with a patient expression, slowly turned to me and waited; 'Your point is?' her look seemed to say. This was a backwater, undisturbed by the dramas of yesterday.

'If what I've written has any real substance, Grace, then Rachel Myer's body would have been buried out here,' I gestured around. 'It must have been near a source of water because it lay there undisturbed, until someone tried to dig for a well in the summer of 1663. Was there, is there a well here?'

'No, not that I know of,' Grace shook her head. 'Though if you are right, could the body still be here?'

'I don't think so. In my story I wrote that her remains were eventually reburied in the local churchyard. To make sure that her last resting place could not be identified, no name was carved on her headstone and rumour was deliberately spread that it was the grave of a drover. If the truth had been known, those who had taken part in the murder and who still needed to believe they had killed a witch and not an innocent woman, would probably have desecrated the grave.'

Oh, I cringed inside, is she believing this? Does it sound sincere or does she think I'm making it up?

Grace led the way indoors but at the threshold I stopped. There was something wrong, out of place, this was not the layout that I had expected to see, and taking a deep sigh of honest relief, I said:

'It's all right, Beryl, it's over. You see, this is wrong, this door should be in line with that staircase,' I pointed to it confidently, through the glass panel.

'It's been moved,' they said in unison and my heart sank. 'It was reorganised, rebuilt years before I came here,' Grace added, and hearing those words, I just gave up the idea of further resistance.

Walking slowly, she showed us into the cosy little sitting room; highly polished, traditionally furnished, spoon backed chairs, small oak tables, broad windowsill, flowers, velvet curtains; all one would expect in a country cottage occupied by a single elderly lady who loved the quiet, orderly life.

Sensitive to my need for silence I think they had moved to the back of the room or perhaps out into the kitchen for I felt no pressure of time, no impatience from them. The house was at rest, the stone structure still as solid and as protective as it always had been, and using the Silva relaxation method, I moved easily into a more intuitive state...

Detached, but aware of my present surroundings, I began to recall memory pictures that I had first viewed in the Middle East. It was here, all around me and easy to replay the shades of that long gone summer when Hannah and Rachel faced a terrifying end. 'Yes, this is it,' I pointed to the iron door of the oven; recessed on the side of the big fireplace, then hovering a hand over the actual brick work I stood up, puzzled.

'These bricks are old, but they're not the original ones.'

'True. They are not,' Grace confirmed. 'The original ones, the ones you must be referring to are underneath. The old hearthstone is there too.'

As Beryl had pointed out earlier; when the ground floor of the cottage had been open as one long room, the oven would have stretched back into her side of the cottage to make full use of the heat from a fire that would have been worked from both sides. Over the centuries the capacity would have been reduced, but in those days, the oven would have been big enough and deep enough to hide a small person, especially one who was pliable, supple in deep sleep. Especially when the alternative was to be butchered to death by a mob, baying for blood!

It was some time later as we wandered out into the sunshine and I stopped to admire the flowers, when Grace suddenly frowned.

'You know, all this talk of the past has caused me to remember something. To my knowledge there has never been a well in this

garden though there is an underground spring just about there.'
She pointed to the exact spot that my attention had first been drawn
to. 'I sometimes hear it gurgling in summer if the water lever is low
in the stream.'

Beryl and I exchanged glances, I, wide eyed at this revelation.
Could this in fact be the place where Rachel Myer had been buried?
The grave would have been shallow, and the first hint of water would
have frustrated the digging. The young Parson, working alone and in
great haste, wouldn't have had time or the emotional and physical
stamina to dig elsewhere. I remembered typing this in the cool of the
morning, thousands of miles away.

Amazing! There was much detail – why? I was past questioning.

Beryl suggested that I might use the divining rods and ask if
anyone had been laid to rest there. I doubted my ability no longer, I
wanted to carry on, I was in the flow, and encouraged by this surge
of confidence I held them out in front and silently asked: Was anyone
buried here?

Without hesitation they reacted and swung across each other. Yes,
was the answer! It was inexplicable. My heart almost stopped. With
every revelation I was being assured of a benign *Intelligence* that I
didn't understand, yet in my innermost heart, I knew it was a force
for good. Thank goodness I had Beryl as a witness; a woman whom
I instinctively and implicitly trusted.

'Now ask how deep the grave was,' she said encouragingly.
'Water levels would have varied over the centuries.'

She stepped back and I set the rods again, asked the question, and
slowly began to count: One foot, two feet, three feet, four feet.
At four feet they came together sharply. It had indeed been a shallow
grave.

Hitting an excessively damp patch must have shaken the poor
Parson rigid. Water! He had to stop digging and with no time to start
again, he would have been distraught.

I decided to ask for more information: Are the remains still here?
The rods swung wide apart: No! 'I suppose they would have used
divining twigs, hazel or something to locate the water,' I offered.

'Anyhow, it supports my story of her body being reburied in the churchyard and that the owner of the Manor and the Parson, footing the cost, perhaps out of Christian respect or for more personal reasons. Maybe we should look for that headstone while things are going well?'

However, time had run out, Beryl was ready to leave for Wales and anyhow, I was emotionally spent.

It had been quite a morning but frustratingly, by the time Beryl returned from Wales, I would be in Saudi Arabia.

My mind was in a whirl as I started the car and drove up the track on to the high road then on impulse, reaching the Manor, I turned down the short lane and parked the car on the grass verge outside the small church. This had to be the place where Rachel Myer was buried. One last try and I would use the pendulum this time, less obvious if anyone saw me. The place was deserted; no one around, no one tidying away dead flowers or walking between the stones, no one to make me feel self-conscious or to question what I was doing.

Just stillness and silence.

I assumed that the little church would at some period have been part of the estate of the Manor House, right next to it. The family and servants would have had access to devotions through the small wooden gate in the long stone wall, now weathered to a soft grey. Perhaps Hannah had used that gate!

Taking my time, walking slowly along the path between the grave stones, relaxing into a receptive frame of mind I entered through the porch into the cool emptiness of the little church; thin cords of sunlight highlighting deep corners, pews polished to a fine patina by the toil of long forgotten hands. I felt them still there, living in their parallel time, aware of me as I was of them. Studying the names on the marble wall plaques and finding none that I recognised, I resorted to seeking help from the crystal that Beryl had given me. Holding the cord in fingertips, I asked: Is there any reference to the person I wish to pay my last respects to, in here? I was a little disappointed when the pendulum immediately circled to the negative. Then where was she? I knew she had to be here, somewhere, and all the happenings of the morning had strengthened my belief in a guiding hand. Why else would I have been given all this information?

Not knowing what to do next, I went out into the sun and walked up the steep little bank just outside the door and wandered aimlessly over to the corner of the wall, nearest the manor house. I was feeling quite weary by now, and with not much hope, I asked my question again. 'Is Rachel Myer here?' and was absolutely amazed when the pendulum gave an instant and positive swing to, Yes. With renewed energy I hurried from grave to grave, scratching away tendrils of ivy, looking across the lawns to other head stones for a likely spot. Rachel Myer was in this graveyard, I was convinced of it, but where? Half an hour later, tired, disappointed and hungry, I got back in the car and drove the long way back to the pub in the medieval village that I had driven through only that morning. It felt like a lifetime ago!

The smallest gravestone on the far right of the row is the unmarked grave of Rachel Myer.

Didn't whoever was guiding me on this mission realize that I would be over three-thousand miles from here by the time Beryl returned from Wales? Oh ye of little faith!

When the pendulum had answered 'Yes' to my question as to the position of Rachel's grave, I hadn't thought to look down at the headstone by my feet! And another 'coincidence' was that I would still be in England when Beryl returned from Wales.

The Cat

One month later, my visa to re-enter the Kingdom of Saudi Arabia had finally arrived and, anxious though I was to get back to my husband and the Middle East, Beryl was home from Wales, and I realized that I could just fit in a quick visit to Sennington. I felt that I needed to regroup my thoughts and conclusions; talk to Beryl and decide where we should go from here. If this whole story that I had called *Unshriven* was going to prove to be fact, (and that seemed a definite and very exciting possibility) then I had to stay in an open and receptive frame of mind. Beryl and I had kept in close contact by phone but after the real drama of our first encounter, neither she nor I knew what to expect. An anti-climax possibly, I thought, heading for the hills.

The month had not been wasted; I had been busy, but at the back of my mind was a nagging dilemma; how to categorize *Unshriven*, when I presented it to a publisher? How could I describe it as fiction, now that I had proof that the 17th century aspect was fact? That wasn't the only difficulty.

I wanted to stay as close to the proven truth as possible; however when writing the story in the Middle East, I hadn't been given all the names of either the places or the people. For the sake of clarity, and only when I had matched the places and situations beyond doubt, I had inserted the real (though old) names, in the fictional novel. There was another problem. Like watching a compelling movie, I had indeed *watched* that mob come down the gully from the settlement above. The gully was there with all the supporting features; photographic evidence of a small village on the hill opposite the manor, the ford, the cottage and its relics etc., but the *emotion* of the crowd, the driving force of hate and terror that had resulted in brutal murder, could not be proven.

So, was I to classify this, too, as fiction just because it had not been documented? If personal relationships were to be ignored because there was no tangible evidence, where was half the story?

Buildings, bricks and stones, records written by hand on parchment, and official church documents had all withstood time and the elements. The physical and emotional experiences however; the joy and the pain and a lifetime of unrequited love that I, like a friend and confidante, had shared, had long drifted into the ether, taking the stories with them. There were no witnesses, no way of confirming the passion – no one left alive to tell their tale...

Hannah Myer must have used my latent powers of clairvoyance (such as they were) to guide me to Sennington. She needed someone, somehow, to tell the outrageous truth of what happened to her sister. As I understood it, once this was done, her soul would be freed, so how could I leave her personal history untold, just because it wasn't written on parchment? And there was another problem. How could I convince a publisher that a book that was half fact and half fiction, was saleable?

What if I presented the whole series of events, including the metaphysical part of the story, as fiction? Would that be good enough to satisfy Hannah and break her emotional bond with this earth? Too much, too much!

I wanted to walk away; yet I just had to know more.

* * * * * * *

It was an exceptionally warm morning for the time of year, with birds singing, making nests and flying in pairs. The drive through the countryside was revealing the best of an English spring; everything fresh, green and sweet-smelling, with early lambs skittering on the steep slopes and I arrived with an open heart and an open mind.

Yet again, when Beryl opened the door, I felt that same mild shock; she was not the person I expected to see. Would this odd feeling ever leave me? Only, perhaps, if 'time' caught up. I smiled at my reasoning as I stepped inside. As welcoming as before, Beryl suggested that after coffee we walk up the steep hills at the back of her cottage to the old Drovers' Track running along the crest; pity to waste such a lovely morning sitting indoors.

We must have been half way up, chatting, walking slowly through rough grass and weeds, and enjoying the warm sun on our backs, when I started to hear the call, quite clear in my mind. There was no one to be seen but it was a woman's voice calling the name. "*John!*" Deep, plaintive, searching, the woman called his name again gradually fading – into a distant past...

The views on the ridge were well worth the effort and we cut to the left, strolling along an arc that would bring us the short walk back, down the hill to the ford running alongside Brook Cottages. We talked about the drovers who had walked this very track, some from as far away as Wales, hoping to sell their geese and sheep at market for a good price or load them on narrow boats and send them up to London from the village of Lechlade, the highest navigable part of the Thames. Sadly, there were stories of the men being robbed or killed for the money from the sale of their stock.

'Think of a spirit trapped up here, unaware of time moving on and still worrying about a family waiting for his return and hungry mouths to be fed,' Beryl said.

'Perhaps that woman's voice I heard calling for John, was that man's wife?' I suggested.

'It could be. The area would have been thickly wooded in those days, easy to hide a body.'

'So what should I do if ever I think that someone is trapped in time?' I asked, wanting to learn from Beryl's vast experience.

'I'll tell you. Some people help such souls to depart by using their own physical bodies as exit channels. I don't do that. I never allow any invasion of my body. I just use the power of my thought to tell them the current date and in a loving way, encourage them to let go and move on to the Light, which to me is Enlightenment; all knowing. Use that as a guideline,' she advised. 'You will soon become confident and do what feels right.'

We made our way home, both deep in personal thoughts, as the track dipped sharply to the left, down towards the stream and Brook Cottages. Tucked along a short lane of fresh, green-leafed trees to our right, were a few scattered stone cottages crouched into the swelling hill. I felt the scrutiny of small windows witness our passing, as they had watched others over several hundred years; one century laying its progress upon another. People pass, time passes, winters follow summers, death follows life, and these cottages, left undisturbed, natural stone upon natural stone, have been and will remain, witness to the drift of life for generations to come.

I felt their mild contempt.

We reached the stream in silence. Everything was still, not a leaf moved. Then – was it my eyes slightly defocusing – or had the light changed? What I can only describe as the Energy of Nature was now visible to me, taking the form of a translucent shimmering haze, completely filling the space from my eyes to its source; the trees and the plants. The Energy of Life, visible like an aura, was everywhere I looked. There was no empty space. Everything was Energy and vibrant with colour. I knew that the aura given off by plants could be photographed with special techniques and here was I, not only sensing it but actually watching this pulsating medium. It was like having a close-up personal demonstration of the Northern Lights! I remembered the paintings of Vincent Van Gogh and of those wild coloured streaks of paint hovering above ripening crops. Had he also witnessed this? Were his senses so heightened that he painted what he actually witnessed?

That feeling again that a door had opened on to something familiar – something I should recall....

I focused for a while longer, concentrating on this other dimension until, gradually, it faded.

The day was getting warmer, still not a breath of wind, nothing disturbing the deep sense of peace, only the stream and the birdsong broke our reverie, and, reluctant to speak, I just touched Beryl's arm as we parted and she went indoors.

No need to explain. She understood.

Grace saw me coming and opened the door and waited patiently as I stopped to absorb the magic from her colourful garden; the energy that seemed to be dancing all around me. I studied Grace more keenly this time, trying to detect the person behind the glasses. Calm, softly spoken, she was the idea of everyone's nice aunt! We exchanged a few quiet words then she turned and led the way indoors, this time through a little kitchen at the back.

Stepping over the threshold of her tiny living room, I paused. I hadn't really noticed on my first visit that it was like the layout for a photograph, one that would go in a coffee table book, and this was no mock-up. The tastefully furnished little sitting room reflected a bygone era: Books, little curios dotted around, fresh flowers from the garden, the smell of lavender, probably from polish, dried grasses in the hearth, an empty china tea cup on a small table and the clock, discreetly ticking away unimportant minutes. Nothing hurried, the room had a settled feel, and everything had its place.

Sun streamed in through small window panes warming the glossy coat of a ginger cat sprawled out on its side, its gently heaving body covering most of the seat of a velvet-covered spoon backed chair. Deeply, deeply asleep, the cat was totally unaware that we had entered the room. Serene, tranquil, at peace, we had not spoken, both of us somehow reluctant to break the spell – and then it happened.

As though a great bolt of electricity had shot through the sleeping cat's body, it sprang to life with an earth shattering screech! Terror in its eyes, tail upright, fur on end, literally standing on its claws, it stared directly at me, screamed again then bolted under the cover of the peripheral furniture, out through the open door and fled into the undergrowth outside, leaving me dumbfounded and poor Grace, visibly shaken.

Astonished, bewildered by the poor creature's reaction, neither of us moved. I didn't know what to say. I felt responsible and not a little embarrassed and had absolutely no idea why it had happened. Grace assured me that her cat had never behaved in that way before; she couldn't understand it either. 'Being involved with the history of this place,' she said in her slow measured way, 'do you think you could have been here before, perhaps in a past life? Could you have been this Rachel Myer, or her sister, and my cat has somehow picked up vibrations, the fear from what happened then?'

Immediately and without hesitation I found myself answering, voicing thought that had never really come to the forefront of my mind.

'No, Grace, I don't think I was either Rachel or Hannah Myer. I don't have any feeling of ever visiting this earth before. I know this might sound strange, and everything to do with this, is indeed strange. It's just that, since my last visit,' I hesitated for a moment then decided to go on.

'I have begun to explore the possibility that I have, with Hannah's consent, taken her place this time round; – her time to *reincarnate*.'

'Why? What do you mean? What makes you say that?'

I took a steadying breath. I really didn't want to go on with this conversation; it was altogether too deep to have with a virtual stranger.

'Well, perhaps it is because I am a writer, spiritually sensitive and able somehow to absorb this information. As for what has just happened, I have no idea why I frightened your poor cat and I'm so sorry.' But in the back of my mind I was wondering if the cat really had sensed some distressing energy connected with this place, which I was somehow channelling.

There was no more time, I had to leave. I called on Beryl to say goodbye and she promised to contact the owners of both manor houses and hopefully arrange for me to visit them, the next time I was home.

I drove away with mixed feelings, wanting to be with my dear husband and wishing too, that I had more time to spend in this atmospheric place. There was so much more to find, I knew it. I was on the tip of a huge breakthrough of understanding – and it all had to be put on hold.

My visa in hand, two days later I was boarding a flight back to Saudi Arabia where I knew I would find the peace and quiet and much needed mental space, to regroup my thoughts.

Music In The Desert

Word went round that there was to be a musical evening in a canyon, out in the desert. (My husband played flute and had joined the Riyadh Concert Band, and as large gatherings were forbidden, practice sessions had to be held in the rather grand American compound.) One late afternoon we all made our separate ways out of town, driving fast along miles of perfect roads cutting straight lines through the desert, all anxious to get to our destination before the light vanished. Leaving the highway we cut off-track into the desert, looking for markers as vague as a strangely shaped hill, or a small clump of bushes with a coca-cola bottle on top; (very *cloak and dagger*.)

We came to a fork in the track, which way? – then a group of Bedouin standing outside wide low tents, pointed us in the right direction with a smile and a wave.

Gestures like that are Universal peace makers. The Bedouin are desert people, who wander great distances to graze their goats and camels. They have chosen not to join in the western way of life or embrace modern values that have totally changed their country's ancient culture. These are not backward looking people and as far back as the nineteen forties, their women did not wear the veil; (impractical for a working woman driving a truck over the rough terrain and also, not law in the Koran – unless a woman is exceptionally beautiful.) What sights those travelling caravans must have seen in the night skies stretching back hundreds, perhaps thousands of years; wonders, mysteries gradually forgotten or passed down as tales to be told, sitting round a fire.

Centuries of desert winds had carved huge caverns and natural acoustics out of the sandstone hills but we were not prepared for such a dramatic scene as we walked through a narrow passage into a vast auditorium: Open to the sky, rugged towering walls, candles burning in every crevice pin-pointing the way to sitting places on slim ledges and, as the sky darkened to indigo, glorious classical music; The Hall of the Mountain King filled our ears and satiated our senses.

We sat spellbound on that *never to be forgotten*, evening, becoming one with the warm night and the breath-taking beauty of it all. It was sheer magic and the wonder of it wrapped itself around me as I studied a myriad of stars, trying to imagine what was out there and – from what dimension Hannah Myer was calling...

How could I not think of her on a night such as this? I thought of Sennington, mysterious and beautiful on a night like this and looking just the way it had done for hundreds of years.

Suppose my discoveries there were just the tip of the iceberg. What if, like the outline of a hand on the wall of a prehistoric cave, the houses where Hannah had lived and that I had been so clearly directed to, were her mark, her 'outline of a hand,' on history. Tangible historic proof that she had been on earth and was now calling across time:

"*I was here. Know me from the things that touched my life. Help me to right the wrong.*"

What more could she do?

Searching the rafters of the sky for answers, I was no longer listening to the music and it was a shock when the audience started to clap, leave their nooks and crannies in the cliffs and head for the cars.

Still absorbed with mental dialogue, when we reached the city I had come to a decision; it was time to get back to the keyboard. The dilemma was how to proceed, when I knew that it was no longer fiction? Alarmed, I rejected the prospect of starting all over again, and this time, writing the hard facts as they had, and probably would continue to emerge.

No! I stamped a mental foot angrily, definitely not. I couldn't just scrap all the work I had already done. It wasn't fair!

My story needed some polishing and editing, though in my

opinion I had written a really good novel, and by this time, in reply to an earlier enquiry, I had received excellent feedback from the Editorial Director of one of the top UK publishing houses. On the other hand, there was no contract on the table; it was always just out of reach. Was there a deeper reason?

"*Write it as fact.*"

There it was again, this nagging persistent thought. It was uncomfortable and it wouldn't go away.

'No, I won't. Get a grip, live in the real world.' (I said to whoever was *Upstairs*) 'I've worked too hard to change in mid-stream. How about a compromise? I will write the factual version – later.

In the mean time, I'll continue with my 1963 version and Stella (my character with clairvoyance) can do research and discover the history of Brook Cottages and the murder. I'll sort of insert the facts into the fiction.

Simple! (It didn't turn out to be simple. I had no idea how difficult the work was going to be and I was later to liken it to changing the pattern on a jumper without first unravelling the garment.)

The Manor at Sennington

I had been abroad for several months and the summer was good as we flew into Heathrow. This wasn't going to be a long visit as we intended to take another holiday on our boat in France before returning to the Middle East.

During the long absence, Beryl and I had corresponded and finally getting a date for my return, she had secured an invitation for me to visit Sennington Manor and meet with the owner, Mrs. C. (whom I will call Catherine).

Accompanied by a friend I set out very early one morning, planning to visit the local historical records office before the meeting at the manor. With names and dates I was able to isolate the necessary files but the search was very difficult. Apart from almost illegible hand-writing and old terminology, there were also huge gaps in the registers of parishes in this area, for when an outbreak of plague occurred, the Parson and his parish clerk, had more important things to do than keep records when people were dropping like flies.

As to the murder of a local woman in the 17th century, we were reminded, this was in an isolated community, the people uneducated and terrified out of their minds. If they had any suspicion of witch craft, they wouldn't have waited for the local magistrate to pronounce judgement. They would have killed savagely to stop the evil. Rational thinking and fear are not good companions.

There was yet another complication; names given at birth were often used time and again for close family members living cheek by jowl. There could be several men called Percy in one family called Smith! We did eventually discover that the name of the mill owner at the time was Myer and, intriguingly, this name still persists in the hamlet.

It was so difficult to make real connections and I was getting cold feet, almost talking myself out of the visit to the manor until my friend reminded me that this wasn't my problem. If more things were to be proven, then they were already in place and all I had to do was to make myself available and receptive and find them.

It was late morning when we arrived at the manor; a long building, well maintained, but the far end was a ruin! Hidden by a wall, the house was set just off the road before the turning to the church. The next turning was the gully, leading to Beryl's cottage. We drove in through big stone pillars then swung along the gravel drive to an imposing front porch. This was the Manor, I reminded myself, where Hannah had been housekeeper. A position she was more than capable of fulfilling having been educated with daughters of the Gentry.

Catherine, our hostess, (slender as a willow with a warm smile and large framed spectacles that couldn't hide eyes bright with laughter) was enthusiastic at the thought of a mystery.

She came out to meet us accompanied by two little silken haired dachshunds, both barking a warning, keeping guard of their beloved mistress who was welcoming and kind and was to allow us, complete strangers, to wander and intimately inspect details of her lovely home.

Once through the porch and inner door, we stepped into a square hall with a wood-blocked floor, an impressive staircase, and a fireplace, shallow and high against the wall. Down two steps, 'That's the cellar,' she pointed underneath the stairs as we followed on through the dining room; a magnificent oak refectory table, daylight straining in from the garden through tiny squares of old glass bound in iron frames then along a flag-stoned hall to the big family kitchen.

From the moment I stepped in through that front door, it was as I had imagined. I had known more or less how the layout of this place would be and sitting at the kitchen table drinking coffee, it was as though Catherine and I had known each other and enjoyed each other's company, for years.

Not wanting to waste time, and with her encouragement, I retraced my steps, out through the dining room, past the door to the cellars, and back into the hall to the main staircase that had featured large in Hannah's time here. It was up there, at the top of the house where Hannah kept her nightly vigil that she had heard young royalist soldiers, loud and foolish from drink, taken away with the clink of chains from some hiding place in the cellars below. I remembered Hannah's mounting tension as, desperate to stop their indiscretions; she started down these very stairs to alert them – too late! The sound of horses clattering into the yard meant that Cromwell's men had arrived. Lawrence was away and, with no one to defend them, they were at the mercy of the Roundheads.

Starting up the staircase, I couldn't hear any talk from the kitchen. The house itself was still and silent as if holding its breath. Ears straining, I found myself listening for something just beyond reach, as though others were there in the shadows, waiting. I passed a corridor of bedrooms and continued the climb, the stairs squaring up to the left as I made my way to the top landing – but I couldn't get there. The staircase had come to an abrupt halt – just as I had written it!

'Catherine, the stairs don't go up to the attics. Why?' I asked, hurrying back into the kitchen.

'I think,' she said slowly, 'that they must have been destroyed when the fire took hold of that wing of the house. That's why the side of the house is a ruin. Go the other way. Carry on down the corridor, stairs on the left, go up to the next floor and you will find back stairs to the top of the attics.'

The attic was spacious and bone dry with a door at the far end that opened on to a large square landing lightened now by a huge side window. And *this* was where Hannah had waited for her Lawrence. *This* was the spot! *This* was proof!

With the dividing door closed at night, the servants would not have known she was there, waiting there in the dark, listening, ears straining to catch the slightest sounds drifting up that staircase from the rooms below. To eavesdrop was not the intention but she had gleaned enough to keep herself and Lawrence secure, should any political scheming threaten.

My reverie was broken as, just at that minute, my friend and our hostess appeared behind me. I hadn't heard them and I was jolted back to the present. 'We've come to find out what you've discovered,' they laughed.

'Then you're just in time to help me.' I pointed to the ceiling. 'What's above our heads?'

'Nothing. There's nothing more.' Catherine answered.

'No other floor, no more rooms?'

'No,' she shook her head. 'Just the roof.'

'Has there ever been?'

'I don't think so. I don't think that the fire that destroyed the end of this house, reached the roof this far. Sorry,'

No rooms! Was that to be it? Something wasn't adding up but facts were facts. Apparently there was nothing above us, nothing more to find up there.

Confused and a bit deflated, I followed them out of the house and into the garden. The ruined part was interesting; inside walls exposed ruined floor levels, and then I saw it; a small window, tucked between the ruin and the main building. It was at an odd angle in the old roof which had been added to over the centuries. 'That window, where is that window?' I asked.

'Ah, yes,' Catherine answered. 'There are two tiny rooms up there a bit higher and to the side of the landing where you were. They're tucked into the eaves. We use them for storage.'

'Yes! I knew it, I knew they had to be there. It's more proof.' I was elated as we hurried back to the attic. 'The view from her room will look out to the hills opposite, where the outline of the old village was photographed. It has to be right, I've already recorded it,' I said confidently as Catherine opened a small door hidden in a shadowy recess. There, up a short flight of steps at the top were the two little rooms I had been searching for, one without a window, the other with a view Hannah would have had of a settlement opposite. No trace of it now and it was reassuring to know that its existence had been proven by an aerial photographer.

Everything was coming together: Meeting Beryl, Brook Cottage, steps in the attic facing a blank wall, the original fireplace, hearth-stone and bread oven and the underground spring in the garden, had held witness to Hannah's existence. Now the rooms that she had occupied, at the Manor, were here, exactly where she had said they were. It was all coming true. I was being constantly reassured, that Hannah Myer really had existed and here was more proof. Dear Hannah was helping me as much as she could and I wouldn't let her down. I was determined to follow this trail to its natural conclusion.

Then I reflected, that if everything is energy, why shouldn't the emotional energy and the binding power of their unrequited love, persist as a force in the home they shared? And why shouldn't their emotional bond be as believable as these bricks and mortar?

'I am fully convinced,' I said later to Catherine, 'that keeping Hannah's history secret from her was a sensible decision on Lawrence's part. Knowing her so intimately he judged her reaction correctly, for when Hannah regained her memory and learned the truth, she really didn't give his impossible position a second thought. All she knew was that her sister had been murdered, the criminals had not been brought to justice, and she had wasted her own life, waiting for a man who was never in a position to claim her.

'It wasn't his fault. He just tried and had succeeded until the end, in making the best of a bad job. Unfortunately, Hannah didn't see it that way. Having focused totally on everything that was negative, she finally died, laying a curse on the date and the cottage where she had lived so comfortably, and blaming Lawrence for her wasted life and for her dying childless.

'Poor man! There is a saying that, *"To know all, is to forgive all."* And I think Hannah just wants to move on now and join her man; her soul-mate?' I added the afterthought.

For some reason I recalled again the evening in Riyadh, that wonderful night of music in the wind-carved cavern open to the sky, when I had felt Hannah's call: *"I was here. Know me from the things that touched my life. Help me to right the wrong."*

'So what's the next step?' Beryl asked as I prepared to leave.

'Well we're going to France in a couple of days but you might be able to set something up for the next time I'm home.

'Hannah was taken to live at another big house in this area, over two hills,' I waved a hand in the general direction.

'Yes, it's over there and there's a small medieval village attached to it, too.'

'That's interesting. Is there any chance of you weaving your magic and arranging a visit the next time I'm home?'

'They are nice people, I'm sure they will agree.' Beryl said confidently. 'What do you hope to find there?'

'Some documentary evidence that would link Hannah to the place would be top of the list of course. She became companion to two daughters of that house so although I don't expect to find Hannah's name there as she wasn't family, the daughters would certainly be on record. I just want the dates to correspond. Not much to ask is it? I just want you to perform another miracle!' I laughed, waving goodbye.

* * * * * * *

Dated: Ann and Apollina Cotton

The months in Saudi Arabia slipped by and I was impatient to be home so that I could continue my research in Sennington. I was therefore delighted when Beryl wrote and said that we had been invited to look through the files and manorial records of Witetune House. It was my belief that Hannah Myer had lived there and had become companion to, and educated alongside, two daughters of the house, and it was evidence of their existence and dates of their marriages, that I hoped to find. (Witetune House is thought to have been built around 1545, and had, over time, been gifted more lands and buildings by Henry 7th, Henry 8th and Elizabeth 1st.)

I will never forget the moment I stood before this impressive Tudor manor. The lovely old house was throwing long shadows across the drive as I stepped out of the car and, delighted to be there, I was quite unprepared for what was about to happen. I barely had time to close the door before the feeling of what I can only describe as a physical weight, like a heavy warm cloak, draped itself across my shoulders. The impression I had was of being drawn towards the house, pulled forward but I felt powerless to move and carry the weight of it and for a few moments, using the pretext of admiring the building (and it was so worthy of admiration) held on to the car for steadying support while mentally struggling to free myself.

Through the heavy ironed oak door, down the short stone-flagged hall, past an impressive dining room and a large comfortable library, stood a magnificent oak staircase with heavy symmetrical newel-posts and the dog-gate, still intact. It was easy to imagine a couple of Irish wolf hounds, in from a day's hunting, wet, and panting, waiting to be fed at the bottom of the stairs. What a place!

We had been welcomed with open-minded acceptance by our hostess; a petite gentlewoman with a serious searching expression and a hesitant warm smile. But it was her eyes that held my attention; looking directly into mine with a kind of open honesty. I liked Gilly immediately and it is a privilege to say that she has become a friend.

With the offer of a tour of the house, we were shown first into a

Witetune Manor

small room where, anticipating my needs, our hostess, her husband and son, had boxes, files and bundles of documents, already piled up on a table in readiness.

So, where to start?

It was our extreme good fortune (another coincidence?) that their friend, a retired archivist, was also there and very willing to help. Having spent much of his retirement collating the history of the house, with patience and good grace, he skilfully steered us through the maze of records not relevant to our investigation, and on to the 17th century pile that might hold some answers. We were extremely glad of his expertise, particularly with cross-referencing, as names in branches of the same family, were repeated over and over. We were encouraged to handle (with great care and with a sense of privilege) private letters, business agreements and official documents, some on rolled parchments, some several hundred years old, held together by simple cords threaded through holes punched at the top and no special care of temperature control; how they had survived the centuries was a miracle. Many were elegantly written in copper-plate, beautifully scripted, with lots of loops and curves and one had to get one's 'eye in' to be able to read most of them. Our archivist, who had spent a lifetime in this world, translated them immediately and with ease but we had found nothing to link Hannah to the house, until:

'Yes, this is it,' I exclaimed aloud. I had never become blasé with the many new discoveries but the one I now held in my hands, took my breath away.

Confirmation and the dates fitted perfectly! Here was documented evidence! There had been two girls living here, daughters of Witetune House: Ann and Apollina Cotton, and Hannah had been their companion. Their ages and the dates of their marriages, would have left Hannah, then in her early twenties; educated, able to keep household books and numbered accounts, free to accept the position of house-keeper at Sennington Manor. At last, she could begin to repay the generosity of her benefactor and he, having waited patiently all these years, could finally take care of her under his own roof. It fitted my calendar perfectly and I could not believe my luck!

As always, time was short and I desperately wanted to see the rest of this house where Hannah had lived out her daily life. Walking through the rooms, we climbed the back staircases that would have been used by the servants, and into the silence of the attics. Here, it was as though decades of thoughts had drifted up and collected like soft curled feathers under the eaves, each one still separate but denuded now of emotion, by long-gone time. (Let me again emphasise the kindness of my hosts; this was their home, yet they had given me permission to go wherever I felt the need.)

As we were leaving the upstairs sitting room, I hesitated. 'Would you mind if I went back in there and had a little time alone,' I asked my host. 'I have no idea why, yet I have the strangest feeling of being needed.' And, as accommodating as ever, he left me to my thoughts.

It was a large room, warm and at rest. The sun was high above the trees, streaming in through the big windows, easing shadows into dark recesses and carving mullioned squares across the faded carpet.

Using my Silva training I became deeply relaxed and focused, gradually becoming at one with the energies in the room. It was as though we were breathing at the same pace as I directed my concentration, relaxing deeper and deeper.

'I have no idea who you are, but I feel that you have been bound to this place for a very long time.' I spoke the words quietly and I had barely finished the sentence when I saw in front of me, suspended in mid-air, four black numbers, at least three feet high. I have to say that I can't remember now if the date was 1762 or 1672. Anyhow, there was this date, several hundred years old, confirming to me that this soul had indeed been trapped there for all that time – yet at no time did I think it was Hannah Myer.

So there was someone else here! From then on I allowed strong intuition to guide me.

Concentrating, centering my attention, I told the Presence (the ghost), the date. (Often they do not realize that time has moved on.) Then I created a picture in my mind of a beech wood in high summer with a shaft of bright sunlight piercing the canopy of leaves, symbolising the path to freedom and Life Beyond. Gently and firmly, I directed the Presence to the path of Light, reassuring, guiding, rather like the firm hand of a parent who knows what is best and wants what is best for the child.

I felt the vibrations, I felt the change, and when it had stopped I directed the energy of pure love into the now empty space.

When I left and closed the door behind me, the room was at peace and so was I.

The clock was moving fast, it was a long difficult drive out of the hills and I needed to take Beryl home first. We had to leave without delay, yet the small private chapel was only yards from the house.

'Pity to miss it,' something seemed to say. I was anxious about the time – yet it wouldn't take more than a couple of minutes; a quick look inside. Just a peep, I reasoned.

I was meant to go into that chapel, for there on the wall was the portrait of a man; Lawrence Roberts, Gent.

I pressed my hands to my cheeks and I couldn't take my eyes off him. Whether this was the man I had written about or (with family names repeated time and again) a close relative, with such strong features, there would surely be a family likeness.

I left the little sanctuary and drove away elated and almost intoxicated with the impossibility of it all. I felt that I had looked upon the likeness of the man Hannah had devoted her life to.

How amazing was that?

The Mill

It was deep autumn before I could visit Beryl and the hamlets again, this time to find the flour mill where Hannah and Rachel Myer had been born. In my research I had found this entry:

Quote from archives and Doomsday Book. There was a Water-Mill, and a wood, one mile long and a half mile broad.

(There was also a small stone quarry that would have supplied the stone for the cottages, built by the people who had fled Prestbury Hill.)

By now I was expecting to identify much of what I was anticipating. Enjoying the colours of autumn and talking as we walked, I told Beryl what I hoped we would find: A mill, mill pond, the sheep dip behind it and behind that, a large clear shallow pool that had a whitish bottom.

Turning off the road we started along the track that ran alongside a rushing stream, turbulent from the recent rain. The sound changed quite subtly as another stream joined ours, adding power to the mill race. I recalled what I had written: "*Two waters meet near the mill,*" and there ahead of us, collecting and spreading the surging streams was a huge basin of water, thundering on and down the side of a derelict mill. There was no sign of life – yet I had a reassuring feeling that we were not alone. Rarely visited, the whole place breathed secrecy, and instinctively lowering our voices, we made our way up past the mill, up the shallow rise – and there was the stone sheep dip. Fine, we are on the right track, I thought, as I moved towards the broad shallow pond beyond, and then I was riveted to the spot. The water was crystal clear – and the bottom of it was white!

'Oh, that is Fuller's Earth,' Beryl enlightened me.

Great Thundering Universe! I looked at the sky, my mind ragged. Why? How could I have visualized a mill and a mill pool with a light base, from over three-thousand miles away? Why such minute detail? Surely a mineral deposit deep in the country wasn't that important to Hannah's story, was it?

Not in isolation perhaps, I seemed to answer myself...

The mineral deposit that formed the base of this pool was indeed

Fuller's Earth. Favoured by drovers for cleaning the wool of their sheep, it also killed ticks and generally smartened and fluffed up the wool before the animals walked the last few miles for sale at the local market or were boarded on to the river boats at Lechlade (then the last navigable part of the Thames) and taken to London.

Another intriguing, rather fanciful, and quite plausible use for the paste that had also formed part of my original novel (when I had thought that what I was writing was pure fiction) was that there was a royal connection. To support this, I had, during my search through various records, found the following beautifully written record.

Quote from Gloucestershire archives:

John Cotton had the honour on 9th September, 1592, of entertaining Queen Elizabeth, in her Progress through Gloucestershire. She was on her way from holding Court at Rendcomb (near Cirencester) to staying with the Duke of Chandos at Sudeley Castle (near Winchcombe) and dyned at Mr. Cotons at Whytington".

So, Elizabeth 1st, *had* travelled these roads on her way to stay with friends at Sudeley Castle – only a few miles further on.

Elizabeth was known as The Virgin Queen, a story that was reinforced when, in her later years, she used a paste made up of Fuller's Earth kept soft by added lanolin (from sheep wool) to smooth and whiten her skin.

This gave the clever ageing Queen an appearance that resembled the white plaster images of The Virgin Mary.

As she waved a hand from her shadowy carriage as her entourage passed through villages and towns, (probably never smiling for fear of creasing the mask) the loyalty of the uneducated, wildly excited and superstitious peasants would have taken on religious fervour. It is not beyond the bounds of probability therefore, that her supply could have been replenished from this clean, unpolluted local source lying only a mile away from Witetune House.

Now, I reasoned, just because I could not prove the royal connection to the pond's properties, the thought, and pictures had still come to my mind, as had the others that are provable. Also, and this is another rather romantic and again quite feasible possibility, the area is not far from Stratford-on-Avon, and bands of travelling actors, knowing of the deposit, could have taken a supply back to Stratford to be used in Shakespeare's theatre productions. He himself could have used it! Why Not?

Another coincidence? Perhaps, though, not being able to prove a truth, doesn't make the truth, untrue.

Cellars in Sennington Manor

My hostess, Catherine, was expecting me, (so were her little dogs it seemed) and we got to work at once.

Opening the door under the staircase, a damp chill seeped up, the dim uncovered light bulb hanging from the ceiling doing little to reassure us as we negotiated the downward spiral of narrow worn steps, shoulders pressed against the spine of brick, curving its way to the rooms below.

'Take care,' Catherine waved the torch. 'These stairs are so narrow you have to step carefully or risk breaking a leg. Just think, with only a taper or candle, searching eyes wouldn't have been on the walls much, would they? And look at this,' she stopped on a slightly broader fan of three brick steps modulating the steep angle and flashed a torch into a large cavity in the wall on the left. 'It would have been cramped, though this space could have hidden about half a dozen men, standing up, don't you think?'

'Cramped – but if your life depended on it...' I said ruefully.

'We think it could have been a priest hole or an escape route into the church. It's in the right direction and not far to tunnel, although as you can see the back is all bricked up now.'

Then I thought of Hannah's words: "*Listening to sounds from the cellars below and young men, loud in drink, being taken away with the clink of chains, across the lawns at night.*"

These cellars, these very walls, the young men drinking to quell their fear which still pervaded these bricks. No wonder there's an oppressive atmosphere down here, I shuddered.

I understood that this was another vital link, one that I had been guided to see, but enough was enough and it was a great relief when we closed the door behind us and felt the reassuring warmth of the house.

I wanted to drive into the hills, find a place for lunch, do anything to clear my head and get away from demands and responsibility that I hadn't volunteered for, but as I got into the car, Catherine hurried over.

'Oh, one more thing. I didn't mention it because we all thought it was my husband, just teasing; but he insists that he has seen a woman in a long grey long dress on the top landing, a number of times – and did I tell you that my dogs won't set foot up there? They follow me all over the house and if I go upstairs the back way they will happily walk along the corridor and past bedrooms that lead out to that landing. At the end though, they come to a full stop and nothing will persuade them out.'

Gripping the steering wheel, I rested my head briefly on my hands, Hannah's words drilling through my brain: "*I will not rest until the truth is told.*"

'And I cannot rest until you are free,' I muttered to myself.

A Gravestone Without a Name

I was due to leave, time was short, yet I could not free myself of the nagging desire to visit Sennington church again. There was unfinished business that I wanted resolved before I left.

Appreciating the pressure on my time, Beryl met me at the churchyard, divining rods in hand. 'We might need them,' she smiled.

The churchyard, siding on to the manor house where Hannah had been housekeeper, was deserted; the headstones, faces to the sun like meditating sentinels, the only things witness to our intrusion.

No one was going to disturb our business.

'She would have walked around many of these old headstones,' Beryl said softly 'perhaps to put flowers on the graves of friends or members of the household. Staying healthy was a precarious business in those days and life expectancy was short. She would have attended some of the big funerals too, and as housekeeper, probably organized the funeral tea, or whatever the equivalent was of sherry and ham sandwiches, in those days!'

I was wandering around, ostensibly studying the architecture of the side and back of the manor, and quietly bracing myself for possible disappointment. On my list visit, the swing of the pendulum that Beryl had given me had indicated that Rachel's remains were in here. It had been a positive response yet I had found nothing. What if there was nothing visible to find? Perhaps there was no gravestone even though I had been told there was. Perhaps if there had been one, it had fallen down or been removed. Three centuries was a long time.

The doubts nagged.

'Beryl, could you use your rods to find out if Rachel Myer is buried in this place? The last time I came here, the pendulum you gave me indicated that she was, and I did look for her grave but for some reason, I just couldn't locate the spot.'

We were now standing in the far corner, on line with the back corner of the manor and about twenty yards away was the side of the church. Without further ado, Beryl raised the rods, mentally asked the question and turning smartly round, strode confidently back the way we had come and without hesitation stopped in front of a line of three graves with small headstones.

'It's this one,' she pointed to one on the end that was shorter than the others, and my heart leapt! Beryl was standing exactly where I had stood when I had asked the same question! The memory of my last visit here came flashing back and with a quiet groan, I whispered, 'I'm so sorry, Rachel,' for I had indeed been given the right answer. How could I have doubted it? I had been shown this grave but instead of looking down by my feet, I had trotted off, peering and scratching at other likely stones until, tired and dispirited, I had given up.

But my work here wasn't finished and I had been patiently steered back to find the last link in the chain; proof that in a tiny churchyard in a remote hamlet, an insignificant grave and a small headstone, *without a name*, did indeed mark the final resting place of a local woman murdered for a crime she did not commit. And I had been told of it and guided back to find it. I had been chosen to finish *unfinished business*.

Photograph showing the back of Sennington Manor, the corner of the Church, Family Vaults and a line of small headstones. The furthest one is Rachel Myer's final resting place.

Being buried without absolution from the Church; the absence of this last public ritual was the crux, the driving force that had crossed three centuries for justice. I was intrigued to see a carved garland of leaves decorating the headstone and a small motif, still in clear relief. The face, sheltered as it was by its close proximity to the wall, was hardly weathered by the years, so the name could not have been so selectively worn away without trace. The two other headstones alongside it were not much later and their names and the dates were still clearly defined.

It is hard to describe my feelings as I gazed at this nondescript little plot. No one else knew the history, the trauma, and the dramas of the life of the person who lay here or of my involvement in bringing closure. No one knew that an *unquiet spirit* still waited patiently for justice and suddenly, I had a lump in my throat.

'What a privilege. Thank you,' I whispered.

Rachel's plot was so small because only her remains were lying here. She had been in the ground for all those years without the protection of a coffin. When they moved her bones, probably under cover of darkness for fear of detection, a bag thrown on a cart would have been easier to disguise.

I became aware that the world around had stilled; no birds sang, no breeze moved the long grasses growing in corners where the mower couldn't reach, the clouds had stopped their drift, the air was warm and still – and kindly. It was as though a collective Presence had moved its stilling hand, to make sure that nothing would interrupt my concentration.

Beryl, bless her, had moved away, leaving me free to whisper my promise:

'I am going to write your Truth, as Fact, Rachel, and I hope it will be enough to clear your family name from any shame you think still attached to it. Although' I added hesitantly, 'I'm still not quite sure if this is what you wanted – or if it is what Hannah thought you wanted. There is no one alive who remembers the cruel injustice you or Hannah suffered. It can't be described as a tragic miscarriage of justice; no *justice* was involved. Fear and suspicion needed an outlet and it was satiated with your murder. Rachel, try to understand that the villagers were not suspicious of *you*. It was your work with herbs, your deep knowledge, and spiritual attuning to nature that unnerved them. Their hate would probably not have lasted the night but once the deed was done, they would have been held silent by shame – and fear of the quarterly judicial session,' I added as an afterthought. 'Be at peace my dear friend and be assured that I will do my best for you. I will do as much as is humanly possible to clear your name.'

Canon H

Trying to find more documentary fact, I made an appointment to see Canon H. at the Vicarage in Sennington. Long since retired but still attending to the spiritual needs of four very small villages, this kindly gentleman listened carefully as I told him the story of *Unshriven*. Finally he shook his head and said that he, a very keen local historian, knew of no such happenings in the hamlet. It was possible of course that some reference to my story could be found, if I had the time to search; he waved a veined hand towards a high steel filing cabinet, the contents bulging from quantity and disarray. Time was my biggest stumbling block and refusing, I thanked him and left. This meant the end of this line of my enquiry, I thought.

Wrong again!

It was a few years later, visiting Beryl in her new home when she told me that shortly before leaving the hamlet, she had called on her old friend, Canon H. In all probability they would never see each other again and perhaps this is what prompted him to tell her, in strict confidence, of a recent discovery. Beryl did not break this confidence until after his death:

"I shouldn't tell anyone about this, Beryl, but I think you should know that I have found written evidence in church records, telling of this murder." He then referred to my visit.

"The Incumbent at the time, having laid out the facts before the head of the Diocese for the area, received special permission to have the body reburied in the churchyard. However, there were conditions.

The first was that the whole procedure was carried out in secret and that there was to be no official ceremony.

Secondly, she had to be placed near the wall, and thirdly, there could be no name on the headstone. Any hint that the church was harbouring the remains of someone once associated with witchcraft, however wickedly untrue, could not be risked."

Canon H., went on to say that he had placed the records of the incident, *"...in the bank, for safe keeping because so many are being stolen.*" (Parish records and registers make fascinating reading, and it is a fact that they are still being stolen to order. The bindings are discarded, the records split up and then the individual pages are framed and sold abroad, to be hung on walls as topics of conversation; their provenance lost forever.)

Unfortunately and sadly, the Canon died soon after Beryl left the area, and we have not, as yet, been able to locate the evidence.

An American in London

Having completed the 'not undemanding task' of writing my story, *Unshriven,* as fact, I had assumed that it not only marked the end of my obligation to Hannah but also to any further emotional involvement with the story. Now, all that I had to do was locate the person who would get it into print and then I could get on with my own life. I didn't worry much on that score either, because I also assumed that the *Powers That Be,* having guided me very firmly to find the relevant information, would also have contacted a willing publisher.

It was over.

Wrong again. It wasn't over! I had overlooked the kernel, the heart's-yearning, that had bound Hannah Myer to this earth for over three hundred years and it was going to take a 'chance' meeting (another co-incidence!) with a complete stranger – an American woman who just happened to be a clairvoyant – to push me right back on track.

Autumn, 2010, strolling past the Oxfam book shop in Marylebone High Street, London, I saw a notice which read:

Book Club This Evening 7.30.
Title of Book Under Review:
"ATONEMENT."
Author, Ian McEwan.

I hadn't read the book and it had been quite a while since I had seen the film, yet for some unexplainable reason, I went in. There were only nine of us and only one man; young, slim and outnumbered. I found myself sitting next to Barbara; a mature, very confident American woman with, as she quickly revealed as we discussed the attitudes of the book, unmovable views on 'right and wrong'.

The messages in the film; forgiveness, making amends, coming to terms; our attitudes varied considerably. For Barbara though, there were no grey areas. I didn't exactly agree yet I admired her; what you saw was what you got, and I felt comfortable with that.

Opinions on the merits of the book were interesting and varied and were to lead to some quite personal revelations, pertinent mostly, to the subject matter of Atonement. We then moved on to déjà vu, and most of the group contributed to this topic with stories of strange happenings; a conversation, a place, a situation that felt almost like the rerun of a film.

Then Barbara took the floor, captivating us with instances of her clairvoyance concerning the welfare of her children and her friends. She was what I would call a 'Wise Woman,' talented and with a great deal of experience of life; one who accepted and balanced her spiritual gift with common sense. She therefore interested me and I instinctively trusted her judgement.

Then I spoke, telling them in broad outline, of *Unshriven*, and how I had somehow channelled this 17th century story, and how 'fiction' finally became traceable and provable 'fact'.

The Book Club was coming to a close and Barbara suggested that we continue our talk outside.

As Barbara and I were heading in the same direction, we said goodbye to the others and chatted as we strolled. She wanted to know more about my story, paying close attention as I explained the reason for the title *Unshriven* and of finding the grave and of Hannah's vow, not to rest until the shame was lifted from the family name.

It was at this point that she suddenly swung to face me, eyes intense: 'That's why you were meant to meet me tonight! Your involvement is not finished. You must get a priest to that grave and in broad daylight. No secrecy. It's been secret too long. That's what this woman wants, public recognition of a wrong, and that's what she is still waiting for.'

When those words rang in my ears, I was rooted to the spot, a sensation sweeping through me that I never thought to experience again. I was back in Beryl's cottage remembering how my involvement with Hannah and Rachel Myer had begun.

Barbara was so obviously right!

'You must get this done, even if you have to drag the priest there. I would!' Barbara called back.

'Of course I have to do this!' I think I might have been speaking aloud but it didn't matter as the cars and taxis sped by. 'Rachel was buried in the churchyard in secret. Permission was obtained from the Church, yes, but still it had been in secret. So, through non-intervention by the authorities, the villagers were allowed to believe that they had murdered a witch.

How foolish of me, how I could have overlooked Hannah's most passionate and adamant demand: public recognition by the Church. She believed that her sister couldn't get into 'Heaven' without it. Getting the Church officially involved was crucial. Prayers needed to be said for Rachel, yes, but only for Rachel? I had long since formed the opinion that the people who killed her weren't wicked or evil; the murder wasn't premeditated. They acted as they did to stop the spread of a rampant disease that was wiping out whole communities.

They were victims too, manipulated by fear and ignorance, though to Hannah, Rachel being buried Unshriven, was a final and calculated insult demanded by the all-powerful, fury-driven, murderous mob. Time had moved on, the story was soon forgotten or had drifted into country legend, the tale to be told and elaborated upon on dark winter nights, sitting round a fire, but the fact was that Hannah's spirit was not at rest. She had died in the 17th century. This was 1963, the 20th century, and her ghost was still being seen on the stairs of the manor, where she had waited a lifetime for her union with Lawrence Roberts.

Now all she wanted was to be free, her problem resolved by the Church, so that she could join him having fulfilled what she felt was her obligation to her sister. I, it seemed, was still the holder of the key to her spiritual freedom and, judging by my 'chance meeting' with Barbara, Hannah had no intention of letting me forget it until I had finished what I had started.

The Last Challenge

How in Heaven's name was I going to make this happen? The prospect of starting all over again and finding an ordained minister of the Church, who would spare the time to listen to my story, and be broad-minded enough not to dismiss it out of hand, just didn't figure on the list of 'things I most wanted to do.' I had no idea how I would make such a contact.

I hadn't however, allowed for yet another 'coincidence'!

Having to make a start somewhere, I wrote to my friends (the owners of the two manor houses involved in my story) and told them about the meeting in London with the American.

Catherine and Gilly were as helpful as ever and soon had the name of a young clergyman whose duties, since the death of Canon H, now included the care of the little church and graveyard at Sennington. (This man had recently arrived back from Africa, having spent some time there, casting out evil spirits. They don't come any more broad-minded than this! Of course, Jesus did the same thing, casting them into pigs that then ran over the cliff edge.

For a people without education, the death of the pigs would have been symbolic and proof positive that the evil had been destroyed. However, I think that Jesus would have mentally directed these poor tortured spirits in the direction of Enlightenment, for they, some-where along the line, had become victims too.)

It took some diary manoeuvring and several calls to the Rev. John B. to agree on a date that suited us both, then following weeks of heavy snow, a day in early March, 2011 found me retracing my first journey, into the Cotswold Hills, with mixed emotions.

Anticipation and apprehension were high on the list yet uncertainty as to the outcome of this very important and conclusive deed, ranked top. Although the Rev. John B. and I had spoken several times on the telephone, had I made my case clearly enough? Would he be attuned to these very special circumstances, or would he just be 'doing his duty'? Humouring this woman with her fanciful story?

Planning to see Catherine and then spend the night at Witetune House, I drove through the now familiar medieval village, busy with local shoppers on this bright early spring morning, then down the hill, left over the little stone bridge, and started the steep twisting climb into the hills. The countryside, just surfacing from a hard winter was already promising a spectacularly beautiful awakening with fresh green shoots in the hedges and spring lambs frisking in a pale sun. It had been late March when I first visited the area and this time I was sad not to the see bright clumps of the weed, coltsfoot, that had dotted the path on my first visit; it was just too early in the month.

* * * * * * *

'I saw her yesterday,' Catherine said, handing me a cup of coffee. 'Hannah,' she clarified, in answer to my puzzled frown. 'For the very first time I saw her here, downstairs. I was kneeling on the floor in the dining room by the door to the passage that leads down to the kitchen. Everything was quiet and still and I was concentrating solely on the job in hand; sorting through books and household papers when, for no reason, I looked up – and there she was, her long dress sweeping behind as she went into the kitchen.'

'Perhaps she is excited or anxious about the ceremony, tomorrow.' I offered, 'It may be that it's made her restless and that's why she is moving around here,' then I reminded Catherine about the builders complaining that while climbing ladders to work on the oldest part of the roof, their shoe laces were being untied and their tools moved just out of reach!'

'Well I'm at ease with Hannah,' Catherine said. 'I really do hope that she doesn't leave us after the service tomorrow. I like having her around. She's a very friendly guest.'

I stayed that night at Witetune House and after dinner with the family, retired to bed. I loved this ground floor room; square and very light, windows on two sides, the big bay with a raised dais in front, big enough for two comfortable chairs and a small writing table. It had a very peaceful ambience and I imagined Hannah sitting by that very same window, reading a book or studying with the daughters of the house. I couldn't resist sitting down and trying to relate to her.

Then, as I recalled the first time I had stayed in here, a night when the energies were so strong in this room, so vibrant, just before I got into bed I spoke out loud:

'Listen, I've a busy day tomorrow so I want a good night's sleep and I don't want any interruptions. No communications. Thank you.' The room was quiet tonight though. I turned off the light and drew back the curtains. Moonlight flooded across the big lawn to the fringe of trees where the shadows hung heavy and dark. It was ethereal; a place where a young girl would dream of slipping out at night to meet with her lover and this was where her love for Lawrence began. Perhaps seeing him arrive, looking so handsome, riding a fine horse, but being a little shy and not wanting to appear obvious; she would have pulled back from the landing window, waiting a while before casually going down to greet him, her heart pounding, hoping she was looking her best. Ah, yes, this could well have been where Hannah's habit of waiting on the landing, listening to conversations drifting up from the rooms below, had begun. On the back stairs here, the route the servants had used so as not to disturb the household. And that was also where my hand and foot had been, oh so gently, positioned into a waiting stance. So, Hannah had been with me, even then! I marvelled.

As any young woman in love, she was anxious to please and willing to wait. Lawrence did love her; his mistake was in assuming their unspoken bond was understood and enough for Hannah. And finally, with the passing of time the needs of passion died.

Somewhere along the way, Hannah had become resigned, taking his unspoken love for granted and she was right to do so, because whatever his failings, Lawrence had been constant in every way. If only he had confirmed it and explained that though it must remain unrequited, he would love and protect her as long as he lived, Hannah would have cherished those sustaining words into her grave. Held tightly in his arms when the truth of her sister's demise was revealed, and given the circumstances of the time, she would have coped and wouldn't have died in shock – and I wouldn't be following a ghost!

The Final Move

I must have drifted into a deep peaceful sleep and woke the next day to a sunny, though very cold, morning. Gilly and I had arranged to have coffee with Catherine at Sennington Manor before meeting the vicar, but needing time alone I went into the churchyard through the little gate in the wall, to find the solitude I needed.

Only then, as I stood alone by the graveside, did I fully anticipate the extent of the change that the next hour could bring. I was about to close a huge chapter on my life, a last link with the Middle East, the end of my involvement with Hannah and Rachel Myer and the end of writing *Unshriven.*

The sun was bright though the wind was like ice and my fingers and toes felt frozen within minutes. Putting the discomfort aside, I concentrated on Hannah and Rachel Myer, acknowledging the enormity of the injustice and what must have been a terrifying ordeal.

Then I voiced my own concern: Were they still nursing anger and hate for the people involved? I didn't think so, yet if they were, what could be a satisfactory outcome?

Hate saps joy and freedom from life. Like fear, it is a greedy parasite that distorts reason and can never be satiated.

Again I felt that other ears were listening and so I addressed my next words quietly to all. 'This has to be the time of reconciliation. The past is the past and cannot be changed. Wicked deeds are often spawned by fear and ignorance. There is always a reason, but whatever it is, we can't put the clock back. Letting go of the past, even if we can't forgive the act, is the only true way to be free.'

I became quiet for a few minutes to give my reasoning time to filter through the air, and then I continued: There would be a religious service though not for the sister alone. It was to include all of the souls who, for whatever reason, were not at rest. This would include any who had taken part in the crime and who might, in retrospect, have doubted the justification for their part in the killing.

'The year is 2011. In the name of Christ, it is surely time to move on.' I finished.

As I stood there, eyes closed, shivering with cold, Gilly and Catherine, accompanied by her two small smooth-haired dachshunds, arrived, followed quickly by the Rev. John B., a bespectacled, tall, slim, rose-cheeked young man with a nice smile, but as he opened the gate I felt a pang of disappointment. He was dressed in jeans and a jumper. Was he going to take this service seriously or was this morning going to end in dissatisfactions – and if so, what then? The question and ramifications sent a shock wave of alarm through my entire system.

I need not have worried for after disappearing into the church for a couple of minutes he emerged in dog collar, cassock and holding a prayer book.

'I thought the full garb was befitting of the occasion,' he smiled, reading the relief on my face. He then produced a printed four page service sheet and, as the congregation, we followed it and made the responses.

The Rev. John B. could not have been more accommodating given the rather unusual nature of the occasion and he didn't seem fazed when, half way though I suddenly felt compelled to speak.

Voice quavering, I once again reminded those listening that this service was for the benefit of everyone involved but most especially for Rachel Myer. Also that this was not a secret gathering; it was being conducted in broad daylight by an ordained minister of the Church, before local witnesses. Throughout the readings I shook with cold and emotion, my words faltering as we gave the responses but I was comforted and reassured by the way Rev. John B. paused,

The Reverend John B. at the gravestone of Rachel Myer
at the back of Sennington Manor

allowing us to reflect on the meaning of his words as they echoed across the small graveyard...

Then the Rev. John B. shook our hands then went to speak to a couple who had just arrived on Church business. Catherine, Gilly and I used the gate in the manor wall and in minutes we were in the warmth of Sennington Manor enjoying a hot drink and talking over our individual feelings and observations.

It had been a long involvement for my two friends who had from the very start taken my story at face value, trusting me by opening their homes for my inspection and never losing interest in my detective work. Above all, they had been kind and encouraging and staunch.

One small disappointment remained however, was that I had not seen the coltsfoot. Had that dear little flower been in bloom, it would have completed the occasion for me. 'They don't grow in my part of the country so I'll have to wait until next spring and make sure I come up later in March,' I said, finishing my coffee.

And so this amazing life-changing experience that had dominated my life for so many years was over. I said goodbye to my dear friends and started for home, my mind trying to come to terms with my new freedom. I should have been truly elated; I had my life back but it took most of the journey to examine my true deeper feelings.

I didn't have the relief or the satisfaction of 'a job well done'.

I didn't know if Hannah was free and happy or even if I had accomplished all she wanted and there was no way of finding out. In short, it was an anti-climax!

Three hours later, safely home, I wandered out into my little courtyard garden; fresh green leaves on every bush, clematis already blooming, birds gathering nesting material – and there in an empty flower pot that was waiting to be replanted with geraniums – was a little bright clump of flowering coltsfoot!

Then it came, like the opening of a great dam; a feeling of immense happiness, a euphoria that sent my spirits soaring. This was, to me, Hannah's way of saying goodbye and of letting me know that all was well. Oh how truly wonderful! And I sent my message back, imagining the words being written large and joyously against the bright blue sky:

'Oh, thank you dear Hannah. Goodbye my dear – and thank you!'

PART THREE

A Life Enriched With Silva

Life is strange! Most of us seem to go along the same track with no real expectation of great change and then one action, one decision, the meeting with that one person that seems like chance or sheer coincidence, can change the course of our lives like the turn of a coin – but as Jose Silva often said:

> *"Call them coincidences and you will be amazed how many coincidences there are"*

Living in Saudi Arabia, over three thousand miles away from my home in England, this is the true story of my 'turning point', and a most remarkable chain of 'coincidences', that introduced me to *The Silva Method* and the subsequent writing of *Unshriven*.

Perfect Time – Perfect Place

I had left the pace and excitement of working in and around New York City to be married in New Orleans. Then with my husband (a physician working in Saudi Arabia) we flew from the Deep South, caught a flight to London, said hello and goodbye to friends and family, collected my entry visa then raced to Heathrow to board a flight to the Middle East. Once aboard we relaxed, cosseted in comfortable seating with soft Arabic music, fat dates and sweet mint tea served from tiny cups. These small pleasures were to become part of daily life over the next ten years. Lie back, enjoy, the pressure is over.

We arrived some six hours later to the call for evening prayer echoing from minaret to minaret, a backdrop of purple pink sky and a sun sinking rapidly into an indigo sea, spilling its gold across the horizon like the pricked yolk of a magnificent egg. This was the view from a picture window of my new home.

There was no evening time, no gentle fading of the light. The day just collapsed into night – an Arabian night, and silhouetted in the last of the stretching rays, a man riding a camel out into the silence of the desert. It was a scene that was to become familiar and one that never lost its magic.

Stepping out of the plane the humidity of the city engulfed me like a soft mist – and I loved it! Time had come to a halt. Time had gone backwards. Here they used the Hajira calendar. The year was 1402. Welcome to the Kingdom of Saudi Arabia.

When the student is ready the teacher appears

I had established a routine, programming myself to wake in the early hours of the morning, (every morning) to direct healing energies and prayers to two dear friends living in England. They had been ill for some time, their prognosis was not good, and my prayers were as much for helping them to cope well with each new day, as for a miraculous healing.

From past experiences I was utterly convinced of the power of mental telepathy. I had been told by my friend and yoga teacher that 2 a.pm. was a good time to communicate (that part of sleep when a person is most relaxed) and as the Middle East was two hours ahead, I would set my alarm clock to go off just before 4 a.m. Then, struggling to surface, I would stumble out of bed and spend the next ten minutes pacing round the sitting room, making myself wake up so that I could concentrate on my friends' needs without yawning or wanting to lie down again. The difficulty was that once the mental work was done, I couldn't get back to sleep. One morning as dawn broke, reaching the point of mental and physical exhaustion I said: "I really cannot do this any longer. I need some help!"

I spoke these words with the utter conviction and absolute certainty that I was entitled to help and that I could expect delivery. It was in a good and just cause and I had done all that I could do, unaided, believing as I did that 'God helps those who help themselves'.

Please do notice the emphasis: I *expected* to receive help. I did not hold *any* thought of doubt or refusal. I gave no *energy* to fear and I wasn't *suppressing* anxiety for I had none. Even so, I could not have anticipated the speed of delivery!

Coincidences?

An English woman, Jennifer E., who had married an Egyptian doctor and emigrated from England to Australia, had arrived in Saudi Arabia with her husband who was to work at our hospital.

Three days after she entered the Kingdom and just hours after I had asked for help, Jennifer knocked on my door.

I can't remember or even now imagine why Jennifer came to see me, yet I found myself explaining to this complete stranger why I was in such a weary state and not very good company.

Jennifer, a really bright, bubbly person, always smiling (she never changed in all the time I knew her) said without hesitation, 'You should take the 'Silva Mind Control' training course.' (The name was later changed as it could have been misinterpreted.) 'Self control over your sleeping pattern is just one of the many techniques you will be taught,' she continued as I made coffee. 'How to put yourself to sleep, how to wake up on time without a clock and, very importantly for you, through developing your creative visualization you will also be taught how to use your mental energy to direct absent healing, to anyone, anywhere in the world. It's only what you are doing now!' she laughed, reading the doubt on my face, 'And you can do it without exhausting yourself.' Quote Jose Silva:

"Do as your doctor instructs and help him and help your body to heal quicker by using the power of your mind."

Only with the benefit of hindsight did I see that the timing of Jennifer's visit had started a chain of almost unbelievable 'coincidences'.

The meeting with Jennifer was the first of the many coincidences that were to change the direction of my life and unlock aptitudes I would never have credited myself with. Now, amazingly others began to fall into place like falling dominos.

The second coincidence was that the name 'Silva' rang a bell. I seemed to recall a friend in England saying that she had taken 'Silva' training and had spoken highly of it.

The third, as luck (?) would have it, I was already booked to fly home that week. (It was as though Universal Intelligence was one step ahead of me, knowing what I would need and organizing the moves and providing the back-up, in advance!)

The fourth: The day I arrived in England I telephoned my friend. 'Yes, I have done the Silva training and I can't recommend it highly enough. It changed my life. It just so happens that there is a seminar in London this next weekend with the introductory meeting on Friday. I'm free. Would you like to go?'

(Would I like to go? You wanna to play me at dominos?)

My Introduction to the Silva Method

That Friday, two friends and I sat in the conference room of a smart London hotel, every seat taken (most surprisingly) by almost equal numbers of men and women, listening intently to the introductory talk given by Paul Fransella. Paul, passionate about his subject, animated as he talked, with eyes so captivating that they held your full attention as he explained the totally logical thinking behind the method.

'You are starting on a wonderful journey of self-development. The training you are about to receive will teach you how to strengthen and direct the power of your mind and imagination, staying focused only on the outcomes you desire, as you gently though firmly move your attention away from fear and lack of success. You will develop a strong mind and a mental discipline that, even in an emergency, will function rationally and help you make the right decisions. You will develop the power of your imagination; your mind will obey your direction, and deliver logical solutions as you access problem solving areas of the brain. Your imagination will no longer be able to manipulate you into emotional panic. You will be in charge of your own mind. The power of your mind is enormous. I am here to teach you how to harness and direct that power. You will learn how to unlock the energy of creative visualization, and how to use your mind in a 'special way', a way that can direct and receive information. You have the innate ability to direct and improve your lives by simply taking charge of your way of thinking.'

Silva Method hand book:

"Tapping the Secrets of Your Mind for Total Self-Mastery"

What Paul was saying was to most of us revolutionary and very exciting. We all wanted to know more and at the end of the talk I joined the queue and signed up without any hesitation. What I had heard made total and logical sense. Everything begins with a thought, so my being able to control the direction of my thinking must be beneficial. (No more lying in bed telling myself I couldn't get back to sleep?) These three points alone had convinced me that this was an honourable organization with integrity its maxim:

A: I was to be taught how to work for MY self-empowerment and for the "Betterment of Mankind" (and not for some brain washing '*ology*' demanding my unquestioning subservience).

B: We were told: "You can reject anything we say, at any level of the mind. You are always in charge." (So no one was going to try and manipulate my subconscious mind.)

C: The Silva Method does not teach you what to think – but how to focus and hold your attention on what you want to think about.

It is this balance of practical teachings, philosophy and integrity that makes The Silva Method unique.

And so I signed up and paid for training that was to enrich every aspect of my life and that was to free my mind of so many ingrained and unquestioned limitations. However, if I had thought that I could sit back, listen to instruction and get a quick fix-it-all, I was in for a sharp awakening.

Second Day

Jose Silva spent 22 years developing techniques that would allow us to use the power of imagination and access unused parts of the brain and in desiring that, we were in good company.

Richard Bach, author of *Jonathan Livingstone Seagull*, and *Illusions, the adventures of a reluctant Messiah*, wrote:

"Whatever you can visualise, you can actualise."

Albert Einstein said:

"Knowledge is wonderful but imagination is everything."

On that first day we were reassured by the science, philosophy, and practical application of the programme. (With your new powers will come a responsibility to use them *"For the betterment of mankind"*.) By the end of that first morning we were beginning to achieve; directing the focus of attention and gaining rapid access into deeper, more concentrated, levels of the mind that would eventually allow us to control pain, quicken healing etc., and sharpen intuition so that the 6th sense would actually become creative. (Amazing!)

Then on to problem-solving and overcoming unwanted habits. Master these, we were assured, and we would achieve inner peace, a quiet optimism, and greater confidence as we took control of our lives and our destinies, in a way we had never imagined possible.

This would prove to be absolutely true, and we were repeatedly and reassuringly told:

"You are in control of your mind and your imagination.
They are your powerful mental tools. You can disregard anything
we say at any level of the mind. You are always in control."

Then we went on to improving general health, the keys to success, self-fulfillment, and personal development: Relax, go deeper, take charge of your thinking, concentrate, meditate, focus your mind, visualize. It didn't stop but by the end of that first day I was really getting the hang of it. No day-dreaming in these classes, they were too exciting.

I went to bed that night quite worn out – and I was awake again at the usual time, just as I had been in Saudi! The difference now was in my attitude. I was motivated to succeed and I understood the process. I really felt that I was in charge and I absolutely expected to stop this cycle of sleep deprivation. Sitting up I said to myself, 'I totally believe that I have power over my mind. I believe in this Silva training because it's so logical. I've travelled thousands of miles to get here and I've paid for this instruction (Payment is a great motivator. People don't value what is free!) so it really has got to work!'

Then, concentrating on my Sleep Control lesson I must have been asleep in seconds! I woke the next morning at 7.30 on the dot as I had told myself to do (another lesson well learned) feeling totally refreshed, invigorated, energized, and confident in my ability to embrace all that Silva had to offer.

Here was I, taking control of my mind and my body, already getting results, and all that was required – was my attention! I was delighted and inspired with my accomplishment, the potential was unlimited and this was only after the first day of the Basic Course!

Day Three

We started the day without preamble and, after a brief recap, began with headache, weight and smoking control, mental house cleaning and becoming aware of, and freeing our mind from, old inhibiting blockages. These were interspersed with deep meditations and visualization designed to strengthened the focus of the mind. (This was to be my most memorable day so far; the day that by deep relaxation, concentration and focus, I would access the "Theta" level; the area of pain control.) This is a strong mental tool in an emergency. After lunch came rapid learning, sharper memory, happier relation-ships, the attaining of new goals then more meditation and an amaz-ing session on dream control. (Using this specific technique I was later able to stop a life-long, intermittent nightmare. Just when it reached the point that I most dreaded, as though watching myself from outside the drama, I told myself to 'Use your Silva Method,' and in an instant I was in control of the nightmare and stopped it in its tracks and I can honestly say that it has never recurred!)

The demanding day ended with a lesson on how to prepare for and take exams, how to sharpen the memory (going back in time and recalling exact details from books) remember lists of things up to 100, and so very much more. We were discovering just some of the many mental powers that are ours by birthright such as our ability to send and receive information telepathically and receive help and guidance on any subject. Call it Divine Intelligence, Intuition, or the Universal Mind, or whatever you are comfortable with, but if you have not yet received the benefit of Silva instruction, just direct your attention to the highest and purest possible source.

Believing that I have the right, I use this 'service' regularly! (Prof. Rupert Sheldrake of Cambridge University has produced over 80 scientific papers on the subject of intuition in humans and animals.)

So another wonderful day came to an end but our most amazing achievement was yet to come.

The Last Exercise of the Final Day

On this last day the air buzzed with excitement and confidence was high. The work we had done on self-improvement was already showing results and we all had positive experiences to relate. There was no point in pretending success. The energy in that room was palpable. We were elated and totally convinced that the program was working. Using the techniques we had learned and practised (practice being the key to success) we were now able to put ourselves to a depth of relaxation where things like dentistry could be performed without pain killers. For me, the energy of intense concentration manifested itself in the form of increasing pressure, like the push of a thumb in the middle of my eyebrows, the feeling becoming stronger the deeper my concentration.

We were coming to the end of the day and I found myself working easily on two levels; my mind sharp and focused, my body relaxed to a point where, as long as I didn't move, I felt detached from it. I had no sensation from my hands or feet and had no idea in what position I had left them. I knew however, that should any emergency present, we had been taught to be wide awake and ready to act in an instant. Even at this deep relaxed level we were in charge at all times; the subconscious mind, like a protective overseer, was always alert. It is a truly wonderful experience to be so deeply relaxed.

The last exercise on the last day was a culmination of all the work we had done. It was designed to strengthen belief in our ability to use the power of the mind, at a distance, and to diagnose physical problems, and then to mentally project healing to the person in mind. This was close to my heart as 'absent healing' had brought Jennifer and the Silva Method, into my life.

All that we, a room full of eager students were told was the age, the sex, and the location of the person that our instructor Paul, had in mind: A 12 year old boy, living in California. We were then told to relax, go down to deep inner conscious level, concentrate on the given facts and wait. There was total silence.

Almost instantly a mental picture began to emerge, fuzzy at first but gradually clearing and then I saw him: a boy, dark wavy hair, walking towards me on a beach. The only puzzling thing was that his right leg was shimmering from the hip line, to the ground. After a few minutes we were quietly and slowly counted back from five to one. When we were wide awake and asked what we had visualized, it was quite startling when other people in that room began to repeat my exact sightings. Others had slight variations on the same picture.

Then Paul told us that the boy in question had had a high leg amputation when he was only two years old!

I looked around the room at the expressions of amazement and incredulity. How mind-blowing was that! If this was the power of the 'directed' mind – it surely knows no man-made boundaries.

I said goodbye to my friends and left London, giving silent thanks to this man, Jose Silva, and his training programmer that had put me in charge of my butterfly mind and free-wheeling imagination, expanding my horizons to a point of liberating excitement. Like being in possession of a wonderful secret, I just couldn't get the smile off my face! With a lot of theory and some actual experience under my belt I felt confident – but little did I know that my confidence and new found beliefs would be challenged that very night.

My First Challenge

Almost home but just before I got off the train, out of the blue: I felt that I had been hit in the eye with a ball – a very hard ball! The pressure and pain were frightening. It was late on Sunday night; I was alone, and not registered with a doctor in the UK. In desperation, as soon as I got indoors, I telephoned one of the friends who had just taken the Silva course with me. She had left London at the same time and would, I hoped, be indoors by now. She had personal experience of using the self-healing techniques and I knew she could help me with distance healing.

'And I'm frightened,' I finished, after explaining my problem.

'I can hear that.' Her voice was calm, 'now I want you to put down the telephone and go into rapid deep relaxation then follow the method for healing. I will meet you at a meditative level (Theta) and work with you – two of us sending the right mental pictures and combining energies, it will be very powerful."

I was really motivated! Putting the receiver down I went to work, putting into practice all that I had learned, following the procedure stage by stage, I accessed the Theta level rapidly and in that deeply relaxed state, visualized total healing. I finished by placing a hand over my physical eye, concentrating on that healing and seeing the outcome I so desired. My concentration was total, motivated by the very human instinct of self preservation. I don't know how long I sat there, five minutes, fifteen? Then a strange sensation like a rapid un-relenting tapping came over the whole eye area – and when it stopped, my eye was healed! The pain had completely gone and as you can imagine, I almost cried with relief. I had no explanation for the sensation so I had to accept it as 'one of those things' and I had no reason to think of it again – until several years later...

Meeting Jose Silva

A great air of excitement: Jose Silva was in London, personally conducting the Advanced Course of the method. Graduates had come from all over the country to hear this remarkable man, on what proved (particularly for me) to be a memorable meeting.

* * * * * * *

It was quite late in the afternoon, Jose had kept us enthralled with details of his many successes, and I was intrigued to hear him declare,

'I have created an electronic sound, a rhythm that stimulates the body's natural immune system. It is called, The Silva Sound.'

Then, placing a tape in the recording machine on the table for us all to see, he went on to tell us of the successes he had had by using it dedicatedly on very difficult health cases.

'If you have a health problem, you should do what your doctor advises but you can aid the doctor and help yourself heal more quickly by relaxing and meditating and by focusing on the outcome you desire. This Silva Sound will greatly assist you. For a serious illness you should use it for fifteen minutes, three times a day and, where possible, play this sound close to the body.'

He then put it on – and I nearly fell off my chair! The sound I was hearing, the Silva Sound, was the audio version of the tapping sensation that I had experienced when meditating on the healing of my eye, all those years ago! I knew this sound and I knew it worked. The threat to my eyesight had been a motivating factor that had sent me into a really deep and instant meditation. I had concentrated on healing with total belief in my ability to instruct my body to heal itself. In those few silent minutes I had worked passionately in another powerful dimension of awareness. By totally believing in my ability and right to access and receive help, I had received the benefits.

My respect and admiration for Jose Silva, already high, now went up to the rafters of the sky as he went on to talk of the power of the mind. And all that it required was our attention.

However, at the time of my first experience of self-healing my eye, my meeting with Jose and this most remarkable repeating of the healing Silva Sound, lay several years in the future.

Writer of *Unshriven*

The Silva Course over, my time in England at an end and heading back to the Middle East, the teachings of the method occupied my thoughts for most of the six hour flight. I was filled with an inner excitement that was hard to contain. Mental barriers had become doors to opportunities and the possibilities were breathtaking. I was surging with energy from this most extraordinary teaching, keen to make these techniques part of my daily life. What fun! How far could the boundaries be pushed? What was I, and what was mankind in general, capable of? And from somewhere deep inside, an inner voice seemed to be urging:

"Get on with it. It is time to move forward"

I didn't go out to work and having the time and the urge to write again, I had started to map out aspects of a strange and rather confusing story that had sort of popped into my head. I had published before; articles or short stories for magazines, newspapers or the B.B.C. This however, was to be my first novel but with my new powers of concentration, I was keen to see if I could put in the hours required for such a project.

The Writing of *Unshriven* the Novel

Dated August 1963, and set in an isolated terrace of four old cottages close to Stratford on Avon, *Unshriven* was to be a tale of interweaving relationships and historical village detection. I had no idea of what would happen, no real plot, no real characters but I was getting mental images; aspects of cottages, the area and people.

Every morning as my husband drove to the hospital, I would put my 'office' out on the patio and before reading yesterday's work or touching the keys, I would do my first directed meditation of the day starting with a deep relaxation. (It is a wonderful experience to be so deeply relaxed). This would be followed by distant healing, a request for guidance, and finally, protection for family and friends. Once this was completed, still deeply relaxed, I would turn my attention to 1963 and my imaginary location and would soon be deeply absorbed in the way the story was developing. Then one day, almost imperceptibly, the date began to change. It was still August, still the same location and cottages – but the year was now, 1663. I didn't realize at the time that this was the start of my channeling historic factual information that was to become the 17th century version of the book.

This past aspect of my story proved to be very powerful; it would not be dismissed. Finally, and by now fascinated, I decided to weave it into my 1963 version as a memory of a past life, recalled by one of my 20th century characters, a clairvoyant named Stella.

Once the decision had been made, the two dates and days seemed to parallel and interweave with each other; developing and interacting with ease and speed. Writing was a joy and there were no distractions. Shaded by bougainvillea and oleander trees with a cooling breeze from the ocean, I typed as though in a light trance, fingers on the keys, interpreting scenes that seemed to be flowing quite freely from my imagination.

Gradually a pattern began to present itself, helping me decide on the day's work. I would 'see' a table with various objects scattered across it. Mentally I would reach out and in no particular order, touch each of them, finally holding one that instantly suggested the theme or character I was to pursue that day. As long as I stayed in this light trance with no distractions, the typed words just poured out across the pages. No writer's block for me. I sometimes had difficulty keeping up with the speed of changing situations.

Hour after hour I sat at my desk, the scenes sharp, the dialogue between the characters, silent yet crystal clear within my thinking as my fingers raced across the keyboard. It was as though my head and my hands on the keyboard were working together and I had no awareness of the rest of my physical body. So completely immersed in the drama, so driven was I, that I didn't notice the backache or tired eyes. I was on a mission; it had become personal. I was taking sides and, like a prosecuting lawyer, I was being driven to tell the truth about an outrageous miscarriage of justice that had blighted the life of a lone survivor.

I was putting in office hours, producing work that was demanding, physically, mentally and emotionally, yet when the subject for that day had run its course, the mind pictures stopped abruptly. It was like turning off the electricity. This happened in exactly the same way when the story finally ended; abruptly, like emptying a vessel, there was nothing left.

I must confess that had I not persevered, had I not used the mental and emotional disciplines of The Silva Method, then *Unshriven* could never have been written. It was very hard work – and it wasn't even half over!

Dyslexia – My Break Through

The principles and self discipline of The Silva Method, were to change the dynamics of my life in a way I could never have foreseen. I could not possibly document or recall all of the achievements, amazing experiences and daily benefits that have helped and guided me over the years. Ranking as one of the most remarkable, and critical to me as a writer, was to be my understanding of and the over-coming of my inability to spell. This was totally due to my previously undiagnosed Dyslexia. Precious years were blighted by it and I was already into my forties when, using a Silva technique, I learned to spell virtually overnight! In my case as it is with so many others, changing my thinking (my concept of my reality) was to change my life.

Aged nine, the girl stood in front of the class, exercise book held high for all to see the spelling mistakes scored through with red ink, slashing marks for an otherwise excellent composition. The teacher, believing that this (quite bright) student was being lazy, had encouraged the other children to laugh at her hopeless attempt at spelling. This was not to humiliate the girl but an effort to make her 'pay attention' and memorize the daily homework list of words. It didn't work, and, confidence shattered, as the years passed there was always a dictionary at hand as every word over three letters was checked again and again before articles could be sold to newspapers or magazines. The conviction that 'I can't spell anything, so how I spell a word, must be wrong,' became an accepted fact of life. I was that child and over thirty years later a sort of miracle happened.

Saudi Arabia – Midnight

It was the Holy month of Ramadan, and I woke because my husband was getting ready to leave for duty at the hospital. During this month, day is turned into night and human nature being what it is, people who have starved all day eat too much and too fast when the setting sun marks the end of the day. As a consequence, the hospital clinics open accordingly.

To put myself back to sleep I was meditating, mentally repeating words of a mantra when, behind closed eyelids I saw the words being written – back to front. Mirror writing? Shocked, eyes wide open I sat up and then told my husband what had happened. He, kind and encouraging as ever, said I should take a pen and see if I could actually reproduce what I had visualized. I was reluctant, this was revolutionary thinking because over the years, proof reading my manuscripts, various people had asked if I could mirror write and, was I dyslexic? "Because there is a pattern here." I had always rejected this idea out of hand having been conditioned to think that dyslexia was an excuse. Embarrassing though it was, I would never give myself an easy way out. No excuses, I couldn't spell and that was a fact.

Now, trying to hold down the excitement, I got out of bed very slowly and, holding the mental picture (Silva discipline), I continued to replay my doing something, that I had assumed totally beyond my capabilities. Picking up pen and note pad I went into the bathroom, turned on the bright light – and wrote as easily right to left as left to right, then upside down, then upside down and back to front! Then, with both hands, I wrote in opposite directions and upside down at the same time! I then held the paper up to the mirror. It was legible! How amazing was that?

The barrier was down! It wasn't an excuse. I really did have a diagnosable problem. I had been struggling valiantly with un-diagnosed dyslexia for a lifetime and the knowledge was so freeing, so overwhelmingly marvelous, that I sobbed like a child! There wasn't a 'blank dumb section' in my brain that couldn't cope with spelling. There had to be a physical explanation: Nystagmus – A slight weakness in holding focus, that flickered and rearranged the letters, had been responsible for all those years of embarrassment, anxiety and misery. Now I was free of it. My subservient acceptance of my limitations, gone!

I still have problems with long division, the numbers are too close together, though algebra proved to be easy-peasy. I've heard the same thing from other dyslexics. Somehow the layout and the patterns make sense to us, partly because of the wider spacing in-between the symbols.

Being able to spell freed my mind from many writing restrictions. If there wasn't a dictionary handy I would make up the text by using the words I could spell, often missing the impact of the point I was trying to make. Now though, accepting this fact that I was dyslexic wasn't enough. It wasn't an end, it was a beginning. I wanted to understand exactly how this weakness in my eye was manifesting – and do something to correct it.

A couple of weeks earlier I had been in a coffee shop. The man next to me opened his newspaper and at the top, in huge banner headlines, I read, 'NIAGARA FALLS TO SELL OIL'

'They've struck oil at Niagara Falls!' I said in amazement to my husband who was sitting opposite – and the man with the newspaper looked at me as if I had gone mad. What the letters actually said were: 'NIGERIA FAILS TO SELL OIL'.

Not only were letters mixing up of their own accord but if they were also being physically moved as was the newspaper, or if I was driving and trying to follow signpost directions, the result was chaos. In that moment, I wanted the floor of the coffee shop to open up and swallow me up.

I had read with confidence from the age of four because I was somehow able to do what I later called block-reading, understanding the meaning of whole pages without actually reading every word. I was called a book-worm, devouring the contents and living in absolute dread of being asked to read aloud. Fortunately, and strangely, I had the ability to correctly interpret the mix of letters on the page.

Unfortunately I wrote down the mixed-up words as I saw them! There was nothing wrong with my memory but I still occasionally put the 'T' in the middle of the word yacht, because that's how I see it. I used to joke that on a good day I could get six letters in the name Jesus. On a bad day it could be as many as seven. If in doubt, put another letter in! The talented actress, writer and fellow dyslexic (!) Susan Hampshire, in *"Every Letter Counts"* (the first of her enlightening and heart warming books) echoed my stressful and ingenious ways of pretending that it had all been a 'silly mistake' and that I did know the answer.

The point of this confession is that the undermining of my confidence as a child and my total acceptance that I couldn't spell (so I couldn't spell anything) was so ingrained that I couldn't think beyond it. I allowed myself no excuses. At spelling I was a duffer, yet it took only minutes to break the stranglehold of a lifetime. Confidence restored and accepting the challenge, I started to read more slowly, giving letters time to settle in the right order and I began to spell correctly, virtually overnight. Amazing. Wonderful!

Yet it still concerns me and I do wonder just how many children have their potential stunted by adults, frustrated by the fact that the accepted ways of teaching are not showing the expected results, shifting the blame by resorting to angry and dismissive comments:

"Oh, don't you understand? I've told you a dozen times. Pay attention. Listen to what I am saying. Oh, I give up with you." Taken up by class mates and repeated often enough, we probably say it to ourselves subconsciously, thus producing a life-long and oh so unnecessary inhibition that can stretch across a lifetime – and yet, as I had proved, by using The Silva Method, if you change your thinking – you can indeed change your life.

* * * * * * *

Since completing the basic Silva Method course, I have graduated in most of the advanced training methods.

We all have the power to change the "Reality" we live

Much later, when the broader picture and the shocking truth of *Unshriven* was revealed, I was to ponder, just how far back do the lines of so-called coincidence reach, coincidence of time and place that present us with fundamental choices and unique opportunities. Is it mere coincidence or fate, or is it as Ernest O'Neil suggested:

> *"There is a destiny that shapes our ends,*
> *rough hew them though we may."*

THE SILVA METHOD

The Silva Method is being taught worldwide.
I cannot recommend it highly enough.

I believe it is time to create a reality worthy of who we really are;
Co-creators of the Society and the World that we live in.
To do this, we have to develop strong minds and imaginations that
are creative and not fear based.

The Silva Method puts you in the driving seat.
The rest is up to you. Have fun!

www.silvamethod.uk.com

U.S.A. Director: Laura Silva Qusade
U.K. Director: Gabriel Ostend